"Author, broadcaster Bob Lee lifts the names and work of contemporaries and ancestors, detailing their courage, skill, plus commitment and lets the world know they were here and are still here with us today. This book, like the traditional spirit word libation water poured down into the earth, grows to guide the generations to come. 'People to Know in Black History & Beyond' will grow, enlighten and inspire generations to come."

Camille Yarbrough
Ancestor House Productions

PEOPLE TO KNOW IN BLACK HISTORY & BEYOND

Recognizing the Heroes and Sheroes
Who Make the Grade

PEOPLE TO KNOW IN BLACK HISTORY & BEYOND

Recognizing the Heroes and Sheroes
Who Make the Grade

Written and Compiled by
Doctor Bob Lee

Edited by
Yvonne Rose

BOB LEE ENTERPRISES
New York City

PEOPLE TO KNOW IN BLACK HISTORY & BEYOND

Published by Bob Lee Enterprises
For Make the Grade Foundation
244 Madison Avenue, #500
New York, NY 10016
Makethegrade4u@gmail.com
www.makethegrade.org

Bob Lee, Publisher & Editorial Director
Yvonne Rose, Editor

Copyright © 2019 by Bob Lee

Paperback ISBN #: 978-0-9970948-9-3

Hardcover ISBN #: 978-0-9970948-7-9

Ebook ISBN #: 978-0-9970948-8-6

Library of Congress Control Number: 2019901082

DEDICATION

I am dedicating this book to the Heroes and Sheroes of the World who have devoted their lives to building a better future for our community with Positivity, Purpose and Progression along with others who continue to Make the Grade.

A SPECIAL ACKNOWLEDGMENT

To my Editor Yvonne Rose

Thank you for your hard work and dedication in helping to edit my fourth published book: *PEOPLE TO KNOW IN BLACK HISTORY & BEYOND.* Your commitment to this project has been second to none, as is my gratitude to you.

CONTENTS

PREFACE

Carter G. Woodson, who is frequently touted as the "Father of Black History," launched Negro History Week in 1926, chosen in the second week of February between the birthdays of Frederick Douglass and Abraham Lincoln. Fifty years later, in 1976 Black History Week evolved into Black History Month.

During the month of February millions of people (both Black and White) reflect on the accomplishments of African Americans. Although there is much pride in celebrating our history, and although the majority of people who celebrate realize that the month is intended to recognize the Black populace, a large percentage of those people do not know the origin of February as "Black History Month."

According to Sherice Torres, Director of Brand Marketing at Google, "Woodson was committed to bringing African-American history front and center and ensuring that it was taught in schools and studied by other scholars." Torres further explained that Woodson served as her inspiration when she said she wanted to attend Harvard and was discouraged by people around her.

Carter G. Woodson was born in 1875 to former slaves. He was unable to attend school for much of his childhood because he had to help his parents financially. He ended up entering high school at the age of 20, completed his studies, and received his diploma two years later. After high school, Woodson taught in West Virginia before earning his undergraduate degree at Berea College. He received a master's degree from the University of Chicago in 1908, and a Doctor of History from Harvard in 1912.

As the second African-American to earn a doctorate from Harvard, Woodson became one of the first scholars of African-American history. During his time spent at Harvard, Woodson also became known for writing the contributions of Black Americans into the national spotlight.

In between teaching and receiving his masters and doctorate, Woodson was a school supervisor in the Philippines. He also founded the Association for the Study of Afro-American Life and History in 1915 and founded the Journal of Negro History in 1916.

Carter G. Woodson is the author of the book, "*The Miseducation of the Negro,*" published in 1933. He died in 1950.

As Carter G. Woodson realized, African American men and women made great contributions to American society throughout the 17th, 18th, 19th, 20th and 21st centuries. ***PEOPLE TO KNOW IN BLACK HISTORY & BEYOND*** brings to light a small percentage of those notable Americans who we should always remember as contributors to our heritage and Black History.

INTRODUCTION

Every year, during Black History Month I always see myself and Ann Tripp, News Director for both WBLS and WLIB, scrambling and looking for black history information. We start looking in the computer and in the history books for details about Black heroes and sheroes: inventors, educators, activists, ministers and other important contributors at the onset of the month of February or whenever we are highlighting people who do great things.

One day, I thought, *you know what? There are so many people who have sacrificed and aspired to greatness, whose shoulders we stand on. By understanding their mission and following their example, we may become inspired enough to build our own legacy and become an example for future generations to follow.* I read about these heroes and sheroes all the time in books and ebooks, on Google, Wikipedia, Twitter, Facebook, Instagram… But then, after I read about them, what do I do with the information? I have compiled some of the information for **PEOPLE TO KNOW IN HISTORY**, in order to give you my legacy about people who you and I believe are notable contributors to *our* Black History.

When I went to school there was a limited amount of Black history taught. That's why I want students to think beyond the few, who we hear about during Black History Month every year. I want students to know that there are people who started out just like them – men and women - who enabled us to go into space, who created life-saving surgical techniques, who propelled us from the 17th century right up to the present by using their wisdom, knowledge and foresight.

There are thousands of brilliant people, who we may or may not be aware of; all are great, in their own right. They all had a strong constitution, a will to overcome obstacles and a burning desire to become successful. For instance, in the recent movie, "Hidden Figures" there were three African American women featured and each had her place in aeronautics history. Who knows how many there actually were, because until the movie was released millions of other people didn't know a thing about these women. "Hidden Figures" was very eye-opening; it was the story of a team of female African-American mathematicians who served a vital role in NASA during the early years of the U.S. space program. (*Isn't it ironic that president Trump is now talking about starting a new branch of the military – the Space Force?...I guess he saw the movie too.*)

If you've seen the film, then you've already felt the impact of knowing Black women were directly responsible for putting the first American astronauts into space. *Hidden Figures* leaves behind a bittersweet taste: a combination of pride for the achievements of these brilliant trailblazers and irritation that this chapter of history is left out of our textbooks. *Hidden Figures*, an adaptation of Margot Lee Shetterly's book of the same name only scratched the surface of these heroic women - Katherine Johnson, Dorothy Vaughan, and Mary Jackson - and their work in NASA's computer section that quite literally catapulted humans into space in 1961.

In 1978, NASA's first three African American astronauts were among the graduating class – Dr. Ronald McNair, Guy Buford and Fred Gregory. In 1983, Guion Stewart Bluford Jr., Ph.D., as a member of the crew of the Orbiter *Challenger* on the mission STS-8, became the first African American in space and Frederick Gregory became the first African American to pilot a space craft, the orbiter Challenger on mission STS-51B. Unfortunately, in 1986 Ronald McNair (at the age of 36) died during the launch of the NASA Space Shuttle Challenger on mission STS-51-L, in which he was serving as one of 3 mission specialists. I remember thinking, *there are so few Black people who will ever make it as an astronaut, and it was such a tragic loss when one who was actually going up to space ended up dying before he could accomplish his ultimate dream.*

The men and women of NASA only touch the tip of the iceberg. Although much of the legacy of Black history is untold, unknown or unrecognized, it spans decades. The Presidential Medal of Freedom serves to recognize the significant cultural achievements by the award winners, spanning areas of arts, entertainment, world peace endeavors, human rights and other arenas.

Similar to the Congressional Gold Medal, the Presidential Medal of Freedom is the highest award given to civilians in the United States.

President, Barack Obama, the nation's first African American President, awarded 16 recipients with the Presidential Medal of Freedom. Of that number, four African-Americans were included: Media mogul Oprah Winfrey, civil rights leader Cordy Tindell "C.T." Vivian, Martin Luther King, Jr. adviser Bayard Rustin, and Chicago Cubs great Ernie Banks. The group joined a distinguished list of past winners such as Jackie Robinson, Sidney Poitier, Muhammad Ali, Maya Angelou, and Dorothy Height, among others. Within these pages, I pay homage to all of the above.

That's the reason I wanted to write this book… there are so many people to honor and recognize. At first, I was doing research for Black History Month, so I could talk about it on my radio show and during my public appearances in the community. Then, I wanted to do something to recognize all those people who have made and continue to make major contributions to our country and throughout the world every day of the year.

3

But then afterwards I thought, *wow there are a lot of people of other colors and ethnicities, who came out with inventions, ideas and discoveries we are using now.* So, I wondered, *how do we work them in there like that. Not just Black history.* Special people doing special things …people that may have been overlooked, particularly because they were minorities… people who have masterminded things that benefit *all* the people of the world.

But now, with **PEOPLE TO KNOW IN HISTORY** you can pay homage to those heroes and sheroes every single day of the year.

Whether you are researching a topic for Black History Month or just want to learn more about your predecessors, we hope this listing of famous and lesser-known African Americans will help you appreciate those people who have truly achieved greatness and given you a foundation upon which to fulfill your dream.

PART ONE

NOTABLE PEOPLE WHO MAKE THE GRADE

Part One of **PEOPLE TO KNOW IN BLACK HISTORY & BEYOND** incorporates those Heroes and Sheroes who have exhibited strong leadership qualities as **Parents, Teachers, Students, Community Activists,** or in the area of **Spirituality**, **Health**, **Science** and **Financial Literacy**.

> *"In the end, that's what being a parent is all about
> — those precious moments with our children that
> fill us with pride and excitement for their future,
> the chances we have to set an example or offer a
> piece of advice, the opportunities to just be there
> and show them that we love them."*
> **– Barack Obama**

CHAPTER ONE – THE PARENT
FEATURING WORLD RENOWNED PARENTS

Although mothers are the primary socializers of children, both parents provide nurturance and discipline. In a study across two generations, it was reported by many fathers that they are more involved with their children than their fathers had been with them. They are taking an active part in their children's care, changing diapers, and playing with their children. This trend is similar in all racial groups and social classes.

In this chapter – THE PARENT – you will see positive role models with both parents participating equally, while nurturing and encouraging their children to become upstanding citizens.

PRESIDENT BARACK OBAMA
& FIRST LADY MICHELLE OBAMA

It's hard to imagine growing up in the White House, let alone parenting as the President and First Lady of the United States of America. Yet, Barack and Michele did just that. The first lady and president are caring parents who put their children first, despite the pressures of the White House.

Barack and Michelle Obama are the proud parents of Malia and Sasha Obama. Michelle LaVaughn Robinson Obama is an American lawyer and writer who was First Lady of the United States from 2009 to 2017. She is married to the 44th President of the United States, Barack Obama.

Prior to giving birth to Malia, Michelle Obama experienced complications and suffered a miscarriage and eventually conceived both of her children through in vitro fertilization.

Malia Ann was born on July 4, 1998 while Natasha (known as Sasha) came into this world on June 10, 2001, just a few months before the world was turned upside down on September 11, 2001. Both the girls were delivered by Anita Blanchard at the University of Chicago Medical Center. Blanchard is also a personal friend of the Obama family.

The Obamas lived in Chicago, where their daughters attended the University of Chicago Laboratory School. Barack always wanted his children to be active, committed and passionate, so he and Michelle designed a busy schedule for their two daughters. Malia was involved with soccer, dance and drama, while Sasha was busy with gymnastics and tap dancing. Both girls learned piano and tennis, as well.

Before winning the election Barack had promised his daughters that he would get a puppy for them. He kept good on his promise and shortly after moving into the White House, the two girls got their puppy, a Portuguese Water dog, named Bo. In 2013, the Obamas got another Portuguese Water dog, named Sunny.

Fatherhood has been a central passion of the President. He was reared without his own father and was often absent when his daughters were very young as he campaigned for office, commuted to his job as an Illinois state legislator and later flew between Chicago and Washington as a U.S. senator. After being elected president, Obama spoke often of his excitement at living full-time under the same roof with his family

After Barack became President of the United States, Malia and Sasha attended the Sidwell Friends School in Washington, D.C., a private school which has enrolled other famous students, as well, such as: Chelsea Clinton, Archibald Roosevelt, Tricia Nixon Cox and the grandchildren of Joe Biden. When he was first elected, Malia was 10 and Sasha was just 7. President Obama's vision for his daughters and for every child in America is that there should be no limits on their dreams and achievements.

Barack deliberately tried to keep his daughters away from the media so that they would have a normal upbringing; but that was not always easy to do, given the newsworthiness of the Obama family.

The Obama daughters have had a unique childhood. They are among the youngest to have grown up in the White House in modern times; but interest in the girls was intensified more by an increasingly ravenous media climate and their historic role as the first black children to grow up in the White House.

By delaying her college enrollment for a year, Malia may have escaped some of the media coverage that follows a sitting president's family. She took a year off after she graduated from high school in 2016, and spent time doing internships at TV studios in New York and Los Angeles. Malia started attending Harvard University in 2017, with aspirations of becoming a filmmaker. Sasha continued her schooling in D.C.; but after graduating high school, she also hopes to attend an Ivy League college – Harvard or Yale.

Barack was determined not to let his job take him away from his children more than necessary; while Michelle pushed and watched her daughters relentlessly. Although Michelle was one of the most active first ladies ever in the White House, she built her schedule entirely around Malia and Sasha, as she strived to give them a normal childhood despite their circumstances.

Michelle bans certain foods from her kitchen, such as potato chips, chocolate, and any snack that is unhealthy. She doesn't want her daughters to become overweight because they're always in the public eye. Malia and Sasha have to eat their vegetables and if they don't, they're not allowed to leave the dinner table. Vegetables consist of green beans, broccoli, cabbage, carrots, and peas. When they want to have a snack, there are limits. They have fruit, some cereals, some crackers, nuts, and dried foods.

Worried that the privileges of the White House could spoil her children, Michelle Obama tried to limit the staff's constant efforts to feed, polish, assist and perfect. Instead she assigned chores to her daughters, which included making their beds daily; and she accordingly gave them a weekly allowance that would be reflected on their assigned tasks...in other words, the First Daughters were not spoiled children.

The girls were not permitted to surf the internet or watch TV during the week, but they took piano lessons, swimming and tennis lessons, and played soccer, lacrosse and basketball.

The President was what his own father had never been, what he had never been, what his wife had always wanted: the dream father, the kind of dad who was around to coach basketball. Barack became one of several parent coaches for Sasha's basketball team; and he and his personal aide put the girls through drill after drill. The President took the job very seriously, even creating special clinics to work on particular skills.

The Obamas encouraged both of their daughters to take an interest in political and policy issues that dovetailed with the girls' own concerns, but they were careful not to force their involvement. They conducted educational conversations at the family dinner table. Most nights at 6:30, he listened to stories about middle-school friendships and shared his on-the-job challenges. Sometimes, his daughters took an interest. In particular, the president has credited conversations with his daughters for his decision to support gay marriage.

Malia sat in on the President's meeting with Malala Yousafzai, the teenage Pakistani activist who advocated for girls' education. Malia has also influenced the President's take on popular culture. He has described himself as sensitive to the messages conveyed by images of women of color in the media and the challenges of those beauty standards for Black women, in part because of conversations with his daughter. Barack has stated that Malia and Sasha have been among the people with whom he can talk about his work.

When President Obama's term ended, Malia was a student at Harvard and Sasha completed high school in Washington, D.C. Barack attended Harvard and he has the same expectations for his daughters. Sasha, like her sister wants to follow in her parents' footsteps and she knows that Harvard is one of the best universities in the world; but if she doesn't get into Harvard, she must strive to attend another credible school, like Yale.

It hasn't been just fun and games for the two girls. They've both had a hand in philanthropic work, as well. They went to Liberia to promote the *Let Girls Learn Peace* initiative. They also went to Morocco to raise money for girls' education. It's really tough to meet your parents' expectations, especially when one of them is the President of the United States! However, Malia and Sasha have done exactly that with great poise.

Michelle LaVaughn Robinson was born on January 17, 1964, in Chicago, Illinois, to Fraser Robinson III, a city water plant employee and Democratic precinct captain, and Marian Shields Robinson, a secretary at Spiegel's catalog store. Her mother was a full-time homemaker until Michelle entered high school.

The Robinson and Shields families trace their roots to pre-Civil War African Americans in the American South. On her father's side, she is descended from the Gullah people of South Carolina's Low Country region. Her paternal great-great grandfather, Jim Robinson, was a slave on Friendfield Plantation in South Carolina, the state where some of her paternal family still reside. Her grandfather Fraser Robinson, Jr. built his own house in South Carolina. He and his wife LaVaughn (Johnson) returned to the Low Country after retirement.

Among her maternal ancestors was her great-great-great-grandmother, Melvinia Shields, a slave on Henry Walls Shields' 200-acre farm in Clayton County, Georgia. Melvinia's first son, Dolphus T. Shields, was biracial and born into slavery about 1860. Based on DNA and other evidence, in 2012 researchers said his father was likely 20-year-old Charles Marion Shields, son of her master. Melvinia did not talk to relatives about Dolphus' father. Dolphus Shields moved to Birmingham, Alabama after the Civil War, and some of his children migrated to Cleveland, Ohio and Chicago.

Raised in Chicago, Illinois, Michelle grew up in a two-story bungalow on Euclid Avenue in Chicago's South Shore community area. Her parents rented a small apartment on the second floor from her great-aunt, who lived downstairs. She was raised in what she describes as a "conventional" home, with "the mother at home, the father works, you have dinner around the table." When the Obama family moved into the White House, Michelle insisted that they have "dinner around the table" as often as possible.

Michelle's father suffered from multiple sclerosis which had a profound emotional effect on her as she was growing up. She was determined to stay out of trouble and be a good student, which was what her father wanted for her. By sixth grade, Michelle joined a gifted class at Bryn Mawr Elementary School (later renamed Bouchet Academy). She attended Whitney Young High School, Chicago's first magnet high school, established as a selective enrollment school. Michelle was on the honor roll for four years, took advanced placement classes, was a member of the National Honor Society, and served as student council treasurer. She graduated in 1981 as the salutatorian of her class.

Michelle was inspired to follow her brother to Princeton University, where he graduated in 1983. While at Princeton, she got involved with the Third World Center (now known as the Carl A. Fields Center), an academic and cultural group that supported minority students, running their day care center, which also included after-school tutoring. She majored in Sociology and minored in African American studies, graduating cum laude with a Bachelor of Arts in 1985.

Michelle went on to earn her Juris Doctor (J.D.) degree from Harvard Law School in 1988. At Harvard she participated in demonstrations advocating the hiring of professors who were members of minorities and worked for the Harvard Legal Aid Bureau, assisting low-income tenants with housing cases. She is the third First Lady with a postgraduate degree, after her two immediate predecessors, Hillary Clinton and Laura Bush.

Following law school, she was an associate at the Chicago office of the law firm, Sidley & Austin, where she first met her future husband. At the firm, she worked on marketing and intellectual property. The couple's relationship started with a business lunch and then a community organization meeting, where he first impressed her. They soon realized that they were quite the opposite from one another - Michelle had stability through her two-parent home, while Barack was "adventurous."

In 1991, Michelle held public sector positions in the Chicago city government as an Assistant to the Mayor, and as Assistant Commissioner of Planning and Development. Barack and Michelle married on October 3, 1992.

In 1993, Michelle became Executive Director for the Chicago office of Public Allies, a non-profit organization encouraging young people to work on social issues in nonprofit groups and government agencies. She worked there nearly four years and set fundraising records for the organization that still stood 12 years after she left.

In 1996, Michelle served as the Associate Dean of Student Services at the University of Chicago, where she developed the University's Community Service Center. By now the Obamas had become parents to two daughters. Malia Ann (born 1998) and Natasha (known as Sasha, born 2001).

In 2002, Michelle began working for the University of Chicago Hospitals, first as executive director for community affairs; and beginning May 2005, as Vice President for Community and External Affairs.

She continued to hold the University of Chicago Hospitals position during the primary campaign but cut back to part-time. After Barack's election to the U.S. Senate, the Obama family continued to live on Chicago's South Side, choosing to remain there, rather than moving to Washington, D.C.

In May 2007, three months after her husband declared his presidential candidacy, Michelle reduced her professional responsibilities by 80 percent while supporting Barack's 2008 Presidential Campaign. Throughout the campaign, Michelle made a "commitment to be away overnight only once a week – to campaign only two days a week and be home by the end of the second day" for their daughters. By early February 2008, things were escalating, and Michelle's participation had increased significantly, attending thirty-three events in eight days. She made several campaign appearances with Oprah Winfrey and delivered a keynote address at the 2008 Democratic National Convention. Michelle wrote her own speeches for her husband's presidential campaign and generally spoke without notes.

The marital relationship has had its ebbs and flows; the combination of an evolving family life and beginning political career led to many arguments about balancing work and family. However, despite their family obligations and careers, they continued to attempt to schedule date nights while they lived in Chicago. After Barack Obama became President of the United States, Marian Robinson, Michelle's mother, moved into the White House to assist with Malia and Sasha's child care.

Michelle returned to speak at the 2012 Democratic National Convention, and again during the 2016 Democratic National Convention in Philadelphia, where she delivered a speech in support of the Democratic presidential nominee, and fellow First Lady, Hillary Clinton.

As First Lady, Michelle Obama became a role model for women, an advocate for poverty awareness, education, nutrition, physical activity and healthy eating, and a fashion icon.

Barack H. Obama was born August 4, 1961 in Hawaii to a mother from Kansas and a father from Kenya, Barack was raised with help from his grandparents, whose generosity of spirit reflected their Midwestern roots. The homespun values they instilled in him, paired with his innate sense of optimism, compelled Obama to devote his life to giving every child, regardless of his or her background, the same chance America gave him.

Few presidents have walked a more improbable path to the White House. After working his way through college with the help of scholarships and student loans, Barack moved to Chicago, where he worked with a group of churches to help rebuild communities devastated by the closure of local steel plants. That experience honed his belief in the power of uniting ordinary people around a politics of purpose, in the hard work of citizenship, to bring about positive change. In law school, he became the first African-American president of the Harvard Law Review, then he returned to Illinois to teach constitutional law at the University of Chicago and begin a career in public service, winning seats in the Illinois State Senate and the United States Senate.

On November 4, 2008, Barack Obama was elected the 44th President of the United States, winning more votes than any candidate in history. He took office at a moment of crisis unlike any America had seen in decades – a nation at war, a planet in peril, the American Dream itself threatened by the worst economic calamity since the Great Depression. And yet, despite all manner of political obstruction, Barack Obama's leadership helped rescue the economy, revitalize the American auto industry, reform the health care system to cover another twenty million Americans, and put the country on a firm course to a clean energy future – all while overseeing the longest stretch of job creation in American history. On the world stage, Obama's belief in America's indispensable leadership and strong, principled diplomacy helped wind down the wars in Iraq and Afghanistan, decimate al Qaeda and eliminate the world's most wanted terrorists, shut down Iran's nuclear weapons program, open up a new chapter with the people of Cuba, and unite humanity in coordinated action to combat a changing climate.

In times of great challenge and change, President Obama's leadership ushered in a stronger economy, a more equal society, a nation more secure at home and more respected around the world. The Obama years were ones in which more people not only began to see themselves in the changing face of America, but to see America the way he always has – as the only place on Earth where so many of our stories could even be possible.

BEYONCE' & JAY-Z

Beyoncé started a relationship with Jay-Z after their collaboration on "Bonnie & Clyde" which appeared on his seventh album *The Blueprint 2: The Gift & The Curse* (2002). Beyoncé appeared as Jay-Z's girlfriend in the music video for the song. On April 4, 2008, Beyoncé and Jay-Z married without publicity.

In April 2011, Beyoncé and Jay-Z traveled to Paris in order to shoot the album cover for *4*, and unexpectedly became pregnant in Paris. In August, the couple attended the 2011 MTV Video Music Awards, at which Beyoncé performed "Love on Top" and ended the performance by coyly revealing that she was pregnant. Her appearance helped that year's MTV Video Music Awards become the most-watched broadcast in MTV history, pulling in 12.4 million viewers; the announcement was listed in *Guinness World Records* for "most tweets per second recorded for a single event" on Twitter, receiving 8,868 tweets per second and "Beyoncé pregnant" was the most Googled term the week of August 29, 2011.

Soon after, Jay-Z posted a new song dedicated to his first-born child on his website, in which he rapped about their pregnancy struggles, including the pain the couple went through with the miscarriage Beyoncé suffered before becoming pregnant with Blue Ivy: "False alarms and false starts, all made better by the sound of your heart." He later adds, "last time the miscarriage was so tragic. We was afraid you disappeared but nah baby, you magic." "Glory feat. B.I.C." Jay-Z also reveals where their first-born daughter was conceived -- "You was made in Paris" – Blue Ivy's cries are included at the end of the song and she was officially credited as "B.I.C." on it.

Glory was released two days after Blue Ivy's birth; thus, at two days old, Blue Ivy became the youngest person ever to appear on a Billboard chart when "Glory" debuted on the Hot R&B/Hip Hop Songs chart. Jay-Z also riffs on her name in the song, rapping "Baby I paint the sky blue, my greatest creation was you" and "The most beautifulest thing in this world, she's daddy's little girl." He later posted the track along with a photo of the Empire State Building lit up in blue.

Blue Ivy was born January 7, 2012 at Lenox Hill Hospital in New York City. When Jay-Z and Beyoncé released their first official statement about Blue Ivy, they said that her "birth was emotional and extremely peaceful, we are in heaven." They added that she was "delivered naturally," weighed seven pounds, and described her arrival as "the best experience of both of our lives." The two-day old baby girl has one thing her parents shed long ago -- a surname. "'Blue Ivy Carter' is the ONLY one in that family with a last name."

In Beyoncé's 2013 HBO documentary *Life Is But a Dream*, she opened up her heart and revealed that she had suffered a miscarriage in 2011 before having daughter Blue Ivy Carter, who was born in 2012. The singer spoke about her first pregnancy, learning she was pregnant and the pain that came when she learned she lost the baby. "About two years ago, I was pregnant for the first time," Beyoncé said. "And I heard the heartbeat, which was the most beautiful music I ever heard in my life." "Being pregnant was very much like falling in love. You are so open. You are so overjoyed. There's no words that can express having a baby growing inside of you, so of course you want to scream it out and tell everyone."

But before she could share the good news, Beyoncé had complications in the early stages. "I flew back to New York to get my check up – and no heartbeat," she said. "Literally the week before I went to the doctor, everything was fine, but there was no heartbeat."

Beyoncé described it as "the saddest thing" she had ever endured; but shortly after, she returned to the studio and wrote music in order to cope with the loss. "And it was actually the first song I wrote for my album. And it was the best form of therapy for me. After the happiness of hearing her baby's heartbeat for the first time, Beyoncé shared that she envisioned what her child would look like and was feeling very maternal. Giving birth is the most powerful thing you can ever do in your life, the most beautiful experience of my life. It was amazing. I felt like God was giving me a chance to assist in a miracle. You're playing a part in a much bigger show.

On February 1, 2017 Beyoncé announced on her Instagram that she was pregnant again; this time, expecting twins with her husband Jay Z. She revealed her pregnancy by telling fans they have been "blessed two times." Her announcement gained over 6.3 million "likes" within eight hours, breaking the world record for the most-liked image on the website at the time. On July 13, 2017, Beyoncé uploaded the first image of herself and the twins onto her Instagram account, confirming their birth date as a month prior, on June 13, 2017 and their names, Rumi and Sir Carter. The twins were born at Ronald Reagan UCLA

Medical Center in California. Rumi, the daughter, was born before Sir, the son.

Jay-Z is one of the country's top business moguls. He realizes that empowerment allows a child to feel in control of their environment and situation. Allowing a child to make a money decision in a safe environment helps them feel competent and powerful in handling funds. Having money and handling it gives a child the sense of, "I can do this. It is my money; I can do it." It also allows a child to think about using money to achieve goals.

It's no wonder that Jay-Z started teaching his daughter Blue Ivy how to be money conscious and philanthropic at a young age. When her parents took Blue Ivy to an auction, the six-year-old daughter of Jay-Z and Beyoncé was bidding up a storm at the Wearable Art Gala at the Waco Theater Center in Los Angeles, where she bought a $10,000 work by Samuel Levi Jones, titled *Composed*, which was made from deconstructed law and medical books. Jay-Z retrieved the paddle, however, before his daughter could top Tyler Perry's $20,000 bid for *Young Sidney*, Tiffanie Anderson's painting of filmmaker Sidney Poitier. Blue Ivy was the underbidder at $19,000.

In Blue Ivy's case, the goal was to collect art, which is an important value in her family. It is key that a child have a goal and it is even better if the goal is reinforced by their closest supporter. For most children, it's their parents.

One of the best goals to consider for a child is that of charity. It is essential and crucial for parents to set the mindset early on. Charity is also good for your child's brain. Beyoncé and Jay-Z used art related to the African American experience, which is something they have probably discussed with their daughter. This approach can easily be applied to whatever issue that resonates with your child.

When children are learning about money and empowerment, it is important that they experience both success and failure. Blue Ivy initially bid $17,000 for the acrylic painting of Sidney Poitier, increased her bid to $19,000, but was eventually outbid. Ideally when children experience disappointing money decisions, they can pick themselves up, consider what went wrong and try for another financial goal. Blue Ivy did just that – she bid on the next lot of art and won.

Ultimately the framework laid out by Beyoncé and Jay-Z with their daughter is one that many parents are working towards for their own children. Raising children today requires parents to focus on how the relationship with money grows. The right teachable moment can leave an imprint that lasts a lifetime.

Rapper **Jay-Z** was born **Shawn Corey Carter** on December 4, 1969, in Brooklyn, New York. Shawn "Jay Z" Carter is a son, brother, husband, father, entrepreneur, mogul, sports agent, rapper, performer, movie producer, author, nightclub owner, Broadway producer, festival organizer, watch designer, soundtrack and video-game executive producer, and art collector. He recently debuted a fragrance (Gold) and a cigar (Comador), and he did a three-month, 49-city world tour. He also partnered with Barneys New York to sell luxury goods from the Shawn Carter Collection during the holiday season. (Twenty-five percent of the Barneys proceeds benefit his foundation, which provides scholarships to students facing socio-economic hardships.)

Shawn Carter grew up in the Marcy Houses—Brooklyn projects that are four and a half miles from his Tribeca loft. The Marcy projects take up six blocks along Flushing and Nostrand Avenues in the Bedford-Stuyvesant section of Brooklyn. He loved to read. He wrote down rhymes, listened to—and imitated—Michael Jackson, and watched *Soul Train*. When Shawn was 11, his father's brother was stabbed and died; his father turned to drugs and left the family. Shawn became withdrawn and, as a teenager, he started to deal drugs.

If you choose the right inspirations, growing up without a dad can be a gift. But, as the title of Jay-Z's album Blueprint 2: The Gift and the Curse suggests, there's a flip side. Many of us who spend Father's Day wishing we had somebody to celebrate with haven't chosen the right influences as substitutes. We might not be making many choices at all.

I grew up without a father regularly in my life. I would leave my mom's house every morning searching for what was missing at home – the role models who could show me how to be a man. Like many kids in the same situation – and many of my peers were fatherless – I found those role models on television and in music. Music helped Shawn Carter survive.

Shawn Carter's first album didn't come out until he was 26 years old, but his whole life [before that] from 15, 16 ... was really hard-core. His mother knew he was dealing drugs, but they never really had those conversations. They just pretty much ignored it.

Since the release of his debut album, *Reasonable Doubt,* in 1996, Jay Z has built an empire and changed the culture. He has collaborated with artists that include Kanye West, Eminem, Nas, Rihanna, Alicia Keys, Coldplay's Chris Martin, Justin Timberlake, and Mary J. Blige. He was a part owner of the Nets basketball team and instrumental in bringing them to Brooklyn, getting the Barclays arena built, and designing the Nets' logo as well as the $600,000 "Vault" luxury suites in the place. In 2007 he sold his Rocawear clothing company for $204 million, and in 2008 made a $150 million deal with Live Nation— which he recently re-upped.

Beyoncé Giselle Knowles Carter was born September 4, 1981 in Houston, Texas, to Celestine "Tina" Knowles, a hairdresser and salon owner, and Mathew Knowles, a Xerox sales manager. Beyoncé's name is a tribute to her mother's maiden name. Mathew is African American, while Tina is of Louisiana Creole descent (African, Native American, and French). Through her mother, Beyoncé is a descendant of Acadian leader Joseph Broussard.

Beyoncé is an American singer, songwriter, actress, record producer, and dancer. Born and raised in Houston, Texas, Beyoncé performed in various singing and dancing competitions as a child. She rose to fame in the late 1990s as lead singer of the R&B girl-group Destiny's Child. Managed by her father, Mathew Knowles, the group became one of the best-selling girl groups in history.

When Beyoncé was eight, she and childhood friend Kelly Rowland met LaTavia Roberson while at an audition for an all-girl entertainment group. They were placed into a group called Girl's Tyme with three other girls, and performed on the talent show circuit in Houston. In 1995 Beyoncé's father resigned from his job to manage the group. He cut the original line-up to four and the group was signed to Elektra Records, and was moved briefly to Atlanta Records. In 1996, under an agreement with Sony Music, the girls began recording their debut album; and soon after, they got a contract with Columbia Records. The group changed their name to Destiny's Child and released their major label debut song "Killing Time" on the soundtrack to the 1997 film, Men in Black.

The following year, the group released their self-titled debut album, scoring their first major hit "No, No, No." Through the years, Destiny's Child has won several awards, including: three Soul Train Lady of Soul Awards for Best R&B/Soul Album of the Year, Best R&B/Soul or Rap New Artist, and Best R&B/Soul Single for "No, No, No." Their Multi-Platinum second album, *The Writing's on the Wall*, which sold more than eight million copies worldwide features some of the group's most widely known songs such as "Bills, Bills, Bills", "Jumpin' Jumpin'" and "Say My Name," which won the Best R&B Performance by a Duo or Group with Vocals and the Best R&B Song at the 43rd Annual Grammy Awards.

In early 2000, two of the girls in the group were replaced and one of the remaining girls quit, leaving the group as a trio. The (new) Destiny's Child third album, *Survivor* (2001), which contains themes the public interpreted as a channel to the group's experience, contains the worldwide hits "Independent Women," "Survivor" and "Bootylicious." In 2002, Destiny's Child announced a hiatus and re-united two years later for the release of their fourth and final studio album, *Destiny Fulfilled*(2004).

In 2001, Beyoncé' became the first black woman and second female lyricist to win the Pop Songwriter of the Year award at the American Society of Composers, Authors, and Publishers Pop Music Awards. Beyoncé was the third woman to have writing credits on three number one songs.

During the Destiny's Child hiatus, Beyoncé made her theatrical film debut in *Austin Powers in Goldmember* (2002) and then she released her first solo album, *Dangerously in Love* (2003), which debuted at number one on the US *Billboard* 200 chart, earned five Grammy Awards, and was featured in the *Billboard* Hot 100 number one singles for "Crazy in Love" and "Baby Boy."

In 2005 Destiny's Child was riding high after releasing their fourth studio LP, *Destiny Fulfilled,* when they decided to take a break. Destiny's Child officially disbanded, stating: "After all these wonderful years working together, we realized that now is the time to pursue our personal goals and solo efforts in earnest."

Following the break-up of Destiny's Child in 2006, Beyoncé released her second solo album, *B'Day* (2006), which contained her fourth number one single, "Irreplaceable", as well as the top ten singles "Déjà Vu" and "Beautiful Liar." Beyoncé also continued her acting career, with starring roles in *The Pink Panther* (2006), *Dreamgirls* (2006), and *Obsessed* (2009).

On April 4, 2008, Beyoncé married Jay-Z. She publicly revealed their marriage in a video montage at the listening party for her third studio album, *I Am... Sasha Fierce*, in Manhattan's Sony Club on October 22, 2008. Beyoncé announced a hiatus from her music career in January 2010, and during the break she and her father parted ways as business partners.

Throughout her career, Beyoncé has sold over 100 million records worldwide, making her one of the world's best-selling music artists. She has won 22 Grammy Awards and is the most nominated woman in the award's history. She is also the most awarded artist at the MTV Video Music Awards, with 24 wins, including the Michael Jackson Video Vanguard Award. *Beyoncé has named Michael Jackson as her major musical influence. At the age of five, she had attended her first-ever concert where Jackson performed, and she claims to have realized her purpose.*

The Recording Industry Association of America recognized Beyoncé as the Top Certified Artist in America, during the 2000s decade. In 2009, *Billboard* named her the Top Radio Songs Artist of the Decade, the Top Female Artist of the 2000s decade, and awarded her their Millennium Award in 2011.

In 2014, Beyoncé became the highest-paid black musician in history and was listed among *Time*'s 100 most influential people in the world for a second year in a row. *Forbes* ranked her as the most powerful female in entertainment on their 2015 and 2017 lists, and in 2016, she occupied the sixth place for *Time*'s Person of the Year. With the release of *Lemonade*, Beyoncé became the first and only musical act in *Billboard* chart history to debut at number one with their first six solo studio albums.

At the 59th Grammy Awards in February 2017, *Lemonade* led the nominations with nine, including Album, Record, and Song of the Year for *Lemonade* and "Formation" respectively. and ultimately won two, Best Urban Contemporary Album for *Lemonade* and Best Music Video for "Formation." On April 14, 2018 Beyoncé became the first African-American woman to headline the Coachella Music and Arts Festival.

The Carters don't make any out-and-out statements about the *right* way to maintain a family. They only describe, in various ways, that they feel stronger together—and that they have decided, "the ups and downs are worth it." As of April 2014, the couple had sold a combined 300 million records together.

To describe Beyoncé and Jay-Z as *rich* is kind of like saying the ocean is big. Technically, it's accurate, but it doesn't even come close to conveying the scope of their wealth.

According to *Forbes*' estimates, "The Carters are more than just multimillionaires—they're bona fide *billionaires*, and their earning potential seems to be perpetually on the rise…their combined wealth was estimated at $1.25 billion in 2018." As Beyoncé puts it, "My great, great, grandchildren are already rich." The power couple, who are the proud parents to daughter Blue Ivy and twins Rumi and Sir, likely will remain in a position to fund future generations of the Carter family.

STEVE AND MARJORIE HARVEY

The love story of **Steve and Marjorie Harvey** had a rough start. The two met at a comedy club in Memphis, Tennessee in 1990. When Steve saw his future wife, he knew it was meant to be. In a later interview, he recalled how the first words he ever spoke to Marjorie were: "I don't know who you are but I'm going to marry you."

The feeling was mutual, as in the same interview Marjorie revealed that she knew "he was the one shortly after I began dating him... but then he just disappeared." That is where the rough start comes in.

After a short relationship the two broke up. They reunited years later, in 2005, just shortly after Steve divorced his second wife. The two became friends and began dating once more.

In June 2007, Steve Harvey married Marjorie Bridges, who he says is responsible for making him a better man and changing his life. Steve Harvey is very big on family. He also *has* a very big family. Steve and his third wife, Marjorie, share seven children together. It is a blended family situation, including Marjorie's three children (Morgan, Jason, and Lori), whom Steve adopted when the couple married. He has since raised them as though they were his own, without prejudice. Steve also has three biological children from his first marriage (Karli, Brandi and Broderick), and one biological child from his second marriage (Wynton). Steve and Marjorie have five grandchildren: three through Jason's marriage to his wife Amanda, one through Morgan's marriage to her husband Kareem, and one through Karli's marriage to husband Ben.

Karli Harvey is one of the twins born to Steve and his first wife, Marcia, in 1982. Karli has made several appearances on her father's talk show, *Steve*, and works as a fitness instructor. She and her twin sister, Brandi, also run a female empowerment group together. Karli is married to Ben Raymond, and the couple have one child together. Benjamin Troy Raymond II made his way into the Harvey family in June of 2016.

Brandi Harvey, along with her twin sister, Karli, runs the female empowerment organization YOUNG, FIT, and FLY. The organization works with underprivileged women to help them take better control over their lives. They teach the women and young girls how to take control over their careers, bodies, finances, and more, in an effort to give them better lives.

Broderick Harvey, Jr., born in 1991, is the son of Steve and his first wife, Marcia. He recently launched a shoe business. Broderick made an appearance on *Family Feud* when the family pitted the girls against the boys in an epic battle.

Wynton Harvey was born on July 18, 1997. He is the son of Steve and his second wife, Mary Lee Harvey. Wynton has been quoted as saying his father is his idol. He has served as a special guest host on his father's talk show, *Steve*, and also appears in some of the YouTube videos on his father's self-titled channel. In addition to these pursuits, he is involved in both modeling and photography.

Morgan Harvey-Hawthorne is Marjorie's first-born. When Marjorie and Steve married, all four of her children took on the Harvey surname and he raised them as his own. Morgan is married to Kareem Hawthorne, and the couple have one child – a daughter named Elle. Morgan also runs the food blog *Give Me Some Mo*.

Lori Harvey was born on January 13, 1997. She takes after her mother, Marjorie, and is pursuing a career in fashion. She is signed to two of the top modeling agencies in the world – LA Models and Select Model Management (in Europe).

Jason Harvey founded the luxury women's footwear company, Yevrah, in 2015. The company outsources all products and materials from Brazil. He is married to model, Amanda Harvey. The couple have three children, including Steve and Marjorie's youngest grandson, Ezra, who was born earlier this year. Ezra's older siblings are Noah and Rose, who made Instagram headlines when a video of them praying was shared.

Steve Harvey, born **Roderick Stephen Harvey** (January 17, 1957) in Welch, West Virginia, is the son of Jesse Harvey, a coal miner, and Eloise Vera. Harvey's family moved to Cleveland, Ohio, living on East 112th Street, which was renamed Steve Harvey Way in 2015. He graduated from Glenville High School in 1974. Shortly after high school, he attended Kent State University and West Virginia University and is a member of Omega Psi Phi fraternity. He has been a boxer, an autoworker, an insurance salesman, a carpet cleaner, and a mailman.

Steve Harvey is an American comedian, television host, producer, radio personality, actor, author and entrepreneur. He hosts *The Steve Harvey Morning Show*, the *Steve* talk show, *Family Feud*, *Celebrity Family Feud*, *Little Big Shots* and its spinoff *Little Big Shots: Forever Young*, *Steve Harvey's Funderdome*, *Showtime at the Apollo*, and since 2015, the Miss Universe pageant. He achieved further critical and commercial success through his book *Act Like a Lady, Think Like a Man* and its subsequent cinematic follow-up, *Think Like a Man*, an ensemble romantic comedy depicting characters taking advice on dating from the book. He is also a six-time Daytime Emmy Award winner and a 14-time NAACP Image Award winner.

Steve Harvey first performed stand-up comedy on October 8, 1985, at the Hilarities Comedy Club in Cleveland, Ohio. In the late '80s, Harvey was homeless for multiple years. He slept in his 1976 Ford when not performing gigs that provided a hotel, and he showered at gas stations or swimming pool showers.

He was a finalist in the Second Annual Johnnie Walker National Comedy Search performing on April 16, 1990, eventually leading to a long stint as host of *It's Showtime at the Apollo*, succeeding Mark Curry in that role. His success as a stand-up comedian led to a starring role on the short-lived ABC show *Me and the Boys* in 1994. He would later star on the WBnetwork show, *The Steve Harvey Show*, which ran from 1996 to 2002.

In 1997, Steve Harvey continued his work in stand-up comedy, performing on the Kings of Comedy tour along with Cedric the Entertainer, D.L. Hughley, and Bernie Mac. The comedy act would later be put together into a film by Spike Lee called *The Original Kings of Comedy*. DVD sales of *The Original Kings of Comedy* and *Don't*

Trip, He Ain't Through with Me Yet increased Harvey's popularity. He released a hip hop and R&B CD on a record label he founded, and authored the book *Steve Harvey's Big Time.*

That title was also used as the name of his comedy and variety television show (later renamed *Steve Harvey's Big Time Challenge*), which aired on The WB network from 2003 until 2005. Harvey launched a clothing line that featured dresswear. In 2005, he co-starred in the movie *Racing Stripes*. He had appeared in the 2003 movie *The Fighting Temptations* alongside Cuba Gooding Jr. and Beyoncé Knowles.

Steve Harvey also hosts, "The Steve Harvey Morning Show*." Ann Tripp and I have the pleasure of working with the "Steve Harvey Morning Show" on WBLS in New York. It is a nationally syndicated radio program, which features him and a team of comedians and commentators.*

Marjorie Harvey was born **Marjorie Elaine Bridges** (October 10, 1964) in Memphis Tennessee to mother Doris Bridges. Marjorie attended the University of Memphis and later pursued a fashion career. She has since become a household name. Marjorie is a popular fashion icon. She is a well-respected member of the fashion community and receives invitations to the majority of high-end social events, as well as invitations to attend Milan's Fashion Weeks.

Marjorie is the owner of online shopping sites, Marjorie Harvey's Closet and Marjorie Harvey handbags, but is perhaps best known as the creator of the fashion blog *Lady Loves Couture* in which she has made a lot of contribution regarding various fashion techniques. She started the blog to address the beauty needs of women and shows them how to lead a lavish life on any budget. The website offers quite a few beauty tips and range of lifestyle products to choose from. This initiative has helped Marjorie Harvey receive a lot of acclaim from all quarters. Marjorie is also a popular internet personality on various social media platforms like Facebook, Twitter, and Instagram with close to 2 million followers. She has fans from around the world.

The Harveys began the Steve and Marjorie Harvey Foundation (SMHF) which is aimed at uplifting the standard of living of children and families in different parts of the world. The Foundation provides youth outreach services that cultivates the next generation of responsible leaders by providing educational enrichment, mentoring, life transformation skills and global service initiatives.

Steve and Marjorie Harvey are model parents. They have accepted one another's children as their own. During an exclusive interview with *PEOPLE* magazine, Marjorie stated: "When you're dealing with a blended family, everyone is coming from a place of broken. I just told [the kids], 'Everyone is included. Everyone has access to their parents. Whatever you didn't have before, don't let that interfere with what you can have now.'"

Both Steve and Marjorie are firm believers that you need to raise children up to pray, believe in God, and of course, be good people. They also believe that you are supposed to do this in a 'lead by example' fashion. The Harveys divide their time between Atlanta, where Steve's radio show is broadcast and *Family Feud* is recorded, and Chicago, where he hosts his talk show for NBC Universal from the company's Chicago studios.

WILL SMITH & JADA PINKETT SMITH

Smith married actress Jada Pinkett on December 31, 1997 (New Year's Eve in 1997) about 100 guests attended their wedding at The Cloisters, near her hometown of Baltimore, Maryland.

Together Will and Jada have two children: Jaden Christopher Syre Smith (born 1998), his co-star in *The Pursuit of Happyness* and *After Earth*; and Willow Camille Reign Smith (born 2000), who appeared as his daughter in *I Am Legend*. Will is also the father and Jada, the stepmother of Trey Smith (born 1992), Will Smith's son with first wife Sheree Zampino.

Trey Smith, his half-brother Jaden, and the only daughter Willow were born to be lucky and famous thanks to their parent's amazing entertainment careers.

Will Smith was the "Fresh Prince" part of the 1980s musical pop duo D.J. Jazzy Jeff and the Fresh Prince, and by 1990 his charisma and infectious enthusiasm had landed him the lead in a TV sitcom, *The Fresh Prince of Bel Air*. Jada met Will Smith in 1994 on the set of Smith's television show *The Fresh Prince of Bel-Air*, when she auditioned for the role of his character's girlfriend, Lisa Wilkes. She was considered too short and the role went to actress Nia Long. Jada and Will became friends and began dating in 1995.

Jada Koren Pinkett Smith (born September 18, 1971) is an American actress, singer-songwriter, and businesswoman, wife of Will Smith. Born in Baltimore, Maryland, Jada Koren Pinkett was named after her mother's favorite soap-opera actress, Jada Rowland. Pinkett Smith is of Jamaican and Barbadian descent on her mother's side and African American descent on her father's side. Her parents are Adrienne Banfield-Norris, the head nurse of an inner-city clinic in Baltimore, and Robsol Pinkett, Jr., who ran a construction company.

Banfield-Norris became pregnant in high school; the couple married but divorced after several months. Banfield-Jones raised Pinkett with the help of her own mother, Marion Martin Banfield, a Boston born daughter of Jamaican immigrants, who was a social worker. Banfield noticed her granddaughter's passion for the performing arts and enrolled her in piano, tap dance, and ballet lessons. She has a younger brother, actor/writer Caleeb Pinkett.

Jada has remained close to her mother. The three generations of women: Jada, along with her mother Adrienne, and daughter Willow co-host a show, *Red Table Talk,* airing on Facebook Watch. The 10-episode series tackled issues such as sex, self-image, past relationships, and more. Jada feels that a mother and daughter's relationship is usually the most honest, and she and her mother are so close. She said that her mother understood what she wanted and never stood in her way.

Jada attended the Baltimore School for the Arts, where she met and became close friends with her classmate, rapper Tupac Shakur. She majored in dance and theatre and graduated in 1989. She continued her education at the North Carolina School of the Arts, and became fully invested in pursuing her acting career, which she began in in 1990 with a guest appearance on the sitcom *True Colors*. She subsequently starred in the television series *A Different World* (1991–1993) and then made her feature film debut in *Menace II Society* (1993). Her breakthrough came opposite Eddie Murphy in *The Nutty Professor* (1996), and she has since starred in more than 20 feature films.

Jada launched her music career in 2002, when she helped create the metal band Wicked Wisdom, for which she is a singer and songwriter. Along with her husband Will Smith, she has a production company, and has had producing credits in films, documentaries, and television series.

Perhaps her best-known role to date is the part of human rebel Niobe in the films *The Matrix Reloaded* (2003) and *The Matrix Revolutions* (2003), sequels to 1999's *The Matrix*, and the related video game *Enter The Matrix* (2003). The character was written specifically with Jada in mind. Directly after she filmed her scenes for *Ali*, Jada flew to Australia to work on the *Matrix* sequels. The sequels earned over $91 million and $48 million during their North American opening weekends, respectively.

Jada next took on the role of a nurse and uptight mom in the comedy *Girls Trip* (2017), alongside Regina Hall, Queen Latifah and Tiffany Haddish. The film was chosen by *Time* magazine as one of its top ten films of 2017, and grossed $140 million worldwide, including over $100 million domestically, the first comedy of 2017 to do so.

After opening her music company, 100% Womon Productions, Jada Pinkett Smith created her own fashion label, Maja, in 1994. The clothing line features women's T-shirts and dresses embellished with the slogan "Sister Power," sold primarily through small catalogs.

Pinkett Smith published her first children's book, *Girls Hold Up This World*, in 2004. She wrote the book for her daughter, Willow and for her friends and for all the little girls in the world who need affirmation about being female in this pretty much masculine world. She tried to capture different sides of femininity and wants girls in the world to feel powerful, to know they have the power to change the world in any way they wish.

Will Smith, born **Willard Carroll Smith Jr.** (September 25, 1968) is an American actor and rapper. In April 2007, *Newsweek* called him "the most powerful actor in Hollywood." Smith has been nominated for five Golden Globe Awards and two Academy Awards, and has won four Grammy Awards.

Smith was born in Philadelphia, Pennsylvania, to Caroline (Bright), a Philadelphia school board administrator and Willard Carroll Smith Sr., U.S. Air Force veteran and refrigeration engineer. He grew up in West Philadelphia's Wynnefield neighborhood, and was raised Baptist. He has an elder sister and two younger siblings (twins). Smith attended Our Lady of Lourdes, a private Catholic elementary school in Philadelphia. His parents separated when he was 13.

In the late 1980s, Smith achieved modest fame as a rapper under the name The Fresh Prince. Based on this success, the duo (DJ Jazzy Jeff & The Fresh Prince) were brought to the attention of Jive Records and Russell Simmons. The duo's first album, Rock the House, which was first released on Word Up in 1986 debuted on Jive in March of 1987. The group received the first Grammy Award for Best Rap Performance in 1989 for "Parents Just Don't Understand" (1988), though their most successful single was "Summertime" (1991), which earned the group their second Grammy and peaked at number 4 on the Billboard Hot 100. Smith and Townes are still friends and claim that they never split up, having made songs under Smith's solo performer credit.

In 1990, his popularity increased dramatically when he starred in the NBC television series *The Fresh Prince of Bel-Air*, which ran for six seasons until 1996. After the series ended, Smith transitioned from television to film, and has gone on to star in numerous blockbuster films. He is the only actor to have eight consecutive films gross over $100 million in the domestic box office, eleven consecutive films gross over $150 million internationally, and eight consecutive films in which he starred, open at the number one spot in the domestic box office tally.

Will Smith's television success led to film roles. His first major roles were in the drama *Six Degrees of Separation* (1993)and he won big at the box office with *Bad Boys* (1995) with Martin Lawrence, *Independence Day* (1996) with Jeff Goldblum, which was a massive blockbuster, becoming the second highest-grossing film in history at the time; and establishing Smith as a prime box office draw, and *Men in Black* (1997) with Tommy Lee Jones.

Smith is primarily known for his action/comic roles, but he's proven himself in dramas — nominated for an Oscar twice, as boxer Muhammad Ali in 2001's *Ali*, and as a down-on-his-luck dad in *The Pursuit of Happyness* (2006).

Smith has been ranked as the most bankable star worldwide by *Forbes*. As of 2014, 17 of the 21 films in which he has had leading roles have accumulated worldwide gross earnings of over $100 million each, five taking in over $500 million each in global box office receipts. As of 2016, his films have grossed $7.5 billion at the global box office. For his performances as boxer Muhammad Ali in *Ali* (2001) and stockbroker Chris Gardner in *The Pursuit of Happyness* (2006), Smith received nominations for the Academy Award for Best Actor.

His other films include *Enemy of the State* (1998) with Gene Hackman; *I, Robot* (2004) based on the novel by Isaac Asimov; *Hitch* (2005); and *I Am Legend* (2007).

Together with Will, Pinkett Smith has created the Will and Jada Smith Family Foundation in Baltimore, Maryland, a charity which focuses on youth in urban inner cities and family support. The charity was awarded the David Angell Humanitarian Award by The American Screenwriters Association (ASA) in 2006.

On December 10, 2007, Smith was honored at Grauman's Chinese Theatre on Hollywood Boulevard. Smith left an imprint of his hands and feet outside the world-renowned theater in front of many fans.

JOHN LEGEND & CHRISSY TEIGEN

Model and bestselling author Chrissy Teigen and R&B and Soul music sensation John Legend are a great image of a healthy relationship. Chrissy and John have two children: their daughter, Luna Simone Stephens born in April 2016 and on May 16, 2018, Teigen gave birth to Miles Theodore Stephens.

Before they got married John wrote the song "All of Me" which was dedicated to Chrissy. It first aired on American mainstream urban radio as the album's third single on August 12, 2013, a month before the wedding. On the week ending May 16, 2014, it peaked at number one on the *Billboard* Hot 100 becoming his first number-one single in the United States.

When Chrissy first heard "All of Me," she immediately knew the song was about her. She loved the song and cried when she heard it. Then starred in the intimate music video, which was filmed in Lake Como, Italy, the same place where they'd have their wedding that fall.

Just a few days before their grand Lake Como nuptials, the two had legally tied the knot in the States. They didn't realize that their Italian wedding would not be recognized unless they had a real ceremony in New York City; so, they went to the courthouse during Fashion Week to make it official.

After trying to have a baby for some time, the couple announced via Instagram that Chrissy was pregnant with their first child, Chrissy later shared that the child was conceived by way of IVF, and that she chose for her baby to be a girl.

Based on all the things that John Legend and Chrissy Teigen have shared about their children on social media so far, there's a lot to love about their kids, Luna and Miles. As they both get older, the family resemblance grows even stronger. What's most striking is exactly how much they look like their parents; in fact, Miles and Luna are basically Legend and Teigen's twins.

Teigen and Legend are both huge celebrities, but it's clear that they're super involved in their children's lives. In fact, John Legend made history as an EGOT (Emmy, Grammy, Oscar and Tony) winner, but the busy musician still makes plenty of time for his family. When Chrissy and John 's daughter, Luna, was in her first year of school, it sent her parents on a roller coaster of emotions that just keeps going, especially when they went to Luna's first parent-teachers conference.

Legend, has spoken out in the past about how important his teachers were to him while he was growing up and that they helped him get through the fact that his parents were getting divorced. He felt that, it was important to have teachers and counselors at school who could give him emotional support and that they took extra time to show him that they cared and were going to hold him accountable.

With parents like John and Chrissy, Luna and Miles will have teachers who are just as caring and kind as it sounds like their dad's teachers were. The two children have plenty of school ahead of them, and it looks like they'll have their parents' support every step of the way.

Chrissy Teigen was born **Christine Diane Teigen** on November 30, 1985, in Delta, Utah. The 5 feet 8 inches tall Chrissy Teigen is a model and television personality who is best known for being the color commentator in Spike TV's 'Lip Sync Battle', and she is a New York Times bestselling author. Her father is Norwegian-American Ron Teigen Sr., who worked as an electrician, and her mother Vilailuck is from Thailand. Chrissy spends much of her spare time on Twitter criticizing United States President Donald Trump. She maintains a very close relationship with her parents, who like their daughter, are very active on social media. Her mother, Vilailuck, better known as Pepper, has over 133,000 followers on Instagram and her father, Ron spends most of his time on Twitter discussing politics.

Chrissy's family lived in Utah, Idaho, and Hawaii; however, most of her childhood was spent in Seattle, Washington before moving to Huntington, California where they eventually settled down. Chrissy took a job at a surf shop to help make ends meet. She did not turn down the opportunity of becoming a model after she was approached by a photographer while working. At the young age of 18, she began the grueling journey to attain supermodel status. Chrissy spent the early years of her career doing catalog shoots and appearing in music videos. She notably appeared on the cover of Maxim's Calendar in 2007 and was used as a substitute model on the reality game show 'Deal or No Deal'.

Chrissy Teigen met John Legend in 2007 when she starred in one of his music videos and soon after started a relationship that lasted for four years before he proposed to her. They exchanged vows two years later in September 2013 at a ceremony held in Como, Italy.

Chrissy's big break came in 2010, at the age of 25, when she was featured as Rookie of the Year in that year's Sports Illustrated swimsuit issue. She went on to appear in the following years' editions, before later making the magazine's 50th-anniversary cover alongside Lily Aldridge and Nina Agdal in 2014. In between those times, Chrissy also appeared in other high-profile magazines, such as Cosmopolitan, Glamour, Esquire, and Italian Vogue.

In 2015, she was made the co-host of 'Lip Sync Battle' alongside LL Cool J after which she co-hosted the Billboard Music Awards with Ludacris. After becoming an established name in the modeling industry, Chrissy branched out to other things she had close to her heart, such as cooking. She further appears as a food stylist on the Tyra Banks talk show FABLife and authored one of the two bestselling cookbooks of 2016.

September 2018, John Legend and Chrissy Teigen celebrated two major milestones: their fifth wedding anniversary and the 12th year since the day they met.

John Legend, born **John Roger Stephens** (December 28, 1978) in Springfield, Ohio, is an American singer, songwriter, record producer and actor. Legend is one of four children of Phyllis Elaine (Lloyd), a seamstress, and Ronald Lamar Stephens, a factory worker at International Harvester. Legend was homeschooled by his mother. At the age of four, he performed with his church choir, and he began playing the piano at age seven. At the age of 12, Legend attended Springfield North High School, from which he graduated salutatorian of his class four years later. He attended the University of Pennsylvania, where he studied English with an emphasis on African-American literature.

While in college, Legend was introduced to Lauryn Hill by a friend. Hill hired him to play piano on "Everything Is Everything," a song from her album *The Miseducation of Lauryn Hill*. After finishing school, he began playing clubs on the east coast of the United States, gaining an audience and getting the notice of recording artists and producers as an accomplished studio musician. His session work in the late '90s and early '00s included guest spots with several top recording acts, but it was Kanye West who helped Legend leap into the spotlight and a deal with Columbia Records. Legend released his debut album, *Get Lifted*, on GOOD Music in December 2004. It featured production by Kanye West, Dave Tozer, and will.i.am, and debuted at number 7 on the US *Billboard* 200, selling 116,000 copies in its first week.

Legend, a piano player and singer who has also worked with Jay-Z and Alicia Keys, chose from the more than three dozen songs he'd been performing in clubs to put together *Get Lifted*, and by the end of 2005 the album had produced hit songs including "Used to Love U" and Song of the Year nominee "Ordinary People." John Legend also co-wrote Janet Jackson's "I Want You," which was certified platinum and received a nomination for Best Female R&B Vocal Performance at the 47th Annual Grammy Awards. A highly sought-after collaborator, Legend was featured on several records the following years.

His next release, *Once Again* (2006), included the singles "Save Room" and "Heaven," and then Legend turned his focus to writing songs for the likes of Whitney Houston, Jennifer Hudson and Aretha Franklin. In 2007, Legend received the Hal David Starlight Award from the Songwriters Hall of Fame. Legend was granted an Honorary Doctorate Degree from Howard University at the 144th Commencement Exercises on Saturday, May 12, 2012.

Legend released his fourth studio album, Love in the Future, on September 3, 2013, debuting number 4 on the Billboard 200, selling

68,000 copies in its first week. The album was nominated for Best R&B album at the 2014 Grammy Awards. Legend's third single from the album, "All of Me," became an international chart success, peaking the Billboard Hot 100 for three consecutive weeks and reaching the top of six national charts and the top ten in numerous other countries, becoming one of the best-selling digital singles of all time. It was ranked the third best-selling song in the United States and the United Kingdom during 2014. The song is a ballad dedicated to his wife, Chrissy Teigen, and was performed at the 56th Annual Grammy Awards.

In 2014, Legend partnered with the rapper Common to write the song "Glory," featured in the film Selma, which chronicled the 1965 Selma to Montgomery marches. The song won the Golden Globe Award for Best Original Song as well as the Academy Award for Best Original Song. Legend and Common performed "Glory" at the 87th Academy Awards on February 22, 2015.

Get Lifted earned Legend a total of eight nominations; he won Best New Artist and Best Male R&B Vocal Performance. He has also won ten Grammy Awards. In 2017, Legend received a Tony Award for co-producing Jitney for the Broadway stage. In 2018, Legend portrayed Jesus Christ in the NBC adaptation of the Andrew Lloyd Webber/Tim Rice rock opera Jesus Christ Superstar. He received a Primetime Emmy Award nomination for his acting role, and won for his role as a producer of the show, making him one of 15 people (and the first black man) to have won an Emmy, Grammy, Oscar and Tony. Legend is also the second youngest to achieve the EGOT status.

> *"I have learned that success is to be measured not so much by the position that one has reached in life as by the obstacles which he has had to overcome while trying to succeed."*
> -Booker T. Washington

CHAPTER TWO – THE TEACHER
FEATURING EDUCATORS THAT INFLUENCED THE NATION

If you are equipped with an education, an opportunity and a purpose, you can begin to lay the foundation to get whatever you want out of life and help others do the same. When you get knocked down, just get up and keep moving forward...there are a lot of hurdles in life...but there are a lot of heroes and sheroes who get over those hurdles. Because of the dedication and commitment of the thousands of teachers throughout the country and the world, our youth have an opportunity to build a meaningful future. Education, however, is but one component that must go into our commitment to give our youth the best possible platform for their successful future. I believe that no matter how long it takes, if you stick with something long enough change will always happens...but make sure it's positive.

BOOKER T. WASHINGTON

Booker T. Washington, born **Booker Taliaferro Washington** (April 5, 1856 – November 14, 1915) was an American educator, author, orator, and advisor to presidents of the United States. Between 1890 and 1915, Washington was the dominant leader in the African-American community.

In 1856, Washington was born into slavery in Virginia as the son of Jane, an African-American slave. After emancipation, she moved the family to West Virginia to join her husband Washington Ferguson.

In 1872, Booker T. Washington left home and walked 500 miles to attend Hampton Normal Agricultural Institute in Virginia. Booker convinced administrators to let him attend Hampton and he took odd jobs working as a janitor to help to support himself and to pay his tuition. The school's founder and headmaster, General Samuel C. Armstrong, soon discovered the hardworking boy and offered him a scholarship.

Armstrong, the son of Hawaiian missionaries, rose through the Union Army during the American Civil War, to become a General leading units of African American soldiers. He was a strong supporter of providing newly freed slaves with a practical education and became best known as an American educator, founding and becoming the first principal of the Hampton Normal Agricultural Institute for African-American and later Native American pupils, which later became Hampton University. Armstrong also founded the Hampton University Museum, which is the oldest African-American museum in the country, and the oldest museum in Virginia. Armstrong became Washington's mentor, strengthening his values of hard work and strong moral character.

Booker T. Washington graduated from Hampton in 1875 with high marks. For a time, he taught at his old grade school in Malden, Virginia, and attended Wayland Seminary in Washington, D.C. (now Virginia Union University).

In 1879, he was chosen to speak at Hampton's graduation ceremonies, where afterward General Armstrong offered Washington a job teaching at Hampton. In 1881, the Alabama legislature approved $2,000 for a "colored" school and Washington founded the Tuskegee Normal and Industrial Institute in Alabama (now known as Tuskegee University). The new school opened on July 4, 1881, initially using space in a local church.

The next year, Washington purchased a former plantation, which became the permanent site of the campus. Under his direction, his students literally built their own school: making bricks, constructing classrooms, barns and outbuildings; and growing their own crops and raising livestock; both for learning and to provide for most of the basic necessities. Washington later furthered his college education at Wayland Seminary.

Washington mobilized a nationwide coalition of middle-class blacks, church leaders, and white philanthropists and politicians, with a long-term goal of building the community's economic strength and pride by a focus on self-help and schooling. But, secretly, he also supported court challenges to segregation and restrictions on voter registration, passing on funds to the NAACP for this purpose.

While Washington traveled all over the countryside promoting Tuskegee Normal and Industrial Institute and raising money, he reassured whites that nothing in the Tuskegee program would threaten white supremacy or pose any economic competition to whites. He believed that by providing needed skills to society, African Americans would play their part, leading to acceptance by white Americans. He believed that Blacks would eventually gain full participation in society by acting as responsible, reliable American citizens.

Shortly after the Spanish–American War, President William McKinley and most of his cabinet visited Booker T. Washington. He led Tuskegee for the rest of his life, more than 30 years. As he developed it, adding to both the curriculum and the facilities on the campus, he became a prominent national leader among African Americans, with considerable influence with wealthy white philanthropists and politicians. He led the school until his death in 1915. By then Tuskegee's endowment had grown to over $1.5 million, compared to its initial $2,000 annual appropriation.

Booker T. Washington was a key proponent of African-American businesses and one of the founders of the National Negro Business League. His base was the Tuskegee Institute. As lynchings in the South reached a peak in 1895, Washington gave a speech, known as the "Atlanta Compromise," which brought him national fame. He called for Black progress through education and entrepreneurship, rather than trying to challenge directly the Jim Crow segregation and the disenfranchisement of Black voters in the South.

Washington played a dominant role in Black politics, winning wide support in the Black community of the South and among more liberal whites (especially rich Northern whites). He gained access to top national leaders in politics, philanthropy and education. Washington's efforts included cooperating with white people and enlisting the support of wealthy philanthropists.

He also gave lectures in support of raising money for the school. On January 23, 1906, he lectured at Carnegie Hall in New York, where he spoke along with great orators of the day, including: Mark Twain, Joseph Hodges Choate, and Robert Curtis Ogden. It was the start of a capital campaign to raise $1,800,000 for the school.

After 1909, Washington was criticized by the leaders of the new NAACP, especially W. E. B. Du Bois, who demanded a stronger tone of protest in order to advance the civil rights agenda. However, while encouraging cooperation with supportive whites, as the only way to overcome pervasive racism in the long run, Washington secretly funded litigation for civil rights cases. At the time, African Americans were strongly affiliated with the Republican Party, and Washington, who was on close terms with national Republican Party leaders, was often asked for political advice by presidents Theodore Roosevelt and William Howard Taft.

In addition to his contributions in education, Washington wrote 14 books. His autobiography, "Up from Slavery", first published in 1901, is still widely read today. During a difficult period of transition, he did much to improve the working relationship between the races. Washington's work greatly helped blacks to achieve higher education, financial power, and understanding of the U.S. legal system. This contributed to Blacks' attaining the skills to create and support the

Civil Rights Movement, leading to the passage of important federal civil rights laws.

Beginning in the 1920s, with the help of Julius Rosenwald, Washington raised funds to build and operate thousands of new, small rural schools and institutions of higher education to improve education for Blacks throughout the South. This work continued for many years after his death.

Despite his travels and widespread work, Washington remained as principal of Tuskegee. His health was deteriorating rapidly; and in 1915 he collapsed in New York City and was brought home to Tuskegee, where he died on November 14, 1915, at the age of 59. Years later, it was determined that examination of medical records indicated that he died of hypertension, with a blood pressure more than twice normal. He was buried on the campus of Tuskegee University near the University Chapel.

At his death Tuskegee's endowment exceeded $1.5 million. Washington's greatest life's work, the education of Blacks in the South, was well underway and expanding. On April 7, 1940, Washington became the first African American to be depicted on a United States postage stamp.

MARY MCLEOD BETHUNE

Mary Jane McLeod Bethune born **Mary Jane McLeod** (July 10, 1875 – May 18, 1955) was an American educator, stateswoman, philanthropist, humanitarian and civil rights activist, best known for starting a private school for African-American students in Daytona Beach, Florida. She attracted donations of time and money and developed the academic school as a college. It later continued to develop as Bethune-Cookman University. She also was appointed as a national adviser to President Franklin D. Roosevelt as part of what was known as his Black Cabinet. She was known as "The First Lady of The Struggle" because of her commitment to gain better lives for African Americans.

McLeod was born in a small log cabin near Mayesville, South Carolina, on a rice and cotton farm in Sumter County. She was the fifteenth of seventeen children born to Sam and Patsy (McIntosh) McLeod, both former slaves. Most of her siblings had been born into slavery. Her mother worked for her former master, and her father farmed cotton near a large house they called "The Homestead."

Mary started working in fields with her family at age five. She took an early interest in becoming educated. Mary attended Mayesville's one-room black schoolhouse, Trinity Mission School, which was run by the Presbyterian Board of Missions of Freedmen. She was the only child in her family to attend school, so each day, she taught her family what she had learned. To get to and from school, Mary walked five miles each day. Her teacher, Emma Jane Wilson, became a significant mentor in her life. Wilson had attended Scotia Seminary (now Barber-Scotia College). She helped McLeod attend the same school on a scholarship, which she did from 1888–1893.

The following year, Mary attended Dwight L. Moody's Institute for Home and Foreign Missions in Chicago (now the Moody Bible Institute), hoping to become a missionary in Africa.

She briefly worked as a teacher at her former elementary school in Sumter County. In 1896, she began teaching at Haines Normal and Industrial Institute in Augusta, Georgia, which was part of a Presbyterian mission organized by northern congregations. It was founded and run by Lucy Craft Laney. As the daughter of former slaves, Laney ran her school with a Christian missionary zeal, emphasizing character and practical education for girls. She also accepted the boys who showed up eager to learn.

Mary married Albertus Bethune in 1898, and they lived for a year in Savannah, Georgia, where she did social work. They had a son, named Albert. Coyden Harold Uggams, a visiting Presbyterian minister, persuaded the couple to relocate to Palatka, Florida, to run a mission school. The Bethunes moved in 1899. Mary ran the mission school and began an outreach to prisoners. Mary's husband, Albertus, left the family in 1907; he never got a divorce but relocated to South Carolina, where he died in 1918 from tuberculosis.

On October 3, 1904, a very determined Mary McLeod Bethune, rented a small house for $11.00 per month. She made benches and desks from discarded crates and acquired other items through charity. Mary used $1.50 to start the Educational and Industrial Training School for Negro Girls. She initially had six students—five girls aged six to twelve: Lena, Lucille, and Ruth Warren, Anna Geiger and Celest Jackson, and her son Albert.

The school bordered Daytona's dump. Bethune, parents of students, and church members raised money by making sweet potato pies, ice cream, and fried fish, and selling them to crews at the dump. In the early days, the students made ink for pens from elderberry juice, and pencils from burned wood; they asked local businesses for furniture. The school received donations of money, equipment, and labor from local black churches. Within a year, Bethune was teaching more than 30 girls at the school. She also courted wealthy white organizations, such as the ladies' Palmetto Club. She invited influential white men to sit on her school board of trustees, gaining participation by James Gamble (of Procter & Gamble) and Thomas H. White (of White Sewing Machines). When Booker T. Washington of Tuskegee Institute visited in 1912, he advised her of the importance of gaining support by white benefactors for funding. Bethune had met with Washington in 1896 and was impressed by his clout with his donors.

The rigorous curriculum had the girls rise at 5:30a.m. for Bible study. The classes in home economics and industrial skills such as dressmaking, millinery, cooking, and other crafts emphasized a life of self-sufficiency for them as women. Students' days ended at 9 pm. Soon Bethune added science and business courses, then high school-level courses of math, English, and foreign languages.

Through Dr. Bethune's lifetime the school underwent several stages of growth and development and on May 24, 1919, the Daytona

Educational and Industrial Institute was changed to Daytona Normal and Industrial Institute. In 1923 the school merged with Cookman Institute of Jacksonville, Florida (founded in 1872) and became co-ed while it also gained the prestigious United Methodist Church affiliation. Although the merger of Bethune's school and Cookman Institute began in 1923, it was not finalized until 1925 when both schools collaborated to become the Daytona-Cookman Collegiate Institute.

Bethune also served as the president of the Southeastern Federation of Colored Women's Clubs from 1920 to 1925, which worked to improve opportunities for black women. She was elected as national president of the NACW in 1924.

Gaining a national reputation, in 1928 Bethune was invited to attend the Child Welfare Conference called by Republican President Calvin Coolidge. In 1930 President Herbert Hoover appointed her to the White House Conference on Child Health.

Bethune was always seeking donations to keep her school operating; as she traveled, she was fundraising. A donation of $62,000 by John D. Rockefeller helped, as did her friendship with Franklin D. Roosevelt and his wife, beginning in the 1930s, who gave her entree to a progressive network.

In 1931, the College became accredited by the Association of Colleges and Secondary Schools of the Southern States, as a Junior College with class B status. On April 27, 1931, the Methodist Church helped the merger of her school with the boys' Cookman Institute, and the school's name was officially changed to Bethune-Cookman College to reflect the leadership of Dr. Mary McLeod Bethune. Thus, Mary became president of the Bethune-Cookman College, a coeducational junior college. Through the Great Depression, Bethune-Cookman

School continued to operate, and met the educational standards of the State of Florida.

Bethune was also active in women's clubs, which were strong civic organizations supporting welfare and other needs, and she became a national leader. After working on the presidential campaign for Franklin D. Roosevelt in 1932, she was invited as a member of his Black Cabinet. She advised him on concerns of Black people and helped share Roosevelt's message and achievements with Blacks, who had historically been Republican voters since the Civil War.

Bethune became a close and loyal friend of Eleanor and Franklin Roosevelt. She had unprecedented access to the White House through her relationship with the First Lady.

The National Youth Administration (NYA) was a federal agency created under Roosevelt's Works Progress Administration (WPA), which provided programs specifically to promote relief and employment for young people. Bethune was appointed to the position of Director of the Division of Negro Affairs, and as such, became the first African-American female division head. She was the only Black agent of the NYA who was a financial manager and she ensured Black colleges participation in the Civilian Pilot Training Program, which graduated some of the first Black pilots. More than 300,000 Black young men and women were given employment and work training on NYA projects.

In 1935 Bethune founded the National Council of Negro Women in New York City (NCNW), bringing together representatives of 28 different organizations to work to improve the lives of Black women and their communities.

In 1938, the NCNW hosted the White House Conference on Negro Women and Children, demonstrating the importance of black women in democratic roles. During World War II, the NCNW gained approval for Black women to be commissioned as officers in the Women's Army Corps. Bethune also served as a political appointee and the Special Assistant to the Secretary of War during the war.

From 1936 to 1942, Bethune had to cut back her time as president of the Bethune-Cookman College because of her duties in Washington, DC. She was one of the few women in the world to serve as a college president at that time. Funding declined during this period of her absence. But, by 1941 the college had developed a four-year curriculum and achieved full college status.

By 1942 Mary gave up the presidency, as her health was being adversely affected by her many responsibilities. However, she resumed responsibilities for a short time from 1946 to 1947.

On May 18, 1955, Bethune died of a heart attack. Her death was followed by editorial tributes in hundreds of newspapers across the United States.

In 1911, because of racial discrimination and serious injustices toward Black people, Mary had also opened the first Black hospital in Daytona, Florida. She found a cabin near the school and through sponsors helping her raise money, she purchased it for five thousand dollars. The hospital started with two beds and within a few years, held twenty. Both white and Black physicians worked at the hospital, along with Bethune's student nurses. This hospital went on to save many Black lives within the twenty years that it operated. In 1931, Daytona's public hospital, Halifax, agreed to open a separate hospital for people of color, but Black people would not fully integrate to the public hospital's main location until the 1960's.

Mary McLeod Bethune's Honors include designation of her home in Daytona Beach as a National Historic Landmark, her house in

Washington, D.C. as a National Historic Site, and the installation of a memorial sculpture of her in Lincoln Park in Washington, D.C. The Legislature of Florida designated her in 2018 as the subject of one of Florida's two statues in the National Statuary Hall Collection.

BETTY SHABAZZ

Betty Shabazz, born **Betty Dean Sanders** (May 28, 1934 – June 23, 1997) and also known as **Betty X**, was an American educator and civil rights advocate. She was the wife of Malcolm X and the mother of six daughters.

Betty Dean Sanders parents were Ollie Mae Sanders and Shelman Sandlin. Sandlin was 21 years old and Ollie Mae Sanders was a teenager; the couple was unmarried. When Betty was about 11 years old, she was taken in by Lorenzo and Helen Malloy, a prominent businessman and his wife. Helen Malloy was a founding member of the Housewives League of Detroit, a group of African-American women who organized campaigns to support Black-owned businesses and boycott stores that refused to hire Black employees. She was also a member of the National Council of Negro Women and the NAACP.

After she graduated from high school, Sanders left her foster parents' home in Detroit to study at the Tuskegee Institute (now Tuskegee University), a historically black college in Alabama that was Lorenzo Malloy's alma mater. She intended to earn a degree in education and become a teacher; but while there, Betty had her first encounters with racism. Unhappy with the situation in Alabama, she moved to New York City, where she became a nurse. It was there that she met Malcolm X and, in 1956, joined the Nation of Islam. The couple married in 1958.

Along with her husband, Malcolm X, Betty left the Nation of Islam on March 8, 1964. He and Betty X, now known as Betty Shabazz, became Sunni Muslims. On February 21, 1965, in Manhattan's Audubon Ballroom, Malcolm X began to speak to a meeting of the Organization of Afro-American Unity when a disturbance broke out in the crowd of 400. Malcom X was assassinated by members of the Nation of Islam, who were later convicted and sentenced to life in prison. Betty Shabazz witnessed her husband's assassination as she attempted to shield her daughters from viewing the horrific scene.

The couple had six daughters. Their names were Attallah, born in 1958 and named after Attila the Hun; Qubilah, born in 1960 and named after Kublai Khan; Ilyasah, born in 1962 and named after Elijah Muhammad; Gamilah Lumumba, born in 1964 and named after Patrice Lumumba; and twins, Malikah and Malaak, born in 1965 after their father's assassination and named for him.

Left with the responsibility of raising six daughters as a single mother, Shabazz pursued a higher education, and went to work at Medgar Evers College in Brooklyn, New York. Actor and activist Ruby Dee and Juanita Poitier (wife of Sidney Poitier) established the Committee of Concerned Mothers, to raise funds to buy a house, and pay educational expenses for the Shabazz family. The Committee held a series of benefit concerts at which they raised $17,000. They bought a large two-family home in Mount Vernon, New York, from Congressmember Bella Abzug.

Shabazz suffered from nightmares in which she relived the death of her husband. She also worried about how she would support herself and her family. In late March 1965, Shabazz made the pilgrimage to Mecca (Hajj), as her husband had the year before. Shabazz returned from Mecca with a new name that a fellow pilgrim had bestowed upon her, Bahiyah.

The publication of The Autobiography of Malcolm X helped, because Shabazz received half of the royalties. Alex Haley, who assisted Malcolm X in writing the book, got the other half. After the publication of his best-seller Roots, Haley signed over his portion of the royalties to Betty. Her share of the royalties from The Autobiography of Malcolm X was equivalent to an annual salary. In 1966, she sold the movie rights to the Autobiography to film-maker Marvin Worth. She began to authorize the publication of Malcolm X's speeches, which provided another source of income.

When her daughters were enrolled in day care, Shabazz became an active member of the day care center's parent's organization. In time, she became the parents' representative on the school board. Several years later, she became president of the Westchester Day Care Council.

Shabazz began to accept speaking engagements at colleges and universities. She often spoke about the black nationalist philosophy of Malcolm X, but she also spoke about her role as a wife and mother. As her daughters grew older, Shabazz sent them to private schools and summer camps. They joined Jack and Jill, a social club for the children of well-off African Americans.

In late 1969, Shabazz enrolled at Jersey City State College (now New Jersey City University) to complete the degree in education she left behind when she became a nurse. She completed her undergraduate studies in one year and decided to earn a master's degree in health administration. In 1972, Shabazz enrolled at the University of Massachusetts Amherst to pursue an Ed.D. in higher education administration and curriculum development. For the next three years, she drove from Mount Vernon, New York to Amherst, Massachusetts, every Monday morning, and returned home Wednesday night. In July 1975, she defended her dissertation and earned her doctorate.

In January 1976, Shabazz became associate professor of health sciences with a concentration in nursing at New York's Medgar Evers College. By 1980, Shabazz was overseeing the health sciences department, and the college president decided she could be more effective in a purely administrative position than she was in the classroom. She was promoted to Director of Institutional Advancement. In her new position, she became a booster and fund-raiser for the college. A year later, she was given tenure. In 1984, Shabazz was given a new title, Director of Institutional Advancement and Public Affairs; she held that position at the college until her death.

During the 1970s and 1980s, Shabazz continued her volunteer activities. In 1975, President Ford invited her to serve on the American Revolution Bicentennial Council. Shabazz served on an advisory committee on family planning for the U.S. Department of Health and Human Services. In 1984, she hosted the New York convention of the National Council of Negro Women. Shabazz became active in the NAACP and the National Urban League. When Nelson and Winnie Mandela visited Harlem during 1990, Shabazz was asked to introduce Winnie Mandela.

Shabazz befriended Myrlie Evers-Williams, the widow of Medgar Evers, and Coretta Scott King, the widow of Martin Luther King Jr. They had the common experience of losing their activist husbands at a young age and raising their children as single mothers. The press came to refer to the three, who made numerous joint public appearances, as the "Movement widows".

For many years, Betty Shabazz harbored resentment toward the Nation of Islam—and Louis Farrakhan in particular—for what she felt was their role in the assassination of her husband.

In January 1995, Qubilah Shabazz was charged with trying to hire an assassin to kill Farrakhan in retaliation for the murder of her father. Farrakhan later defended Qubilah, saying he did not think she was guilty, and that May, Betty Shabazz and Farrakhan shook hands on the stage of the Apollo Theater during a public event intended to raise money for Qubilah's legal defense. Nearly $250,000 was raised that evening. In the aftermath, Shabazz agreed to speak at his Million Man March that October.

Following the arrest of her daughter Qubilah for allegedly conspiring to murder Louis Farrakhan, Betty Shabazz took in her ten-year-old grandson Malcolm. On June 1, 1997, young Malcolm set a fire in Shabazz's apartment. Shabazz suffered burns over 80 percent of her body, and remained in intensive care for three weeks, at Jacobi Medical Center in the Bronx, New York. She died of her injuries on June 23, 1997. Shabazz was buried next to her husband, El-Hajj Malik El-Shabazz (Malcolm X), at Ferncliff Cemetery in Hartsdale, New York.

There are many memorials honoring Betty Shabazz: In late 1997, the Community Healthcare Network renamed one of its Brooklyn, New York, clinics the Dr. Betty Shabazz Health Center, in honor of Shabazz. The Betty Shabazz International Charter School was founded in Chicago, Illinois, in 1998 and named in her honor. In 2005, Columbia University announced the opening of the Malcolm X and Dr. Betty Shabazz Memorial and Educational Center. The memorial is located in the Audubon Ballroom, where Malcolm X was assassinated. In March 2012, New York City co-named Broadway at the corner of West 165th Street, the corner in front of the Audubon Ballroom, Betty Shabazz Way.

BOBBY AUSTIN

Bobby William Austin (December 29, 1944) founded the Village Foundation, an organization dedicated to "repairing the breach" between African American males and the rest of society. Its mission is to engage African American young men and boys in American society, by reconnecting them first to their local communities and then to the larger society. One of the leading initiatives of the Village Foundation today is the Give a Boy a Book Day campaign. This program is designed to encourage reading and literacy in young African American men. He continues to serve there as the president and CEO.

Austin was born in Jonesville, Kentucky. His father, Herschel, worked as a porter on the L&N Railroad, and his mother, Mary, was a homemaker. His mother instilled in him a passion that would remain with Austin throughout his life: literature. As a child, he would receive books for Christmas instead of toys, and he would carry them everywhere with him. After graduating from the High Street High School in Bowling Green, Kentucky, Austin went on to attend Western Kentucky University, also in Bowling Green, earning his B.A. degree in economics and sociology in 1966. From there, he attended Fisk University, earning his master's degree in sociology in 1968 and then went on to earn his Ph.D. from McMaster University in Hamilton, Ontario, Canada in 1972.

After completing his doctoral studies, Austin relocated to Washington, D.C., where he became involved with a number of organizations. He was the founder and editor of the *Urban League Review*, and he also served as a partner with Austin Ford Associates, a Washington, D.C. based consulting firm. Following these positions, Austin became an executive assistant to the president of the University of the District of Columbia (UDC), and later served as an assistant to the UDC Board of Trustees and the late Secretary of Commerce Ron Brown. He has also worked as a speechwriter for former Housing and Urban Development Secretary Patricia Roberts Harris and the former mayor of Washington, D.C. Sharon Pratt Kelly. From 1986 until 1998, Austin was the program director for the W.K. Kellogg Foundation.

In 1997, Austin founded the Village Foundation. He also serves as the Mohatma M.K. Gandhi Fellow of the American Academy of Political and Social Science, and on the boards of the National Housing Trust and the National Institute for Urban Wildlife.

RAMONA EDELIN

Ramona Edelin (September 4, 1945) was born in Los Angeles, California. At an early age, Edelin's family relocated to Atlanta, Georgia, where she attended elementary school. She went on to Carbondale, Illinois, for some high school; then she graduated from Stockbridge High School in Massachusetts in 1963. Following graduation, Edelin attended Fisk University in Nashville, Tennessee, earning her B.A. degree in 1967, and then studied at the University of East Anglia in Norwich, England, for her M.A. degree, completing the program in 1969. Edelin later resumed her education, completing her Ph.D. degree at Boston University in 1981.

After earning her master's degree, Edelin became the founder and chair of the Department of African American Studies at Northeastern University. In 1977, Edelin joined the National Urban Coalition, where she eventually rose to the positions of president and CEO, which she maintained from 1988 until 1998. Under Edelin's guidance, the NUC initiated the *Say Yes to a Youngster's Future* program, which provided math, science, and technology assistance to youth and teachers of color in urban settings.

Under the National Science Foundation's Urban Systemic Initiative, this program was brought to more than two hundred schools nationwide and was eventually partnered with the *Laboratory for Student Success* within the United States Department of Education. Edelin also created the M. Carl Holman Leadership Development Institute and the Executive Leadership Program, bringing minorities into leadership development opportunities.

She was elected a member of the Board of Directors of the Congressional Black Caucus Foundation, Inc. in 1991, was elected its Executive Director in February of 1998 and served in that capacity until June of 2002.

In 1998, President Bill Clinton appointed Edelin to the Presidential Board on Historically Black Colleges and Universities; she also accompanied the President on his trip to South Africa that same year. Edelin went on to serve as treasurer of the Black Leadership Forum, which she co-founded.

Dr. Edelin served as Vice President, Policy and Outreach of the Corporation for Enterprise Development (CFED) from September of 2003 through August of 2004. She also served on a wide array of committees and boards of directors, having chaired the District of Columbia Educational Goals 2000 Panel; sitting on the board of the Federal Advisory Committee for the Black Community Crusade for Children; and chairing the board of the D.C. Community Humanities Council.

A resident of Washington, D.C., Edelin was recognized by Ebony as one of the 100 Most Influential Black Americans; earned the Southern Christian Leadership Award for Progressive Leadership; and received the IBM Community Executive Program Award.

CORNEL WEST

Cornel West, (June 2, 1953) was born in Tulsa, Oklahoma. Dr. West is an American philosopher, scholar of African American studies, and political activist. His influential book *Race Matters* (1993) lamented what he saw as the spiritual impoverishment of the African American underclass and critically examined the "crisis of black leadership" in the United States.

West grew up in Sacramento, California, where he graduated from John F. Kennedy High School. His mother, Irene, was a teacher and principal, and his father, Clifton Louis West Jr., was a general contractor for the Defense Department. Irene B. West Elementary School in Elk Grove, California, is named for his mother.

During West's childhood the family settled in an African American working-class neighborhood in Sacramento, California. There West regularly attended services at the local Baptist church, where he listened to moving testimonials of privation, struggle, and faith from parishioners whose grandparents had been slaves. Another influence on West during this time was the Black Panther Party, whose Sacramento offices were near the church he attended. The Panthers impressed upon him the importance of political activism at the local level and introduced him to the writings of Karl Marx.

As a young man, West marched in civil rights demonstrations and organized protests demanding black studies courses at his high school, where he was class president.

In 1970, at age 17, West entered Harvard University on a scholarship and took classes from philosophers Robert Nozick and Stanley Cavell. He graduated magna cum laude three years later with a bachelor's degree in Middle Eastern languages and literature. He credits Harvard with exposing him to a broader range of ideas, influenced by his professors as well as the Black Panther Party.

He attended graduate school in philosophy at Princeton University, where he was influenced by the American pragmatist philosopher Richard Rorty. In his late-20s, he returned to Harvard as a W. E. B. Du Bois Fellow.

In 1984, he went to Yale Divinity School in what eventually became a joint appointment in American Studies. While at Yale, he participated in campus protests for a clerical labor union and divestment from apartheid South Africa. One of the protests resulted in his being arrested and jailed. As punishment, the University administration canceled his leave for the spring term in 1987, leading him to commute from Yale in New Haven, Connecticut, where he was teaching two classes, across the Atlantic Ocean to the University of Paris.

He then returned to Union Theological Seminary for one year before going to Princeton to become a professor of religion and director of the Program in African-American Studies from 1988 to 1994. After Princeton, he accepted an appointment as professor of African-American studies at Harvard University, with a joint appointment at the Harvard Divinity School. West taught one of the University's most popular courses, an introductory class on African-American studies. In 1998, he was appointed the first Alphonse Fletcher University Professor. West utilized this new position to teach in not only African-American studies, but also in divinity, religion, and philosophy. West left Harvard after a widely publicized dispute with then-President Lawrence Summers in 2002.

That year, West returned to Princeton, where he helped create "one of the world's leading centers for African-American studies" according to Shirley Tilghman, Princeton's president in 2011. In 2012, West left Princeton and returned to the institution where he began his teaching career, Union Theological Seminary. His departure from Princeton, unlike his departure from Harvard, was quite amicable. As of 2017, he continues to teach occasional courses at Princeton in an emeritus capacity as the Class of 1943 University Professor in the Center for African American Studies.

The recipient of more than 20 honorary degrees and an American Book Award, Cornel West has written 20 books and edited 13. He has a passion to communicate to a vast variety of publics in order to keep alive the legacy of Martin Luther King, Jr. – a legacy of telling the truth and bearing witness to love and justice West is an outspoken voice in American leftist politics, and as such has been critical of members of the Democratic Party. From 2010 through 2013, West co-hosted a radio program with Tavis Smiley, called Smiley and West.

JOE LOUIS CLARK

Joe Louis Clark (May 7, 1938) was born in Rochelle, Georgia and grew up in Newark, New Jersey where he attended Central High School. Clark worked while attending high school to support his mother and siblings. He then went on to get his bachelor's degree from William Paterson College and a master's degree from Seton Hall University. In addition, Clark received an honorary doctorate from the U.S. Sports Academy.

Joe Louis Clark is a former Army drill instructor and has always seen education as a mission. As the former principal of Eastside High School in Paterson, one of New Jersey's toughest inner-city schools, he is referred to as the "bat-toting principal." A 20-year veteran of the Paterson school system, he had taken the helm of Eastside High in 1982 until 1990, and restored order with a bullhorn and a baseball bat.

Clark's experience is that young people, who are notoriously susceptible to outside pressures, have a way of meeting adult expectations of them, so such expectations should be set high. He argues that by making excuses for young blacks, society has set lower expectations for them.

Clark disagrees with those who believe the learning process is disrupted by tough discipline. Clark said he held high expectations for students, challenging them to develop habits for success and confronting them when they failed to perform. On a single day during his first week at Eastside, **without asking the school board's approval**, Clark expelled 300 students for fighting, vandalism, drug possession, profanity, or abusing teachers; in other words, "hoodlums" who were frequently tardy or absent from school, sold or used drugs in school, or caused trouble in school. Clark was seen as an educator who was not afraid to get tough on difficult students.

He deliberately disobeyed fire codes by keeping school exit doors chained to keep the dealers from coming back. He announced his own dress code and suspension policies, and he fired administrators who dared to challenge him. His practices did result in slightly higher average test scores for Eastside High during the 1980s.

Clark is the subject of the 1989 film "Lean on Me", starring Morgan Freeman. He gained public attention in the 1980s for his unconventional and controversial disciplinary measures as the principal of Eastside High.

February 1, 1988, Joe Clark was on the cover of *Time magazine*. Criticism focused on the social impact of expelling delinquent students to improve test scores, claiming that "tossing out the troublesome low achievers" simply moved the problems from the school onto the street. Clark defended the practice, saying teachers should not have to waste their time on students who do not want to learn.

Time magazine noted that the national dropout rate for such students remained high across the country, with few alternatives available, and that each inner-city school that had been able to reverse the trend had done so through "a bold, enduring principal" such as Clark who was "able to maintain or restore order without abandoning the students who are in trouble."

However, even as Clark was being cheered by U.S. Education Secretary William J. Bennett for his tough policies, the critics moved in. The teachers' union accused the principal of "making teen-agers the enemy."

Despite the controversy, President Ronald Reagan named him a model educator and offered him a White House post as a policy adviser. Clark turned it down.

Clark used the publicity to make his argument for more rigorous academic standards. He was widely quoted as saying that some students would have to fail for others to succeed. His bullheadedness attracted Hollywood, with Morgan Freeman playing him in the 1989 movie "Lean on Me." However, the publicity, combined with heart problems, forced him out of the Eastside job. So, he turned to the lecture circuit for six years, though Clark says he yearned for a new challenge and venue to fight against what he calls "institutional racism."

After retiring from Eastside High, against the advice of officials who thought he would be unmanageable, Essex County Executive James Treffinger offered Clark a job at a decaying, inner-city the juvenile detention center. When he accepted the offer, the irony that he would now be responsible for the kind of teen-agers he once threw out of Eastside was not lost on Clark. He decided to take a more spiritual tact, bringing in ministers and encouraging inmates to study the Bible.

In 1993, a federal court had appointed a master to oversee the rat-infested center. Despite some improvements, Essex County's youth detention facility was a disgrace, and any director seemed doomed to fail. But Clark said that Master Bennet Zurofsky helped turn the center around. There were visits from ministers and teachers. A new boot camp and discipline that is unusual for such a facility.

In August 1995, he was appointed director of Essex County Detention House, a juvenile detention center in Newark, NJ, which housed teen-agers accused of murder, theft, rape, and more. During his six years as the center's director, he continued his challenging work to bring change to the community that brought him up. Some of Clark's old critics were happy to see him take a job in a field in which he had no experience. The Essex County youth center houses more than 200 teen-agers in a facility built for half that. The inmates are 95 percent black and 5 percent Hispanic. The average stay, as the young people await trial, is 60 days.

The state of New Jersey may have held the deed, but the building belonged to Joe Clark. A list of rules, signed by Clark and posted at the entrance, noted that even state officials must comply, and concluded with a favorite phrase of the director: "No exceptions will be tolerated."

He also issued new rules banning packages to detainees (a common drug entry method) and establishing a dress code for visitors to the center.

He has been writing and speaking more, advocating orphanages as a way to reduce the prison population. Sometimes he thinks about his days at Eastside High School, and about how very little has changed. "My tactics are still the same," he says. "There's very little difference between a school and a jail, when you think about it. The only real difference is that many people in the schools have not been incarcerated yet."

When Clark accepted the position as director of Essex County Detention House, he said, "I will stay until I have brought about change. I can't think of anything more noble." He retired in 2001 at the age of 73.

Clark is the father of Olympic track athletes Joetta Clark Diggs and Hazel Clark, and the father-in-law of Olympic track athlete Jearl Miles Clark. His son, JJ Clark, was their coach. Joe Louis Clark currently resides in Newberry, Florida.

ALEXANDER TWILIGHT

Alexander Lucius Twilight (September 23, 1795 - June 19, 1857) was an American educator, minister and politician. Alexander Lucius Twilight was born, at Corinth, Vermont. Both his parents were free and mixed race, of African and English descent. It is unknown if they were born free; they were likely descendants of African slaves and English ancestors. His father Ichabod Twilight was a Revolutionary War veteran from New Hampshire. His mother Mary was described as 'white' or 'light-skinned,' implying she was of partial African descent. His parents were both listed in the Corinth town history as "the first negroes to settle in Corinth."

Starting around 1802 when he was eight years old, Twilight worked for a neighboring farmer in Corinth. Working from an early age was typical of working-class children of his era. For the next 12 years he read, studied, and learned mathematics while working in various farm labor positions. Twilight enrolled in Randolph's Orange County Grammar School in 1815 at the age of 20. From 1815 to 1821, he completed all the institution's secondary school courses as well as the first two years of a college-level curriculum. He enrolled in

Middlebury College in 1821, where he graduated in 1823 with a Bachelor of Arts degree.

Alexander Twilight is the first African-American man known to have earned a bachelor's degree from an American college or university, graduating from Middlebury College in 1823. He was licensed as a Congregational preacher and worked in education and ministry all his career. His first job was teaching in Peru, New York. Twilight also studied for the ministry with the Congregational Church and served several Congregational churches. He occasionally led worship services and delivered sermons. The Champlain Presbytery of Plattsburgh licensed him to preach. Twilight taught for four years in Peru, then moved to Vergennes, Vermont in 1828 to teach during the week and hold weekend church services in Waltham and Ferrisburg.

In 1829 Twilight became principal of the Orleans County Grammar School. Wanting to create a residence dormitory to accommodate out of town students, from 1834-1836 Twilight designed, raised funds for, and had built a massive four-story granite building which he called Athenian Hall. The first granite public building in Vermont, it served as a dormitory for the co-educational school, also known as the Brownington Academy. Both his home and Athenian Hall are today part of a historic district listed on the National Register of Historic Places.

In 1836 Alexander Twilight was the first African-American elected as a state legislator, serving in the Vermont House of Representatives; he was also the only African-American ever elected to a state legislature before the Civil War.

Twilight left his job as headmaster in 1847, and taught school in Shipton and Hatley, Quebec. Without Twilight's leadership, the school in Brownington experienced declining enrollment, and it was closed in 1852. Persuaded to return to Brownington, Twilight resumed his duties as principal and pastor. He resigned as pastor in 1853, and continued as principal until 1855, when he suffered a stroke which left him partially paralyzed and caused him to retire as principal of the Brownington school. Alexander Twilight died on June 19, 1857 and was buried at the Congregational church in Brownington.

In 1826, Twilight married Mercy Ladd Merrill of Unity, New Hampshire. They remained married until his death and had no children. Mercy Twilight died in 1878.

CHARLOTTE FORTEN GRIMKÉ

Charlotte Louise Bridges Forten Grimké (August 17, 1837 – July 23, 1914) was an African-American anti-slavery activist, poet, and educator. She grew up in a prominent abolitionist family in Philadelphia. She taught school for years, including during the Civil War, to freedmen in South Carolina. Later in life she married Francis James Grimké, a Presbyterian minister who led a major church in Washington, DC, for decades. He was a nephew of the abolitionist Grimké sisters and active in civil rights.

Charlotte's diaries, written before the end of the Civil War have been published in numerous editions in the 20th century and are significant as a rare record of the life of a free Black woman in the North in the antebellum years.

Charlotte, known as "Lottie," was born in Philadelphia, Pennsylvania, to Mary Virginia Wood (1815-1840) and Robert Bridges Forten (1813-1864), members of the prominent Black Forten-Purvis clan of Philadelphia. Robert Forten and his brother-in-law Robert Purvis were abolitionists and members of the Philadelphia Vigilance Committee, an anti-slavery network that rendered assistance to escaped slaves. Charlotte 's mother, paternal aunts Margaretta Forten and Harriet Forten Purvis, and grandmother, Charlotte Vandine Forten, were all founding members of the Philadelphia Female Anti-Slavery Society. Her grandfather, wealthy sailmaker James Forten, Sr., was an early equal rights activist in Philadelphia.

While the Fortens were free northern Blacks, Charlotte's mother, Mary Virginia Wood, was the daughter of wealthy planter, James Cathcart Johnston of Hayes Plantation, Edenton, North Carolina, and granddaughter of Governor Samuel Johnston of North Carolina. Mary and her mother, Edith "Edy" Wood (1795-1846) were the slaves of Captain James Wood, owner of the Eagle Inn and Tavern in Hertford, Perquimans County, North Carolina.

Edy Wood and James Cathcart Johnston carried on a longstanding relationship and had four daughters: Mary Virginia, Caroline (1827-1836), Louisa (1828-1836), and Annie E. (1831-1879). Johnston emancipated Edy and their children in 1832 and settled them in Philadelphia in 1833 where they rented a Pine Street home for two years from Sarah Allen, widow of Richard Allen of Philadelphia's Mother Bethel A.M.E. Church. The following year, from 1835 through 1836, Edy Wood and her children boarded with Elizabeth Willson, mother of Joseph Willson, author of "Sketches of Black Upper-Class Life in Antebellum Philadelphia."

After Mary Virginia Wood's 1836 marriage to Robert B. Forten, her mother Edy joined the Forten household and paid board to her son-in-law. When Mary Wood Forten died of tuberculosis in 1840, Edy Wood continued to care for her grandchild Charlotte alongside Charlotte's young aunt, Annie Wood, who was only six years older. Upon Edy Wood's death in 1846, Charlotte was raised by various members of the

Forten-Purvis family, and her aunt Annie lived at the Cassey House where she was adopted by Amy Matilda Cassey.

In 1854, Charlotte joined the household of Amy Matilda Cassey and her second husband, Charles Lenox Remond, in Salem, Massachusetts, where she attended the Higginson Grammar School, a private academy for young women. She was the only non-white student in a class of 200. Known for emphasis in critical thinking, the school had classes in history, geography, drawing and cartography, and placed an emphasis on critical thinking skills. After Higginson, Charlotte studied literature and teaching at the Salem Normal School, which trained teachers. Charlotte cited William Shakespeare, John Milton, Margaret Fuller and William Wordsworth as some of her favorite authors.

In 1856, finances forced Charlotte to take a teaching position at Eppes Grammar School in Salem. She was the first African American teacher hired to teach white students in a Salem public school. She was well received as a teacher but returned to Philadelphia after two years due to tuberculosis. At this point, Charlotte began writing poetry, much of which was activist in theme. Her poetry was published in The Liberator and Anglo African magazines.

Charlotte became a member of the Salem female Anti-Slavery Society, where she was involved in coalition building and fundraising. She proved to be influential as an activist and leader on civil rights. She occasionally spoke to public groups on abolitionist issues. In addition, she arranged for lectures by prominent speakers and writers, including Ralph Waldo Emerson and Senator Charles Sumner. Charlotte was acquainted with many other anti-slavery proponents, including William Lloyd Garrison, editor of The Liberator, and the orators and activists Wendell Phillips, Maria Weston Chapman and William Wells Brown.

During the American Civil War, Charlotte was the first black teacher to join the mission to the South Carolina Sea Islands known as the Port Royal Experiment. The Union allowed Northerners to set up schools to begin teaching freedmen who remained on the islands, which had been devoted to large plantations for cotton and rice. The Union forces divided the land, giving freedmen families plots to work independently. Charlotte worked with many freedmen and their children on St. Helena Island. During this time, she resided at Seaside Plantation. She chronicled this time in her essays, entitled "Life on the Sea Islands", which were published in Atlantic Monthly in the May and June issues of 1864. Charlotte struck up a deep friendship with Robert Gould Shaw, the Commander of the all-black 54th Massachusetts Regiment during the Sea Islands Campaign. She was present when the 54th stormed Fort Wagner on the night of July 18, 1863. Shaw was killed in the battle, and Forten volunteered as a nurse to the surviving members of the 54th.

Following the war in the late 1860s, Charlotte worked for the U.S. Treasury Department in Washington, DC, recruiting teachers. In 1873 she became a clerk in the Department.

In December 1878, Charlotte Forten married Presbyterian minister Francis J. Grimké, pastor of the prominent Fifteenth Street Presbyterian Church in Washington, D.C., a major African-American congregation. He was a mixed-race nephew of white abolitionists Sarah and Angelina Grimké of South Carolina. Francis and his brother Archibald Grimké were the sons of Henry Grimke and Nancy Weston (a woman of color). At the time of their marriage, Forten was 41 years old and Grimke was 28.

On January 1, 1880, Charlotte and Francis' daughter Theodora Cornelia was born, but the child died less than five months later. Charlotte Forten Grimké helped her husband in his ministry at

Fifteenth Street Presbyterian Church in Washington, DC., helping create important networks in the community, including providing charity and education. Many church members were leaders in the African-American community in the capital. She organized a women's missionary group and continued her "racial uplift" efforts.

FANNY JACKSON COPPIN

Fanny Jackson Coppin (January 8, 1837 – January 21, 1913) was an African-American educator and missionary and a lifelong advocate for female higher education.

Born an American slave, Fanny Jackson's freedom was purchased by her aunt at age 12. Fanny Jackson spent the rest of her youth working as a servant for author George Henry Calvert, studying at every opportunity. In 1860, she enrolled in Oberlin College in Ohio, the first college in the United States to accept both black and female students.

Fanny writes in her autobiography: "The faculty did not forbid a woman to take the gentleman's course, but they did not advise it. There was plenty of Latin and Greek in it, and as much mathematics as one could shoulder. Now, I took a long breath and prepared for a delightful contest. All went smoothly until I was in the junior year in College. Then, one day, the Faculty sent for me--ominous request--and I was not slow in obeying it. It was a custom in Oberlin that forty students from the junior and senior classes were employed to teach the preparatory classes.

As it was now time for the juniors to begin their work, the Faculty informed me that it was their purpose to give me a class, but I was to distinctly understand that if the pupils rebelled against my teaching, they did not intend to force it. Fortunately for my training at the normal school, and my own dear love of teaching, though there was a little surprise on the faces of some when they came into the class, and saw the teacher, there were no signs of rebellion. The class went on increasing in numbers until it had to be divided, and I was given both divisions. One of the divisions ran up again, but the Faculty decided that I had as much as I could do, and it would not allow me to take any more work."

During her years as a student at Oberlin College, she taught an evening course for free African Americans in reading and writing, and she graduated with a Bachelor's degree in 1865.

In 1865, Fanny Jackson accepted a position at Philadelphia's Institute for Colored Youth (now Cheyney University of Pennsylvania). She served as the principal of the Ladies Department and taught Greek, Latin, and Mathematics. In 1869, Fanny Jackson was appointed as the principal of the Institute after the departure of Ebenezer Bassett, becoming the first African American woman to become a school principal.

In her 37 years at the Institute, Fanny Jackson was responsible for vast educational improvements in Philadelphia. During her years as principal, she was promoted by the board of education to superintendent. She was the first African American superintendent of a school district in the United States, but soon went back to be a school principal.

On December 21, 1881, Fanny married Reverend Levi Jenkins Coppin, a minister of the African Methodist Episcopal Church, pastor of Bethel AME Church, Baltimore. Fanny Jackson Coppin started to become very involved with her husband's missionary work, and in 1902 the couple went to South Africa and performed a variety of missionary work, including the founding of the Bethel Institute, a missionary school with self-help programs.

In 1893, Coppin was one of five African American women invited to speak at the World's Congress of Representative Women in Chicago, with Anna Julia Cooper, Sarah Jane Woodson Early, Fannie Barrier Williams, and Hallie Quinn Brown.

After almost a decade of missionary work, Fanny Jackson Coppin's declining health forced her to return to Philadelphia, and she died on January 21, 1913. In 1926, a Baltimore teacher training school was named the Fanny Jackson Coppin Normal School (now Coppin State University).

> *Don't follow the path. Go where there is no path
> and begin the trail. When you start a new trail
> equipped with courage, strength and conviction, the
> only thing that can stop you is you!*
> **- Ruby Bridges**

CHAPTER THREE – THE STUDENT
FEATURING STUDENTS THAT MADE A DIFFERENCE

In modern day society, having a high school education as well as a college education is one of the most important things a person could do for themselves. For an individual to earn a college degree would mean that they have devoted a large amount of time, effort and money on their career goal and are deserving of a large amount of respect.

I believe that every adult who is in a position to help young people learn to become more knowledgeable and successful students should take this responsibility upon themselves whenever possible. First and foremost, we must teach young people to step up to the plate and not just stay in one place and think everything will come to them.

The people who are featured in this chapter have sacrificed, studied and shared their talents as students who made the grade and became role models for those who would follow in their footsteps.

CARLOTTA WALLS LANIER

Carlotta Walls LaNier (December 18, 1942) was the youngest of the Little Rock Nine, a group of African-American students who, in 1957, were the first black students ever to attend classes at Little Rock Central High School in Little Rock, Arkansas. She was the first black female to graduate from Central High School. In 1999, LaNier and the other people of the Little Rock Nine were awarded the Congressional Gold Medal by President Bill Clinton.

Carlotta Walls LaNier was born in Little Rock, Arkansas to Juanita and Cartelyou Walls. Cartelyou was a brick mason and a World War II veteran, while Juanita was a secretary in the Office of Public Housing.

Carlotta first attended Dunbar Junior High School, a segregated school in Little Rock. However, after graduating, she volunteered to be one of the first African-Americans to attend Central High School. She married Ira (Ike) LaNier in 1968 with whom she had two children, Whitney and Brooke. She currently resides in Englewood, Colorado.

On September 4, 1957, the Little Rock Nine made an unsuccessful attempt to enter Central High School, which had been segregated. The Arkansas National Guard, under orders from the governor, and an angry mob of about 400 surrounded the school and prevented them from going in. On September 23, 1957, a mob of about 1000 people surrounded the school again as the students attempted to enter. The following day, President Dwight D. Eisenhower took control of the Arkansas National Guard from the governor and sent soldiers to accompany the students to school for protection. Soldiers were deployed at the school for the entirety of the school year, although they were unable to prevent incidents of violence against the group inside.

The crisis resulted on all of Little Rock's high schools being closed during that year. Despite this, Carlotta returned to Central High in 1959 and graduated in 1960.

Following her graduation from Central High in 1960, Walls attended Michigan State University for two years. However, her father was unable to find a job because of the crisis surrounding his daughter, and they moved to Denver, Colorado. LaNier graduated from Colorado State College (now the University of Northern Colorado) and began working at the YWCA as a program administrator for teens. In 1977, she founded LaNier and Company, a real estate brokerage company.

LaNier and the Little Rock Nine have received numerous awards and recognition, including the prestigious Spingarn Medal from the NAACP in 1958, and the nation's highest civilian award, the Congressional Gold Medal, which was bestowed upon them in 1999 by President Bill Clinton. Other prestigious recognition includes the Pierre Marquette Award and recently the Lincoln Leadership Prize from the Abraham Lincoln Library Foundation. She has been a member of the Urban League, NAACP, and is currently president of the Little Rock Nine Foundation, a scholarship organization dedicated to ensuring equal access to education for African Americans. She has served as a trustee for the Iliff School of Theology in Denver, and the University of Northern Colorado.

LaNier was named a "Woman of Distinction" by the Girl Scouts in 2000 and was inducted into the Colorado Women's Hall of Fame in 2004. She was inducted into the National Women's Hall of Fame in October 2015. She recently received the National Shining Star Award from NOBEL/Women (National Organization of Black Elected Legislative Women).

Carlotta Walls LaNier is the co-author of A Mighty Long Way: My Journey to Justice at Little Rock Central High School, with Lisa Frazier Page.

NATHAN HARE

Nathan Hare (April 9, 1933) is an American sociologist, activist, academic, and psychologist. In 1968 he was the first person hired to coordinate a black studies program at the university level in the United States, which he set up at San Francisco State University. A graduate of Langston University and the University of Chicago, he had become involved in the Black Power movement while teaching at Howard University.

After being fired as chair of the Black Studies program at San Francisco State, in November 1969 Hare and Robert Chrisman co-founded the journal, The Negro Scholar (now The Black Scholar: A Journal of Black Studies and Research). They worked together for several years.

After earning his second Ph.D., in clinical psychology, Hare set up a private practice in Oakland and San Francisco. Together with his wife,

Dr. Julia Hare, in 1979, he founded the Black Think Tank and for several years published a periodical, Black Male/Female Relationships. He and his wife have written and published several books together on black families and history.

Hare was born on his parents' sharecropper farm near the Creek County town of Slick, Oklahoma, on April 9, 1933. He attended segregated public schools, L'Ouverture Elementary School and L'Ouverture High School. The two schools were named after the Haitian revolutionary and general Toussaint Louverture; they were part of the so-called "Slick Separate Schools" in the late 1930s and 1940s.

When Hare was eleven years old, his family migrated to San Diego, California during the defense buildup related to World War II. His single mother took a civilian janitorial job with the Navy air station. Hundreds of thousands of blacks left the South to go to California and the West Coast, in the Great Migration through 1970, totaling 5 million in all. As World War II ended and his mother was laid off, she brought her family back to Oklahoma. This put on hold Hare's ambition to become a professional boxer, an idea he had picked up after adult neighbors in San Diego assured him that writers all starve to death.

Hare's life changed in high school after he was selected in ninth grade to represent the class at the annual statewide "Interscholastic Meet" of the black students held at Oklahoma's Langston University. (His English teacher had administered standardized tests in English Composition and selected him for his score on the test.) Hare won first prize at the meet, with more prizes to come in ensuing years. The L'Ouverture principal encouraged him to go to college and arranged for him to start at Langston with a full-time job working in the University Dining Hall to pay his way. By his junior year, Hare was working as a Dormitory Proctor of the University Men, and as a Freshman Tutor in his senior year.

When Hare enrolled at Langston University, it was the only college to admit Black students in the state of Oklahoma. The town of Langston and the college were named for John Mercer Langston, one of five African Americans elected to Congress from the South in the late 19th century, before the former Confederate states passed constitutions that effectively disenfranchised most Blacks and ended their participation in politics for decades. The town was founded by Black nationalists hoping to make the Oklahoma Territory an all-Black state. Langston, Oklahoma claimed to be the first all-Black town established in the United States.

One of Hare's professors was the poet Melvin B. Tolson. He was also elected mayor of the town for four terms and was named poet laureate of Liberia. His spectacular style of teaching would be portrayed in The Great Debaters. Graduating from Langston with an AB in Sociology, Hare won a Danforth Fellowship to continue his education; he obtained an MA (1957) and PhD in Sociology (1962) from the University of Chicago.

Hare started his academic career in 1961 as an assistant sociology professor at Howard University, a historically Black university in Washington, DC. He was dismissed in June 1967 after becoming increasingly involved with the Black Power movement on campus and leading student-faculty protests.

In 1966 he wrote a letter to the campus newspaper, The Hilltop, mocking Howard president James Nabrit's statement to the Washington Post on September 3, 1966 that he hoped to increase white enrollment at Howard to as much as 60%. Nabrit had been part of the NAACP legal team to successfully argue the 1954 Brown vs. Board of Education case before the U.S. Supreme Court, which ruled that segregation of public schools was unconstitutional. By 1966, the civil rights movement had achieved passage of the Civil Rights Act of 1964 and Voting Rights Act of 1965. After that, some activists were seeking "Black Power," as declared Stokely Carmichael in Montgomery, Alabama, who was a former student of Hare. (Hare had also taught Claude Brown, future author of "Manchild in the Promised Land").

On February 22, 1967, Hare held a press conference, with students identified as "The Black Power Committee," and read "The Black University Manifesto." It called for "the overthrow of the Negro college with white innards and to raise in its place a Black university, relevant to the Black community and its needs."

In the spring of 1967, Hare invited the champion fighter Muhammad Ali to speak at Howard. He was controversial for statements about Black power and as one of numerous opponents to the Vietnam War. Hare was dismissed effective in June 1967. Hare briefly resumed his own aborted professional boxing efforts. He won his last fight by a knockout in the first round in the Washington Coliseum on December 5, 1967.

Hare was recruited to San Francisco State in February 1968 by John Summerskill, the college's liberal president, and the Black Student Union leader Jimmy Garrett.

At San Francisco State, the Black Student Union demanded an "autonomous Department of Black Studies." Hare was soon involved in a five-month strike to establish such a department. He was at the center of the longest student strike in American academic history. Ultimately he was removed as Chair, but the strike of Black and Third World students established Black and Ethnic Studies at SFSU. The strike was led by The Black Student Union and backed by the Third World Liberation Front and the local chapter of the American Federation of Teachers. The student-faculty strike disrupted university operations and contributed to the firing of the president John Summerskill and resignation of his successor, Robert Smith. The next president was S. I. Hayakawa, a semantics scholar. Weeks later, on February 28, 1969, Hayakawa dismissed Hare as chairman of the newly formed black studies department, the first in the United States, effective June 1 of that year. Dr. Nathan Hare is considered the *Father of Black Studies* since he was the first chair of a Black Studies Department on a major university at San Francisco State College/now University.

Months after being fired from San Francisco State, Hare teamed with Robert Chrisman, a black faculty member of the college's English Department, and Allen Ross who owned the Graphic Arts of Marin printing company. They founded the journal, The Black Scholar: A Journal of Black Studies and Research in November 1969. Hare and Chrisman chipped in $300 each to launch the journal. Other early members of the editorial board included Shirley Chisholm, later elected to the US Congress; Imamu Baraka, a noted playwright; Angela Davis, scholar and activist; Dempsey Travis, Max Roach, John Oliver Killens, Ossie Davis, Shirley Graham Du Bois, Ron Karenga, and Lerone Bennett.

Hare left what The Black Scholar in 1975 and changed fields to psychology. By 1979, in collaboration with his wife, Dr. Julia Hare, he founded the Black Think Tank. Throughout his career, Hare has served as a consultant and given numerous lectures and presentations. He has written several books and articles and has been the recipient of many awards including the National Council for Black Studies National Award for his distinguished scholarly contributions to Black Studies. Throughout his life, his love of boxing and learning has helped him to fight for social justice.

INEZ BEVERLY PROSSER

Inez Beverly Prosser, (1895–1934) teacher and school administrator, is often regarded as the first African-American woman to earn a doctorate in psychology. Prosser was one of the key figures in the debate on how to best educate Black students.

Inez was born to Samuel Andrew and Veola Hamilton Beverly in Yoakum, Texas on December 30, 1897. Her mother was a homemaker and her father was a waiter. Inez was the eldest daughter and the second of eleven children. During her youth, there were few educational opportunities for African-Americans, and her family moved many times to seek the best education they could find for their children.

To contribute to the household, Inez started a college fund to support her younger siblings' education. Of the eleven children, all graduated from high school and six earned college degrees. She graduated as valedictorian from Yoakum Colored High School in 1912 and then received a degree in teacher training from Prairie View Normal

College (now Prairie View A&M University), where she was also valedictorian.

Inez returned to Yoakum and taught for a short time at their segregated schools. Then, she became an assistant principal at Clayton Industrial School in Manor, Texas, before accepting a more long-term position at Anderson High School. Throughout her time at Anderson, she taught English and coached for the Interscholastic League, an organization that sponsored events for Black high school students throughout the state.

During this period, Inez met and married Allen Rufus Prosser, who worked as an elevator operator at a department store in Austin, and the two were married in 1916. She received several awards and embraced the opportunity to continue her education. She went on to receive a master's degree in educational psychology from the University of Colorado.

At Colorado, Prosser took several courses that were particularly relevant to her master's thesis whose subject areas include mental tests, tests and measurement, and research methods. Her thesis, "The Comparative Reliability of Objective Tests in English Grammar", examined four kinds of English grammar tests (using the standards proposed by the National Education Association). Her four test types included true-false, multiple choice, completion, and matching questions. All tests covered the same subject areas and difficulty levels as well as comparable numbers of factual and reasoning questions.

Upon receiving her master's degree, Inez left Anderson High School in 1927 to accept a position as a faculty member at Tillotson College, a Black college in Austin. At Tillotson, she not only displayed her teaching and leadership skills but truly dedicated herself to the educational and psychological development of Black students. She was given the opportunity to organize a series of lectures from 1929 to 1930, which even featured a lecture by George Washington Carver. Overall, Inez Prosser was at Tillotson College from 1921 to 1930, serving as "Dean, Registrar and Professor of Education. Her influences extended well beyond the classroom walls or administrative offices. Inez was eventually transferred to another dual teaching and administrative position at Tougaloo College in Tougaloo, Mississippi. Even as Dean and Registrar of Tougaloo College, Inez accepted the position as Principal of Tougaloo High School.

Her career took an important turn when she applied for and was awarded aid from the General Education Board (established by John D. Rockefeller in 1902). She received $1,000 to apply towards another year of graduate studies. Inez Prosser continued her education and became one of the first Black women to earn a PhD in psychology.

Prosser arrived at the University of Cincinnati as a candidate for a PhD in educational psychology in 1931, graduating from the University of Cincinnati in 1933. She arrived at a time when there was a research program that "focused on African Americans in different school environments." The general consensus in the department at this time was that "all-Black schools with Black teachers could best provide the skills Black students needed to survive in a society where most faced limited opportunities...segregated schools, by insulating Black students from white abuse.

Inez Prosser's dissertation, *The Non-Academic Development of Negro Children in Mixed and Segregated Schools*, completed in 1933, examined personality differences in Black children attending either voluntarily segregated or integrated schools and concluded that Black children were better served in segregated schools. It became an important text for issues relating to education, reform, social development, racial identity, and other prominent topics related to segregation. It was a "companion study" to Mary Crowley's 1931 dissertation, "A Comparison of the Academic Achievement of Cincinnati Negroes in Segregated and Mixed Schools" Prosser's interest in the topic "grew out of a desire to determine objectively, so far as possible, the degree of truth in the often repeated statement that the Negro child develops superior character traits, more racial self-respect, and a greater concomitants of a well-rounded education when he is placed under the direction of Negro teachers during his formative years." She took Crowley's research a step further by considering the demographics of the student body in the schools as well.

Although Inez's dissertation research was in psychology, her doctoral mentor and other members of her committee were psychologists, and much of her coursework was in psychology, she is often denied her well-deserved title of psychologist.

Inez Prosser's dissertation research remains unpublished; yet it was one of several studies in the 1920s and 1930s that was part of the debate on segregated schools as maintained in the United States under the "separate but equal" doctrine of Plessy v. Ferguson (1896). This article examines the life and career of Inez Prosser in the context of educational barriers and opportunities for African Americans in the early part of the twentieth century and explores the arguments that pitted African Americans against one another in determining how best to educate Black children, arguments that eventually led to the desegregation decision of Brown v. Board of Education (1954).

Inez Prosser died in a car accident in 1934, a short time after earning her doctorate. She was a critical voice for the African-American community at a time when women in academics were scarce. Inez Prosser's contributions to the improvement of education for all students can be felt in many policies still being used throughout the teaching community today.

RUBY BRIDGES

Ruby Nell Bridges Hall (September 8, 1954) is an American civil rights activist. She was the first African-American child to desegregate the all-white William Frantz Elementary School in Louisiana during the New Orleans school desegregation crisis in 1960.

Ruby Bridges was the oldest of five children born to Abon and Lucille Bridges. As a child, she spent much time taking care of her younger siblings, though she also enjoyed playing jump rope, softball and climbing trees. When she was four years old, the family relocated from Tylertown, Mississippi, where Ruby was born, to New Orleans, Louisiana. In 1960, when she was six years old, her parents responded to a request from the National Association for the Advancement of Colored People (NAACP) and volunteered her to participate in the integration of the New Orleans school system, even though her father was hesitant.

Ruby was born during the middle of the Civil Rights Movement. *Brown v. Board of Education* was decided eight months and nine days after Ruby's birth. The famous court ruling declared the process of separating schools for Black children and white children unconstitutional. Though the *Brown v. Board of Education* decision was finalized in 1954, southern states were extremely resistant to the decision that they must integrate for the six following years.

Many white people did not want schools to be integrated and, though it was a federal ruling, state governments were not doing their part in enforcing the new laws. In 1957, federal troops stationed in Little Rock, Arkansas were ordered to combat violence that occurred as a result of the decision. Under significant pressure from the federal government, the Orleans Parish School Board administered an entrance exam to students at Ruby's school with the intention of keeping black people out of white schools.

Ruby attended a segregated kindergarten in 1959. In early 1960, Ruby was one of six black children in New Orleans to pass the test that determined whether they could go to the all-white William Frantz Elementary School. Two of the six decided to stay at their old school, Bridges went to Frantz by herself, and three children were transferred to McDonogh No. 19 and became known as the McDonogh Three. Ruby and her mother were escorted to school by four federal marshals during the first day that Ruby attended William Frantz Elementary. In the following days of that year, federal marshals continued to escort her, though her mom stayed behind to take care of her younger siblings.

Ruby's father was initially reluctant, but her mother felt strongly that the move was needed, not only to give her own daughter a better education, but to "take this step forward for all African-American children. Ruby's mother finally convinced her father to let her go to the school.

Judge J. Skelly Wright's court order for the first day of integrated schools in New Orleans on Monday, November 14, 1960, was commemorated by Norman Rockwell in the painting, *The Problem We All Live With* (published in *Look* magazine on January 14, 1964). As Ruby describes it, "Driving up I could see the crowd, but living in New Orleans, I actually thought it was Mardi Gras. There was a large crowd of people outside of the school. They were throwing things and shouting, and that sort of thing goes on in New Orleans at Mardi Gras." Former United States Deputy Marshal Charles Burks later recalled, "She showed a lot of courage. She never cried. She didn't whimper. She just marched along like a little soldier, and we're all very very proud of her."

As soon as Ruby entered the school, white parents pulled their own children out; all the teachers except for one refused to teach while a Black child was enrolled. Only one person agreed to teach Ruby and that was Barbara Henry, from Boston, Massachusetts, and for over a year Henry taught her alone, "as if she were teaching a whole class."

That first day, Ruby and her mother spent the entire day in the principal's office; the chaos of the school prevented their moving to the classroom until the second day. On the second day, however, a white student broke the boycott and entered the school when a 34-year-old Methodist minister, Lloyd Anderson Foreman, walked his 5-year-old daughter Pam through the angry mob, saying, "I simply want the privilege of taking my child to school ..." A few days later, other white parents began bringing their children, and the protests began to subside. Yet, still, Ruby remained the only child in her class, as she would until the following year. Every morning, as she walked to school, one woman would threaten to poison her, while another held up a Black baby doll in a coffin; because of this, the U.S. Marshals dispatched by President Eisenhower, who were overseeing her safety, allowed Ruby to eat only the food that she brought from home.

Child psychiatrist Robert Coles volunteered to provide counseling to Ruby during her first year at Frantz. He met with her weekly in the Bridges' home, later writing a children's book, *The Story of Ruby Bridges*, to acquaint other children with Ruby's story. Coles donated the royalties from the sale of that book to the Ruby Bridges Foundation, to provide money for school supplies or other educational needs for impoverished New Orleans school children.

The Bridges family suffered for their decision to send her to William Frantz Elementary: her father lost his job as a gas station attendant; the grocery store the family shopped at would no longer let them shop there; her grandparents, who were sharecroppers in Mississippi, were turned off their land; and Abon and Lucille Bridges separated.

Ruby Bridges has noted that many others in the community, both Black and white, showed support in a variety of ways. Some white families continued to send their children to Frantz despite the protests, a neighbor provided her father with a new job, and local people babysat, watched the house as protectors, and walked behind the federal marshals' car on the trips to school. It wasn't until Ruby was an adult that she learned that the immaculate clothing she wore to school in those first weeks at Frantz was sent to her family by a relative of Dr. Coles.

Ruby says her family could never have afforded the dresses, socks, and shoes that are documented in photographs of her escort by U.S. Marshals to and from the school.

Ruby, now Ruby Bridges Hall, still lives in New Orleans with her husband, Malcolm Hall, and their four sons. After graduating from a desegregated high school, she worked as a travel agent for 15 years and later became a full-time parent. She is now chair of the Ruby Bridges Foundation, which she formed in 1999 to promote "the values of tolerance, respect, and appreciation of all differences." Describing the mission of the group, she says, "racism is a grown-up disease and we must stop using our children to spread it."

Like hundreds of thousands of others in the greater New Orleans area, Bridges Hall lost her home (in Eastern New Orleans) to the catastrophic flooding in the failure of the levee system during Hurricane Katrina in 2005. Hurricane Katrina also significantly damaged William Frantz Elementary School, and Ruby played a significant role in fighting for the school to remain open.

In November 2007, the Children's Museum of Indianapolis unveiled a new permanent exhibit documenting her life, along with the lives of Anne Frank and Ryan White. The exhibit, called "The Power of Children: Making a Difference," cost $6 million to install and includes an authentic re-creation of Bridges' first grade classroom.

In 2010, Ruby had a 50th year reunion at William Frantz Elementary with Pam Foreman Testroet, who, at age five, was the first white child to break the boycott that ensued from Bridges' attendance at that school.

On July 15, 2011, Bridges met with President Barack Obama at the White House, and while viewing the Norman Rockwell painting of her on display he told her, "I think it's fair to say that if it hadn't been for you guys, I might not be here and we wouldn't be looking at this together." The Rockwell painting was displayed in the West Wing of the White House, just outside the Oval Office, from June through October 2011.

In September 1995, Ruby Bridges Hall and Dr. Robert Coles were awarded honorary degrees from Connecticut College and appeared together in public for the first time to accept the awards. On January 8, 2001, Bridges Hall was awarded the Presidential Citizens Medal by President Bill Clinton. In October 2006, the Alameda Unified School

District in California named a new elementary school for Ruby Bridges, and issued a proclamation in her honor. In November 2006 she was honored as a "Hero Against Racism" at the 12th annual Anti-Defamation League "Concert Against Hate" with the National Symphony Orchestra, held at the Kennedy Center in DC. On May 19, 2012, Bridges Hall received an Honorary Degree from Tulane University at the annual graduation ceremony at the Superdome. In 2014, a statue of Bridges was unveiled in the courtyard of William Frantz Elementary School.

JAMES MEREDITH

James Howard Meredith (June 25, 1933) is an African-American Civil Rights Movement figure, writer, political adviser and Air Force veteran. Meredith was born in Kosciusko, Mississippi, the son of Roxie (Patterson) and Moses Meredith, who is of African-American, British Canadian, Scots and Choctaw heritage.

James Meredith was raised on a farm with nine brothers and sisters, largely insulated from the racism of the time. His first experience with institutionalized racism occurred while he was riding a train from Chicago with his brother. When the train arrived in Memphis, Tennessee, Meredith was ordered to give up his seat and move to the crowded black section of the train, where he had to stand for the rest of his trip home. He vowed then that he would dedicate his life to ensuring equal treatment for African Americans.

Meredith completed the 11th grade at Attala County Training School (which was segregated as "white" and "colored" under the state's Jim

Crow laws) and he completed the 12th grade at Gibbs High School in St. Petersburg, Florida. He graduated from high school in 1951 and then, enlisted in the United States Air Force. Meredith spent nine years in the United States Air Force where he served from 1951 to 1960. He attended the all-black Jackson State College, for a year.

In 1961, inspired by President John F. Kennedy, Meredith started to apply to the University of Mississippi, intending to insist on his civil rights to attend the state-funded university. It still admitted only white students under the state's culture of racial segregation, although the US Supreme Court ruled in Brown v. Board of Education (1954) that segregation of public schools was unconstitutional, as they are supported by all the taxpayers.

When Meredith applied to the all-white University of Mississippi, he was initially accepted; but his admission was later withdrawn when the registrar discovered his race. Since all public educational institutions had been ordered to desegregate by this time, Meredith filed a suit alleging discrimination.

On May 31, 1961, Meredith, with backing of the NAACP Legal Defense and Educational Fund, filed suit in the U.S. District Court for the Southern District of Mississippi, alleging that the university had rejected him only because of his race, as he had a highly successful record of military service and academic courses. Although the state courts ruled against him, the case made its way to the U.S. Supreme Court, which ruled in his favor.

When Meredith arrived at the university to register for classes on September 20, 1962, he found the entrance blocked. Rioting soon erupted, and Attorney General Robert Kennedy sent 500 U.S. Marshals to the scene. Additionally, President John F. Kennedy sent military police, troops from the Mississippi National Guard and officials from the U.S. Border Patrol to keep the peace. On October 1,

1962, James Meredith became the first black student to enroll at the University of Mississippi after the intervention of the federal government, an event that was a flashpoint in the Civil Rights Movement.

In 1963, Meredith graduated with a degree in political science. He wrote an account of his experience, titled *Three Years in Mississippi*, which was published in 1966. Meredith planned a solo 220-mile March Against Fear from Memphis, Tennessee, to Jackson, Mississippi; he wanted to highlight continuing racism in the South and encourage voter registration after passage of the Voting Rights Act of 1965. He did not want major civil rights organizations involved. The second day, Meredith suffered numerous wounds when he was shot by a white unemployed hardware clerk named Aubrey James Norvell, who was apprehended and sentenced to five years in prison. (He would ultimately serve just 18 months.).

Leaders of major organizations vowed to complete the march in his name after he was taken to the hospital. While Meredith was recovering, more people from across the country became involved as marchers. He rejoined the march and when Meredith and other leaders entered Jackson on June 26, 1966 they were leading an estimated 15,000 marchers, in what was the largest civil rights march in Mississippi. During the course of it, more than 4,000 African Americans had registered to vote, and the march was a catalyst to continued community organizing and additional registration.

Meredith eventually recovered from his injuries and went on to receive a master's degree in economics from the University of Ibadan in Nigeria. He then received a law degree from Columbia University in 1968.

In 2002 and again in 2012, the University of Mississippi led year-long series of events to celebrate the 40th and 50th anniversaries of

Meredith's integration of the institution. He was among numerous speakers invited to the campus, where a statue of him commemorates his role. The Lyceum-The Circle Historic District at the center of the campus has been designated as a National Historic Landmark for these events. James Meredith lives in Jackson, Mississippi, and continues to be active in civil rights.

> *"The man who is right is a majority. He who has God and conscience on his side, has a majority against the universe."*
> **-Frederick Douglass**

CHAPTER FOUR - THE COMMUNITY
FEATURING CIVIL RIGHTS LEADERS AND ACTIVISTS

18TH - 19TH CENTURY

If you feel like you're not doing enough, that you could do more to make a difference, step out on faith and fight for what you know is right. Never hesitate to reach out to the community to give back.

African Americans have advocated for civil rights since the earliest days of the founding of the United States. Leaders like Martin Luther King, Jr., and Malcolm X are two of the best-known civil rights leaders of the 20th century. But in the century before the Civil Rights Movement there were thousands of brave souls who were willing to fight until death in order to set a new standard of living, to gain freedom and equal rights for the generations to come.

CRISPUS ATTUCKS

Crispus Attucks (1723—March 5, 1770) is remembered as the first American to die in Boston, Massachusetts in the colonists' fight for freedom from Britain. Crispus Attucks was an escaped slave of African and Native American (Wampanoag) descent, but not much else is known about him. Apparently, young Attucks developed a longing for freedom at an early age.

According to *The Black Presence in the Era of the American Revolution,* historians believe that an advertisement placed in the *Boston Gazette* on October 2, 1750, referred to him: "Ran away from his Master *William Brown from Framingham,* on the 30th of *Sept.* last, a Molatto Fellow, about 27 Years of age, named Crispas, 6 Feet two

Inches high, short curl'd Hair, his Knees nearer together than common: had on a light colour'd Bearskin Coat."

Assuming that the *Boston Gazette* advertisement did refer to Crispus Attucks, he would have been about 47-years old at the time of his death. Attucks' occupation made him particularly vulnerable to the presence of the British. As a seaman, he felt the ever-present danger of impressment into the British navy. As a laborer, he felt the competition from British troops, who often took part-time jobs during their off-duty hours and worked for lower wages.

Historians definitely place Attucks in Boston in March of 1770. Although nothing is known definitively about his ancestry, his father is thought to be Prince Yonger, a slave who was brought to America, while his mother is thought to be Nancy Attucks, a Natick Indian. The family, which may have included an older sister named Phebe, lived in Framingham, Massachusetts.

On Friday, March 2, 1770 a fight between Boston rope makers and three British soldiers set the stage for a later confrontation. After dusk on Monday, March 5, 1770, a crowd of colonists confronted a sentry who had struck a boy for complaining that an officer was late in paying a barber bill. As anger escalated, a church bell rang, which drew people out of their homes. Toward evening that day, a crowd of colonists gathered and began taunting a small group of British soldiers of the 29th Regiment of Foot, who were called to duty.

Violence soon erupted, and the townspeople responded by hurling snowballs and debris at the soldiers. A group of men led by Attucks approached the vicinity of the government building with clubs in hand, and a soldier was struck with a thrown piece of wood. Some accounts named Attucks as the person responsible for throwing the wood. Other witnesses stated that Attucks as "leaning upon a stick" when the soldiers opened fire.

Tension mounted rapidly, and, when the soldier was struck, the others fired their muskets. Five Americans were killed and six were wounded. Attucks was the first one killed; he took two bullets in the chest. Rope maker Samuel Gray and sailor James Caldwell also died in the incident. Samuel Maverick, a 17-year-old joiner's apprentice, died the next day. Irish leather worker Patrick Carr died nine days later. Attucks' body was carried to Faneuil Hall, where it lay in state until Thursday, March 8, when he and the other victims were buried in a common grave.

Attucks was the first to fall, thus becoming one of the first men to lose his life in the cause of American independence. The shootings were quickly dubbed "The Boston Massacre" and seized on by angry colonists as a case of brutality by heavy-handed British rulers.

Attucks was the only victim of the Boston Massacre whose name was widely remembered. In 1888 the Crispus Attucks monument was unveiled in the Boston Common.

John Adams, later the second president of the United States, defended the British soldiers at trial and won an acquittal for them by arguing that Crispus Attucks and the others were common thugs, not political freedom-fighters. After the trial, patriots said it proved that even a British soldier could get a fair trial in independence-minded Boston. Despite that result, Crispus Attucks was held up as a martyr for defending political liberty.

Crispus Attucks became the first casualty of the American Revolution when he was shot and killed. Although Attucks was credited as the leader and instigator of the event, debate raged for over a century as to whether he was a hero and a patriot, or a rabble-rousing villain. The debate notwithstanding, Attucks, immortalized as "the first to defy, the first to die," has been lauded as a true martyr, "the first to pour out his blood as a precious libation on the altar of a people's rights."

Martin Luther King, Jr., referred to Crispus Attucks in the introduction of *Why We Can't Wait* (1964) as an example of a man whose contribution to history, though much-overlooked by standard histories, provided a potent message of moral courage.

He is one of the most important figures in African-American history, not for what he did for his own race but for what he did for all oppressed people everywhere. He is a reminder that the African-American heritage is not only African but American and it is a heritage that begins with the beginning of America.

TOUSSAINT LOUVERTURE

Toussaint Louverture (May 20, 1743 - April 7, 1803) was born with the name **François Dominique Toussaint**. He was a former Haitian slave who led the only successful slave revolt in modern history. It is believed his father was Gaou Guinou, the younger son of the king of Allada, a West African kingdom. His father was an African prisoner of war who was sold into slavery, along with his family, in Saint-Dominque. Toussaint was the eldest of eight children.

Saint-Domingue, located in the western region of the island of Hispaniola, was a prized possession of France, due to the wealth derived from the labor of a half-million enslaved people, working primarily in sugarcane and coffee cultivation. In 1791, after the French Revolution, the enslaved people of Saint-Domingue and their allies began a revolution that would last twelve years.

As a child, Toussaint was fortunate to be owned by enlightened masters who allowed him to learn to read and write French and Haitian patois, and he enjoyed access to books and schooling. The classics as well as political philosophers deeply influenced him. He also developed a deep devotion to the teachings of Catholicism. Toussaint's father taught him the use of traditional medicine and he became an expert in medicinal plants and horsemanship. Recognized by his master for his abilities, he quickly rose to become the plantation's chief steward. It is said that he was given his freedom in 1776, the same year the United States declared its independence from Great Britain.

Toussaint continued to work for his former owner and married Suzanne Simone Baptiste in 1782. The couple had three children: Placide, Isaac, and Saint-Jean. Before becoming a coachman for his master, Toussaint herded livestock. By his mid-thirties, he was free and working toward becoming a property owner.

On August 22, 1791, slaves rebelled in the French colony of Saint-Domingue on the western half of Hispaniola. Inspired by the French Revolution, and angered by generations of abuse, slaves began slaughtering whites with impunity. At first, François Toussaint was uncommitted and reluctant to join the revolt in the northern province.. He was nearly fifty years-old and married with a family, farming a small plot of land and running a plantation for his former master. But the rebellion began to expand and eventually it migrated to where Toussaint was living. Despite being free himself, Toussaint saw opportunity in the slave rebellion and joined the fight for liberation. His decision to join the rebellion wasn't only driven by the desire to defend his way of life. Toussaint was also deeply influenced by his Catholic religion, which condemned slavery.

Toussaint first secured the safety of his wife and family in the Spanish-controlled eastern half of the island, away from the rebellion. He then saw to it that his former master's family was on a boat bound for the United States. Toussaint joined Georges Biassou's rebels who had allied with the Spanish against France. During his time in slavery, Toussaint had learned African and Creole herbal-medical techniques. He now served as a doctor to the troops, as well as a soldier.

Toussaint quickly developed a reputation and was given command of 600 black former slaves. His determination and leadership earned him a promotion to general. His forces were well-organized and steadily grew to 4,000 men. Jean-Jacques Dessalines, an escaped slave, joined Toussaint and quickly became a close confident and able lieutenant.

In 1793, warfare between France and Spain provided an opportunity for Louverture to form an alliance with the Spanish, who controlled the eastern side of the island of Hispaniola. That year, he had added "Louverture" (French for "opening") to his name, presumably for his skill in finding or creating openings in enemy lines.

The British government was concerned that the slave revolt would spread to their neighboring colony of Jamaica. Seeking an opportunity to harass the French, the British sent troops to put down the slave revolt. Fearing defeat, the French National Convention acted to preserve its colonial rule and secure the loyalty of the black population. In 1794 France abolished slavery in the empire, granting freedom and citizenship to all Blacks in the Empire. But the British troops remained determined to wreak havoc on France's tenuous hold on Saint-Domingue.

Louverture then reversed his allegiance and joined the French military and helped to repel British and Spanish attempts to take the island. His first mission was to attack Spanish-controlled Santa Domingo on the eastern side of the island. Forming an army of former slaves and deserters from the French and Spanish armies, he trained his followers in guerrilla warfare. He was now fighting his former Black colleagues, who were still loyal to Spain. Under his leadership, Toussaint's troops were able to capture Santa Domingo and successfully ended slavery in Hispaniola.

The Treaty of Basel, in July 1795, ended the hostilities between France and Spain and the Spanish pulled out of Hispaniola. Toussaint contained the remaining British troops, rendering them ineffective and soon they too withdrew from the island.

Toussaint Louverture and the Haitian Revolution inspired millions of free and enslaved people of African descent to seek freedom and equality throughout the Atlantic world. Toussaint and other Black leaders of Saint-Domingue helped to lead the only Atlantic slave society which successfully defeated its oppressors. The former slaves were able to achieve freedom and equality by political and military force, when they defeated the advances of French, British, and Spanish troops.

In 1799 Napoleon Bonaparte gained control of France, amidst the chaos of the French Revolutionary government. He issued a new constitution that declared all French colonies would be ruled under special laws. Toussaint and others suspected this would mean the return of slavery. Through a series of political maneuvers and power grabs, Louverture gained control of the whole island and sought to gain French support for his authority. He was careful not to declare full independence and professed himself a Frenchman to convince Napoleon of his loyalty.

In an 1801 Toussaint introduced a constitution, which reiterated the abolition of slavery. Toussaint was now the de facto ruler of the entire island of Hispaniola, named himself as leader for life of a free, autonomous, multiracial Saint-Domingue and declared himself Governor-General for Life, with nearly absolute powers.

Hoping to bring some stability back to Hispaniola, he set out to reestablish agriculture and improve the economic conditions. Toussaint established trade agreements with the British and the Americans, who supplied his forces with arms and goods in exchange for sugar and the promise not to invade Jamaica or the American South. Defying French Revolutionary laws, he allowed plantation owners, who had fled during the rebellion, to return. He imposed military discipline on the workforce, while at the same established reforms that improved workers' conditions.

Napoleon confirmed Toussaint's position as colonial governor and promised not to reinstate slavery. Napoleon also forbade Toussaint from invading Santo Domingo, the eastern half of the island, where he had French authorities, trying to restore order after the Spanish departure.

The temptation to have complete control over the entire island was too tempting for Toussaint. In January 1801, his armies invaded Santo Domingo and took control with little effort. He instituted French law, abolished slavery, and set out to modernize the country. Angered by Toussaint's boldness, in 1802, Napoleon sent his brother-in-law, General Charles Emanuel Leclerc, with 20,000 French troops to apprehend Toussaint, regain control and restore plantation slavery. These men were hand-picked for their experience in the campaigns in Europe and would be a formidable force against Toussaint.

Though Toussaint was able to put up strong resistance for several months, eventually his coalition fell apart. Most Europeans and mulattos living on the island sided with the French. In time, even Toussaint's best generals, Henri Christophe and Dessalines joined Leclerc. After many weeks of fighting, General Charles Leclerc captured Louverture and deported him to the French Alps.

By June 1802, the end was near. Under the pretense of discussing peace, French General Jean-Baptiste Brunet sent a letter to Toussaint inviting him to his quarters. There Toussaint was arrested and sent to Fort-de-Joux in the Jura Mountains of France. He died of pneumonia and starvation on April 7, 1803.

With Toussaint Louverture removed from power, Napoleon Bonaparte decreed that slavery be reinstated in all the French colonies in the Americas in 1802. Soon after, Jean-Jacques Dessalines switched sides again and commanded rebel forces against the French. Dessalines' coalition of Blacks and mulattos were successful in forcing the French to surrender and leave the island. By 1803 rebel forces were victorious and in 1804 Dessalines proclaimed independence and declared himself emperor. The new and independent Republic of Haiti emerged when Hispaniola became the first Black independent republic in the world.

Though he didn't live to see it, Francois Toussaint's actions set in motion a series of global events that changed the geography of the western hemisphere and spelled the beginning of the end for European colonial domination in the Americas. Frustrated by a rebellion he couldn't control in Hispaniola, Napoleon Bonaparte decided not to expand his empire into North America and sold the Louisiana territory to the United States in 1803. This paved the way for western expansion throughout the 19th century.

Toussaint's actions also inspired revolutions in several Latin American countries over the next 100 years and American abolitionists, both Black and white, to fight for an end to slavery.

JEAN BAPTISTE POINTE DUSABLE

Jean Baptiste Point du Sable (1745-1818) (or Point de Sable, Point au Sable, Point Sable, Pointe DuSable) was born on the island of St. Marc, Saint Dominique (Haiti). around 1745 to a French mariner and a mother who was a slave of African descent.

DuSable was a famous frontier trader, fur trapper, farmer, international scout, businessman, and authenticated father, regarded as the first permanent resident of what became Chicago, Illinois the nation's third largest city in America. The original name of Chicago was then called Checagou, meaning wild onions.

It is widely believed, that DuSable's mother was probably killed by the Spanish when he was around ten years old. DuSable's father took him to France to be educated. He worked as a seaman on his father's ships. He had a love for European art and, at one time, owned twenty-three Old World art treasures. He spoke French, English, Spanish and several Indian dialects.

At the age of twenty, DuSable arrived in New Orleans, Louisiana whereupon he learned the colony had become a Spanish possession. Having lost his identification papers and been injured on the voyage to New Orleans, DuSable was almost enslaved.

French Jesuit priests protected him until he was healthy enough to travel. It is believed Du Sable and his childhood friend Jacques Clemorgan sailed from Haiti to New Orleans. DuSable was eventually thankful for moving to New Orleans because it was there that he and his friend Clemorgan met their future partner of a trading post in New Orleans, and later in what would become Peoria, Illinois. The young man Du Sable and Clemorgan met was a Native American Indian named Choctaw, from the Great Lakes. At the time, Choctaw was working at a Catholic mission. Du Sable, Clemorgan, and Choctaw later moved to an Indian River settlement in Peoria Illinois.

Choctaw taught DuSable and Clemorgan things of value for their entire life. They learned how to set traps and where to find martens, small animals trapped for their fur. The three men started a trading post. Du Sable and Choctaw spent their time trapping in the woods, while Clemorgan devoted his time to hauling pelts downstream to New Orleans.

DuSable migrated north, up the Mississippi River, later settling in an area near present-day Peoria, Illinois. He also lived in what is now Michigan and Indiana as well during the 1770s.

In the early 1770's, DuSable built a cabin and eventually owned more than 800 acres of land in Peoria. He enjoyed a special relationship with Illinois territorial Indians. where he met and married a Potawatomi woman named Catherine (Kittihawa), in a tribal ceremony. The couple had two children, Jean Baptiste Point DuSable, Jr. and Suzanne. The marriage was formally recognized before a Catholic priest in Cahokia, Illinois on October 27, 1778.

In 1779 DuSable was arrested at what is now Michigan City, Indiana by British troops who considered him a spy and was imprisoned briefly at Fort Michilimackinac before being released to manage a tract of woodlands claimed by British Lt. Patrick Sinclair on the St. Clair River in Eastern Michigan.

DuSable settled along the northern bank of the Chicago River near Lake Michigan in 1779 in a marshy area the Indians called Eschikagu, "the place of bad smells." Despite the disadvantages, DuSable developed a prosperous trading post established a dairy farm and planted fruit orchards and fields of corn, hay and alfalfa. Starting from scratch, DuSable built the first permanent home on the north bank of the Chicago River, where the present-day Chicago Tribune Tower stands. His land extended onto the present Wrigley Building site and beyond, on the Chicago River front. It was a well-constructed house consisting of five rooms and equipped with all the modern conveniences of the times. The construction of DuSable's home was the first European scale permanent architectural structure in the area.

DuSable's home was well-constructed, consisting of five rooms and equipped with all the modern conveniences of the time. Jean Baptiste Pointe DuSable became the first real estate developer and builder when he established a permanent settlement for himself and his newly arrived wife, and about one hundred other Pottawatomie.

The trading post consisted of a mill, bake house, dairy, smokehouse, workshop, poultry-house, horse stable, barn and several other smaller buildings. His post was the main supply station for white trappers, traders, woodsmen and the Indians. The Chicago portage boomed. It became the key route for merchant trading, and DuSable sent wheat, breads, meats, and furs to trading posts in Detroit and Canada. DuSable became a man of considerable wealth and means.

In a short time, DuSable became well-known as far away as Wisconsin, Detroit and Canada. At his trading post, DuSable served Native Americans, British, and French explorers. He spoke Spanish, French, English, and several Native American dialects, which served him well as an entrepreneur and mediator. He also owned a substantial quantity of field and carpentry tools, which indicated that he must have hired men for fieldwork and building assignments. In addition, he owned an appreciable quantity of livestock, poultry, and hogs.

Du Sable's settlement was the model that later created the beginning of a new multi-cultural society that would come to be called Chicago. DuSable also was the first permanent immigrant, entrepreneur and non-native leader in the Chicago area. The promise of greatness of the "Chicago" area, where DuSable decided to settle, had been passed over by others who arrived before him. None had the foresight to look beyond its barren, damp, marsh condition, nor did they have fortitude to make "nothing" into one of the greatest locations in the Western Hemisphere

In 1784 DuSable brought his wife and children to Chicago. And, as DuSable was a devout Catholic, he waited for the first Catholic priest to come in the area to marry him to his wife Catherine in a Catholic ceremony. In 1796, their granddaughter became the first born in the city of Chicago.

On May 7, 1800, DuSable sold his entire wealth for a mere $1,200 and returned to Peoria, Illinois. DuSable sold his estate on May 7, 1800 and returned to Peoria, Illinois. He later moved to St. Charles, Missouri, where he continued as a farmer and trader until his death on August 28, 1818. DuSable was buried in a Catholic cemetery in St. Charles, Missouri. In 1968, the State of Illinois recognized Jean Baptiste Pointe DuSable as being the founder of Chicago.

SOJOURNER TRUTH

Sojourner Truth (1797 – November 26, 1883) was born Isabella Baumfree in the town of Swartekill, in Ulster County, New York. She was born into slavery, but escaped with her infant daughter to freedom in 1826. After going to court to recover her son in 1828, she became the first black woman to win a case against a white man.

Even in abolitionist circles, some of Truth's opinions were considered radical. She sought political equality for all women and chastised the abolitionist community for failing to seek civil rights for Black women as well as men. She openly expressed concern that the movement would fizzle after achieving victories for Black men, leaving both white and black women without suffrage and other key political rights.

During the Civil War, Truth helped recruit black troops for the Union Army. After the war, she tried unsuccessfully to secure land grants from the federal government for former slaves.

Sojourner Truth was one of as many as 12 children born to James and Elizabeth Baumfree. Her father, James Baumfree, was a slave captured in modern-day Ghana; Elizabeth Baumfree, also known as Mau-Mau Bet, was the daughter of slaves from Guinea. Charles Hardenbergh inherited his father's estate and continued to enslave people as a part of that estate's property. Colonel Hardenbergh bought James and Elizabeth Baumfree from slave traders and kept the Baumfree family at his estate in a big hilly area in Esopus, New York, 95 miles north of New York City, called by the Dutch name Swartekill (just north of present-day Rifton). The area had once been under Dutch control, and both the Baumfrees and the Hardenbaughs spoke Dutch in their daily lives.

When Charles Hardenbergh died in 1806, nine-year-old Sojourner (known as Belle), was sold at an auction with a flock of sheep for $100 to John Neely, near Kingston, New York. Until that time, Truth spoke only Dutch. She later described Neely as cruel and harsh, relating how he beat her daily and once even with a bundle of rods. Neely sold her in 1808, for $105, to Martinus Schryver of Port Ewen, a tavern keeper, who owned her for eighteen months. Schryver sold her in 1810 to John Dumont of West Park, New York. Although this fourth owner was kindly disposed toward her, considerable tension existed between Truth and Dumont's second wife, Elizabeth Waring Dumont, who harassed her and made her life more difficult.

Around 1815, Truth met and fell in love with a slave named Robert from a neighboring farm. The two had a daughter, Diana. Robert's owner (Charles Catton, Jr., a landscape painter) forbade their relationship. He did not want the people he enslaved to have children with people he was not enslaving, because he would not own the children. Diana and any subsequent children produced by the union would be the property of John Dumont rather than himself. One day Robert snuck over to see Truth. When Catton and his son found him, they savagely beat Robert until Dumont finally intervened, and Truth never saw Robert again. He died some years later, perhaps as a result of the injuries, and the experience haunted Truth throughout her life.

In 1817, Dumont compelled Truth to marry an older slave named Thomas. She bore five children: James, her firstborn, who died in childhood, Diana (1815), fathered by either Robert or John Dumont, and Peter (1821), Elizabeth (1825), and Sophia (ca. 1826), all born after she and Thomas united.

The state of New York, which had begun to negotiate the abolition of slavery in 1799, emancipated all slaves on July 4, 1827. The shift did not come soon enough for Sojourner. After John Dumont reneged on a promise to emancipate Sojourner, in late 1826, she escaped to freedom with her infant daughter, Sophia. She had to leave her other children behind because they were not legally freed in the emancipation order until they had served as bound servants into their twenties.

She found her way to the home of Isaac and Maria Van Wagenen in New Paltz, who took her and her baby in. Isaac offered to buy her services for the remainder of the year (until the state's emancipation took effect), which Dumont accepted for $20. She lived there until the New York State Emancipation Act was approved a year later.

Shortly after her escape, Sojourner learned that her son Peter, then five years old, had been illegally sold by Dumont to an owner in Alabama. With the help of the Van Wagenens, she took the issue to court and in 1828, after months of legal proceedings, she got back her son, who had been abused by those who were enslaving him, securing his return from the South. The case was one of the first in which a black woman successfully challenged a white man in a United States court.

Sojourner had a life-changing religious experience during her stay with the Van Wagenens and became a devout Christian. In 1829 she moved with her son Peter to New York City, where she worked as a housekeeper for Elijah Pierson, a Christian Evangelist. While in New York, she befriended Mary Simpson, a grocer on John Street who claimed she had once been enslaved by George Washington. They shared an interest in charity for the poor and became intimate friends. In 1832, she met Robert Matthews, also known as Prophet Matthias, and went to work for him as a housekeeper at the Matthias Kingdom communal colony.

Shortly after Sojourner changed households, Elijah Pierson died. Robert Matthews was accused of poisoning Pierson in order to benefit from his personal fortune, and the Folgers, a couple who were members of his cult, attempted to implicate Sojourner in the crime. In the absence of adequate evidence, both were acquitted of the murder, though Matthews was convicted of lesser crimes and served time. Matthews had a growing reputation as a con man and a cult leader. Because he had become a favorite subject of the penny press, he decided to move west. In 1835 Truth brought a slander suit against the Folgers and won.

After Truth's successful rescue of her son, Peter, from slavery in Alabama, mother and son stayed together until 1839. At that time, Peter took a job on a whaling ship called the Zone of Nantucket. From 1840 to 1841, she received three letters from him, though in his third letter he told her he had sent five. Peter said he also never received any of her letters. When the ship returned to port in 1842, Peter was not on board and Truth never heard from him again.

In 1840, in Boston, Massachusetts, William Lloyd Garrison invited Sojourner Truth to give a speech at an annual antislavery convention. Wendell Phillips was supposed to speak after her, which made her nervous since he was known as such a good orator. So Truth sang a song, "I am Pleading for My people," which was her own original composition sung to the tune of Auld Lang Syne

1843 was a turning point for Isabella Baumfree when she became a Methodist, and on June 1, she changed her name to Sojourner Truth. She told friends: "The Spirit calls me, and I must go" and left to make her way traveling and preaching about the abolition of slavery. At that time, Truth began attending Millerite Adventist camp meetings. However, that did not last since Jesus failed to appear in 1843 and then again in 1844. Like many others, disappointed, Truth distanced herself from her Millerite friends for a while.

In 1844, she joined the Northampton Association of Education and Industry in Northampton, Massachusetts. Founded by abolitionists, the organization supported women's rights and religious tolerance as well as pacifism. There were, in its four-and-a-half-year history, a total of 240 members, though no more than 120 at any one time. They lived on 470 acres, raising livestock, running a sawmill, a gristmill, and a silk factory. While there, Truth met William Lloyd Garrison, Frederick Douglass, and David Ruggles. In 1846, the group disbanded, unable to support itself. In 1845, she joined the household of George Benson, the brother-in-law of William Lloyd Garrison. In 1849, she visited John Dumont before he moved west.

Truth started dictating her memoirs to her friend Olive Gilbert, and in 1850 William Lloyd Garrison privately published her book, *The Narrative of Sojourner Truth: A Northern Slave*. That same year, she purchased a home in what would become the village of Florence in Northampton for $300, and spoke at the first National Women's Rights Convention in Worcester, Massachusetts. In 1854, with proceeds from sales of the Narrative and cartes-de-visite entitled "I sell the shadow to support the substance," she paid off the mortgage held by her friend from the Community, Samuel L. Hill.

In 1851, Truth joined George Thompson, an abolitionist and speaker, on a lecture tour through central and western New York State. In May, she attended the Ohio Women's Rights Convention in Akron, Ohio, where she delivered her famous extemporaneous speech on women's rights, later known as "Ain't I a Woman." Her speech demanded equal human rights for all women as well as for all blacks. Advocating for women and African Americans was dangerous and challenging enough, but being one and doing so, was far more difficult.

The first version of the speech was published a month later by Marius Robinson, editor of Ohio newspaper *The Anti-Slavery Bugle*, who had attended the convention and recorded Truth's words himself. It did not include the question "Ain't I a woman?" even once. The famous phrase would appear in print 12 years later, as the refrain of a Southern-tinged version of the speech. It is unlikely that Sojourner Truth, a native of New York whose first language was Dutch, would have spoken in this Southern idiom.

In 1853, she spoke at a suffragist "mob convention" at the Broadway Tabernacle in New York City; that year she also met Harriet Beecher Stowe. In 1856, she traveled to Battle Creek, Michigan, to speak to a group called the "Friends of Human Progress." In 1858, someone interrupted a speech and accused her of being a man; Truth opened her blouse and revealed her breasts.

In 1856, Sojourner bought property in Northampton, but she did not keep the new property for long. On September 3, 1857, she sold all her possessions, new and old, to Daniel Ives and moved to Battle Creek, Michigan, where she rejoined former members of the Millerite Movement who had formed the Seventh-day Adventist Church. Antislavery movements had begun early in Michigan and Ohio. Here, she also joined the nucleus of the Michigan abolitionists, the Progressive Friends, some who she had already met at national conventions.

During the Civil War, Sojourner helped recruit black troops for the Union Army. Her grandson, James Caldwell, enlisted in the 54th Massachusetts Regiment. In 1864, Truth was employed by the National Freedman's Relief Association in Washington, D.C., where she worked diligently to improve conditions for African-Americans. In October of that year, President Abraham Lincoln received her at the White House. In 1865, while working at the Freedman's Hospital in Washington, Sojourner rode in the streetcars to help force their desegregation.

May 9–10, 1867: Her speech was addressed to the American Equal Rights Association, and divided into three sessions. Sojourner was received with loud cheers. The Call had advertised her name as one of the main convention speakers. For the first part of her speech, she spoke mainly about the rights of black women. Sojourner argued that because the push for equal rights had led to Black men winning new rights, now was the best time to give Black women the rights they deserve too.

In the second sessions of Sojourner's speech, she utilized a story from the Bible to help strengthen her argument for equal rights for women. She ended her argument by accusing men of being self-centered, saying, "man is so selfish that he has got women's rights and his own too, and yet he won't give women their rights. He keeps them all to himself."

For the final session of Sojourner's speech, the center of her attention was mainly on women's right to vote. Sojourner told her audience that she owned her own house, as did other women, and must therefore pay taxes. Nevertheless, they were still unable to vote because they were women. Black women who were enslaved were made to do hard manual work, such as building roads. Sojourner argues that if these women were able to perform such tasks, then they should be allowed to vote because surely voting is easier than building roads.

In 1870, Sojourner tried to secure land grants from the federal government to former enslaved people, a project she pursued for seven years without success. While in Washington, D.C., she had a meeting with President Ulysses S. Grant in the White House. In 1872, she returned to Battle Creek, became active in Grant's presidential re-election campaign, and even tried to vote on Election Day, but was turned away at the polling place.

A major project of Truth's later life was the movement to secure land grants from the federal government for former slaves. She argued that ownership of private property, and particularly land, would give African Americans self-sufficiency and free them from a kind of indentured servitude to wealthy landowners. Although Truth pursued this goal forcefully for many years, she was unable to sway Congress.

Sojourner spoke about abolition, women's rights, prison reform, and preached to the Michigan Legislature against capital punishment. She had many friends and staunch support among many influential people at the time, including Amy Post, Parker Pillsbury, Frances Gage, Wendell Phillips, William Lloyd Garrison, Laura Smith Haviland, Lucretia Mott, Ellen G. White, and Susan B. Anthony."

As Sojourner's reputation grew and the abolition movement gained momentum, she drew increasingly larger and more hospitable audiences. She was one of several escaped slaves, along with Frederick Douglass and Harriet Tubman, to rise to prominence as an abolitionist leader and a testament to the humanity of enslaved people.

While always controversial, Truth was embraced by a community of reformers including Amy Post, Wendell Phillips, William Lloyd Garrison, Lucretia Mott and Susan B. Anthony — friends with whom she collaborated until the end of her life. Until old age intervened, Truth continued to speak passionately on the subjects of women's rights, universal suffrage and prison reform.

Sojourner died at her Battle Creek home on November 26, 1883. On November 28 her funeral was held at the Congregational-Presbyterian Church officiated by its pastor, the Reverend Reed Stuart. Some of the prominent citizens of Battle Creek acted as pall-bearers. Truth was buried alongside her family in the city's Oak Hill Cemetery.

A larger-than-life sculpture of Sojourner Truth by artist Tina Allen, was dedicated in 1999, which is the estimated bicentennial of Sojourner's birth. The 12-foot tall Sojourner monument is cast bronze.

Sojourner Truth is remembered as one of the foremost leaders of the abolition movement and an early advocate of women's rights. Abolition was one of the few causes that Sojourner was able to see realized in her lifetime. The 19th Amendment to the constitution, which enabled women to vote, was not ratified until 1920, nearly four decades after Sojourner Truth's death.

NAT TURNER

Nat Turner (October 2, 1800 - November 11, 1831) was born in Southampton County, Virginia on a small plantation, owned by slaveholder Benjamin Turner. Nat's mother was born in Africa and had been shipped to the United States as a slave. She taught her son to hate slavery. While still a young child, Nat was overheard describing events that had happened before he was born. Nat's master's son taught him to read.

Nat grew up involved deeply in religion and served as a preacher to the slaves around him. This, along with his keen intelligence, and other signs marked him in the eyes of his people as a prophet "intended for some great purpose." Some of the slaves he preached to, began to call him "the Prophet," owing to some of his visions that he thought God had communicated to him in dreams.

In 1821, Nat ran away from his overseer, returning after thirty days because of a vision in which the Spirit had told him to "return to the service of my earthly master." The next year, following the death of his master, Samuel Turner, Nat was sold to Thomas Moore.

Three years later, Nat Turner had another vision. He saw lights in the sky and prayed to find out what they meant. Then "... while laboring in the field, I discovered drops of blood on the corn, as though it were dew from heaven, and I communicated it to many, both white and Black, in the neighborhood; and then I found on the leaves in the woods hieroglyphic characters and numbers, with the forms of men in different attitudes, portrayed in blood, and representing the figures I had seen before in the heavens."

On May 12, 1828, Turner had his third vision: "I heard a loud noise in the heavens, and the Spirit instantly appeared to me and said the Serpent was loosened, and Christ had laid down the yoke he had borne for the sins of men, and that I should take it on and fight against the Serpent, for the time was fast approaching when the first should be last and the last should be first... And by signs in the heavens that it would make known to me when I should commence the great work, and until the first sign appeared I should conceal it from the knowledge of men; and on the appearance of the sign... I should arise and prepare myself and slay my enemies with their own weapons."

At the beginning of the year 1830, Turner was moved to the home of plantation owner and slaveholder Joseph Travis, the new husband of Thomas Moore's widow. His official owner was Putnum Moore, still a young child. Turner described Travis as a kind master, against whom he had no complaints.

Then, in February 1831, there was an eclipse of the sun. Turner took this to be the promised sign from God to start an insurrection and lead his people out of slavery. He confided his plan to the four men he trusted the most: Henry, Hark, Nelson, and Sam. They decided to hold the insurrection on the 4th of July and began planning a strategy. However, they had to postpone action because Turner became ill.

On August 13, there was an atmospheric disturbance in which the sun appeared bluish-green, served as another sign from God for Turner to commence his uprising. This was the final sign, and a week later, on August 21, Turner and the four other slaves met in the woods to eat a dinner and make their plans. At 2:00 that morning, they set out to the Travis household, where they killed the entire family (men, women and children) as they lay sleeping. They continued on, from house to house, killing all of the white people they encountered. Turner's force eventually consisted of more than 40 slaves, most on horseback.

By about mid-day on August 22, Turner decided to march toward Jerusalem, the closest town. By then, word of the rebellion had gotten out to the whites; confronted by a group of militia, the rebels scattered, and Turner's force became disorganized. After spending the night near some slave cabins, Turner and his men attempted to attack another house, but were repulsed. Several of the rebels were captured. In the end, the rebels had stabbed, shot and clubbed at least 55 white people to death.

The remaining rebel force then met the state and federal troops in a final skirmish, in which one slave was killed and many escaped. Turner had escaped and hid in several different places near the Travis farm; but on October 30th he was discovered and eventually captured in October. Turner was tried, hanged and skinned on November 11, 1831.

In total, the state executed 55 people, banished many more, and acquitted a few. The state reimbursed the slaveholders for their slaves. But in the hysterical climate that followed the rebellion, close to 200 Black people, many of whom had nothing to do with the rebellion, were murdered by white mobs. In addition, slaves as far away as North

Carolina were accused of having a connection with the insurrection and were subsequently tried and executed.

The state legislature of Virginia considered abolishing slavery, but in a close vote decided to retain slavery and to support a repressive policy against Black people, slave and free.

DRED SCOTT

Dred Scott (1800 - September 1858) migrated westward with his master, Peter Blow. They travelled from Scott's home state of Virginia to Alabama and then, in 1830, to St. Louis, Missouri. Two years later Peter Blow died; Scott was subsequently bought by army surgeon Dr. John Emerson, who later took Scott to the free state of Illinois. In the spring of 1836, after a stay of two and a half years, Emerson moved to a fort in the Wisconsin Territory, taking Scott along. While there, Scott met and married Harriet Robinson, a slave owned by a local justice of the peace. Ownership of Harriet was transferred to Emerson.

Scott's extended stay in Illinois, a free state, gave him the legal standing to make a claim for freedom, as did his extended stay in Wisconsin, where slavery was also prohibited. But Scott never made the claim while living in the free lands -- perhaps because he was unaware of his rights at the time, or perhaps because he was content with his master. After two years, the army transferred Emerson to the south: first to St Louis, then to Louisiana.

A little over a year later, a recently-married Emerson summoned his slave couple. Instead of staying in the free territory of Wisconsin, or going to the free state of Illinois, the two travelled over a thousand miles, apparently unaccompanied, down the Mississippi River to meet their master. Only after Emerson's death in 1843, after Emerson's widow hired Scott out to an army captain, did Scott seek freedom for himself and his wife. First he offered to buy his freedom from Mrs. Emerson -- then living in St. Louis -- for $300. The offer was refused. Scott then sought freedom through the courts.

Scott went to trial in June 1847 but lost on a technicality -- he couldn't prove that he and Harriet were owned by Emerson's widow. The following year, the Missouri Supreme Court decided that the case should be retried. In an 1850 retrial, the St Louis circuit court ruled that Scott and his family were free. Two years later the Missouri Supreme Court stepped in again, reversing the decision of the lower court. Scott and his lawyers then brought his case to a federal court, the United States Circuit Court in Missouri. In 1854, the Circuit Court upheld the decision of the Missouri Supreme Court. There was now only one other place to go. Scott appealed his case to the United States Supreme Court.

The nine justices of the Supreme Court of 1856 certainly had biases regarding slavery. Seven had been appointed by pro-slavery presidents from the South, and of these, five were from slave-holding families. Still, if the case had gone directly from the state supreme court to the federal supreme court, the federal court probably would have upheld the state's ruling, citing a previously established decision that gave states the authority to determine the status of its inhabitants.

But, in his attempt to bring his case to the federal courts, Scott had claimed that he and the case's defendant (Mrs. Emerson's brother, John Sanford, who lived in New York) were citizens from different states. The main issues for the Supreme Court, therefore, were whether it had jurisdiction to try the case and whether Scott was indeed a citizen.

The decision of the court was read in March of 1857. Chief Justice Roger B. Taney -- a staunch supporter of slavery -- wrote the "majority opinion" for the court. It stated that because Scott was Black, he was not a citizen and therefore had no right to sue. The decision also declared the Missouri Compromise of 1820, legislation which restricted slavery in certain territories, unconstitutional.

While the decision was well-received by slaveholders in the South, many northerners were outraged. The decision greatly influenced the nomination of Abraham Lincoln to the Republican Party and his subsequent election, which in turn led to the South's secession from the Union.

Peter Blow's sons, childhood friends of Scott, had helped pay Scott's legal fees through the years. After the Supreme Court's decision, the former master's sons purchased Scott and his wife and set them free on May 26, 1857.

Scott worked as a porter in a St. Louis hotel, but his freedom was short-lived. He died nine months later from tuberculosis in September 1858. He was survived by his wife and his two daughters.

The newspaper coverage of the court ruling, and the 10-year legal battle raised awareness of slavery in non-slave states. The arguments for freedom were later used by U.S. President Abraham Lincoln.

The harsh words of the decision built popular opinion and voter sentiment for his Emancipation Proclamation and the three constitutional amendments ratified shortly after the Civil War: the Thirteenth, Fourteenth and Fifteenth amendments, abolishing slavery, granting former slaves citizenship, and conferring citizenship to anyone born in the United States and "subject to the jurisdiction thereof" (excluding those subject to a foreign power such as children of foreign ambassadors).

JOHN BROWN

John Brown (May 9, 1800 – December 2, 1859) was an American abolitionist who believed in and advocated armed insurrection as the only way to overthrow the institution of slavery in the United States.

Moving about restlessly through Ohio, Pennsylvania, Massachusetts, and New York, Brown was barely able to support his large family in any of several vocations at which he tried his hand: tanner, sheep drover, wool merchant, farmer, and land speculator. Though he was white, in 1849 Brown settled with his family in a Black community founded at North Elba, New York, on land donated by the New York antislavery philanthropist Gerrit Smith.

Long a foe of slavery, Brown became obsessed with the idea of taking overt action to help win justice for enslaved Black people. In 1855 he followed five of his sons to the Kansas Territory to assist antislavery forces struggling for control there, a conflict that became known as

Bleeding Kansas. With a wagon laden with guns and ammunition, Brown settled in Osawatomie and soon became the leader of antislavery guerrillas in the area.

Brooding over the sack of the town of Lawrence by a mob of slavery sympathizers (May 21, 1856), Brown concluded that he had a divine mission to take vengeance. Three days later he led a nighttime retaliatory raid on a proslavery settlement at Pottawatomie Creek, in which five men were dragged out of their cabins and hacked to death during the raid, which became known as the Pottawatomie Massacre. Brown then commanded anti-slavery forces at the Battle of Black Jack (June 2) and the Battle of Osawatomie (August 30, 1856). The name of "Old Osawatomie Brown" conjured up a fearful image among local slavery apologists.

In the spring of 1858, Brown convened a meeting of Blacks and whites in Chatham, Ontario, Canada, at which he announced his intention of establishing in the Maryland and Virginia mountains a stronghold for escaping slaves. He proposed, and the convention adopted, a provisional constitution for the people of the United States. He was elected commander in chief of this paper government while gaining the moral and financial support of Gerrit Smith and several prominent Boston abolitionists. In addition to Smith, this group, later referred to as the "Secret Six," comprised physician and educator Samuel Gridley Howe, teacher and later journalist Franklin Benjamin Sanborn, industrialist George L. Stearns, and ministers Thomas Wentworth Higginson and Theodore Parker. Some of them had provided financial support for Brown's efforts in Kansas, and they would back his next and most famous undertaking, too.

In the summer of 1859, with an armed band of 16 whites and 5 blacks, Brown set up a headquarters in a rented farmhouse in Maryland, across the Potomac from Harpers Ferry, the site of a federal armory.

On the night of October 16, 1859 Brown led a raid on the federal armory at Harpers Ferry, Virginia (today West Virginia) to start a liberation movement among the slaves there. He took this desperate action in the hope that escaped slaves would join his rebellion, forming an "army of emancipation" with which to liberate their fellow slaves. He quickly took the armory and rounded up some 60 leading men from the area as hostages, but Brown himself was wounded, and 10 of his followers (including two sons) were killed. Brown intended to arm slaves with weapons from the arsenal, but the attack failed. Throughout the next day and night he and his men held out against the local militia; however within 36 hours, Brown's men had fled or been killed or captured by local farmers, militiamen and a contingency of troops under the command of Colonel Robert E. Lee, including a small force of U.S. Marines that had broken into the armory and overpowered Brown and his comrades.

He was tried for treason against the Commonwealth of Virginia, the murder of five men (including 3 Blacks), and inciting a slave insurrection, was found guilty on all counts, and was hanged. John Wilkes Booth, later Abraham Lincoln's assassin, was present at the execution as a militiaman.

The 1859 raid made him a martyr to the antislavery cause and was instrumental in heightening sectional animosities that led to the American Civil War (1861–65). Although Brown failed to spark a general slave revolt, the high moral tone of his defense helped to immortalize him and to hasten the war that would bring emancipation. As they marched into battle during the Civil War, Union soldiers sang a song called "John Brown's Body" that would later provide the tune for the "Battle Hymn of the Republic."

FREDERICK DOUGLASS

Frederick Douglass born **Frederick Augustus Washington Bailey** (February 1818 – February 20, 1895) was born on a plantation was between Hillsboro and Cordova on the Eastern Shore of the Chesapeake Bay in Talbot County, Maryland. Born into slavery, Frederick's birthplace was likely his grandmother's cabin, east of Tappers Corner, and west of Tuckahoe Creek. The exact date of his birth is unknown, and he later chose to celebrate his birthday on February 14th.

Frederick Douglass was an American social reformer, abolitionist, orator, writer, and statesman.

After escaping from slavery in Maryland, he became a national leader of the abolitionist movement in Massachusetts and New York, gaining note for his oratory and incisive antislavery writings. In his time, he was described by abolitionists as a living counter-example to slaveholders' arguments that slaves lacked the intellectual capacity to function as independent American citizens. Northerners at the time found it hard to believe that such a great orator had once been a slave.

Douglass was of mixed race, which likely included Native American and African on his mother's side, as well as European. According to historian, David W. Blight, Douglass's father was "almost certainly white." His mother Harriet Bailey gave him his name. After escaping to the North years later, he took the surname Douglass, having already dropped his two middle names.

Douglass did not recollect ever seeing his mother by the light of day. At night, she would lie down with him, and get him to sleep, but long before he waked she was gone.

After this early separation from his mother, young Frederick lived with his maternal grandmother, Betty Bailey. At the age of six, he was separated from his grandmother and moved to the Wye House plantation, where Aaron Anthony worked as overseer. Douglass's mother died when he was about ten. After Anthony died, Douglass was given to Lucretia Auld, wife of Thomas Auld, who sent him to serve Thomas' brother Hugh Auld in Baltimore.

When Douglass was about twelve, Hugh Auld's wife Sophia started teaching him the alphabet. Hugh Auld disapproved of the tutoring, feeling that literacy would encourage slaves to desire freedom. Under her husband's influence, Sophia came to believe that education and slavery were incompatible and one day snatched a newspaper away from Douglass.

However, Douglass continued, secretly, to teach himself how to read and write. When he was hired out to William Freeland, he taught other slaves on the plantation to read the New Testament at a weekly Sunday school. As word spread, the interest among slaves in learning to read was so great that in any week, more than 40 slaves would attend lessons. While Freeland remained complacent about their activities, other plantation owners became incensed about their slaves being educated; and they burst in on a gathering, armed with clubs and stones, to disperse the congregation permanently.

Douglass had spent seven relatively comfortable years in Baltimore before being sent back to the country. In 1833, as punishment for giving reading lessons to the other slaves, Thomas Auld took Douglass back from Hugh and sent Douglass to work for Edward Covey, a poor farmer who had a reputation as a notorious "slave-breaker." The treatment Douglass received was brutal. Whipped daily and barely fed, he was "broken in body, soul, and spirit."

The sixteen-year-old Douglass finally rebelled against the beatings and fought back. After Douglass won a physical confrontation, Covey never tried to beat him again.

Frederick tried to escape with three others in 1833, but the plot was discovered before they could get away. On January 1, 1836, Douglass made a resolution that he would be free by the end of the year. He planned an escape. But early in April he was jailed after his plan was discovered. Two years later, while living in Baltimore and working at a shipyard, Douglass would finally realize his dream: he fled the city on September 3, 1838. Travelling by train, then steamboat, then train, he arrived in New York City the following day. Several weeks later he had settled in New Bedford, Massachusetts, living with his newlywed bride (whom he met in Baltimore and married in New York). In New Bedford, he worked as a labourer for three years, eluding slave hunters by changing his surname to Douglass.

Five years later, however, he fled to New York City and then to New Bedford, Massachusetts, where Douglass was a firm believer in the equality of all peoples, whether B, female, Native American, or recent immigrant. He was also a believer in dialogue and in making alliances across racial and ideological divides, and in the liberal values of the U.S. Constitution.

Always striving to educate himself, Douglass continued his reading. He joined various organizations in New Bedford, including a Black church. He attended Abolitionists' meetings. He subscribed to William Lloyd Garrison's weekly journal, the *Liberator*. Garrison soon became impressed with Douglass, mentioning him in the *Liberator*.

At the age of 23, Frederick Douglass traveled to Nantucket, an island in Massachusetts, where he gave a stirring, eloquent speech to abolitionists at the Massachusetts Anti-Slavery Society's annual convention, about his life as a slave. Before leaving the island, Douglass was asked to become a lecturer for the Society for three years. It was the launch of a career and Douglass would become a leading spokesperson for the abolition of slavery and for racial equality and he would continue to give speeches for the rest of his life.

To avoid recapture by his former owner, whose name and location he had given in a narrative, Douglass left on a two-year speaking tour of Great Britain and Ireland. Abroad, Douglass helped to win many new friends for the abolition movement and to cement the bonds of humanitarian reform between the continents.

Douglass returned with funds to purchase his freedom and also to start his own antislavery newspaper, the *North Star* (later *Frederick Douglass's Paper*), which he published from 1847 to 1860 in Rochester, New York.

During the Civil War (1861–65) Douglass became a consultant to President Abraham Lincoln, advocating that former slaves be armed for the North and that the war be made a direct confrontation against slavery. Throughout Reconstruction (1865–77), Douglass fought for full civil rights for freedmen and vigorously supported the women's rights movement.

After Reconstruction, Douglass served as assistant secretary of the Santo Domingo Commission (1871), and in the District of Columbia he was marshal (1877–81) and recorder of deeds (1881–86). Finally, he was appointed U.S. minister and consul general to Haiti (1889–91).

Frederick Douglass was one of the most eminent human rights leaders of the 19th century. He held several public offices. His oratorical and literary brilliance thrust him into the forefront of the U.S. abolition movement, and he became the first black citizen to hold high rank in the U.S. government. Without his approval, Douglass became the first African American nominated for Vice President of the United States as the running mate and Vice Presidential nominee with Victoria Woodhull, on the Equal Rights Party ticket.

Douglass remained an active campaigner against slavery and wrote his autobiography, *Life and Times of Frederick Douglass*. First published in 1881 and revised in 1892, three years before his death, Douglass died from a heart attack at the age of 77 on February 20, 1895.

HARRIET TUBMAN

Harriet Tubman (1820 - March 10, 1913) was born a slave on a plantation in Dorchester County, Maryland. Her parents, Harriet ("Rit") Green and Benjamin Ross, named her **Araminta Ross** and called her "Minty." Harriet's mother, Rit, worked as a cook in the plantation's "big house," and her father, Benjamin, was a timber worker. Araminta later changed her first name to Harriet in honor of her mother.

Harriet had eight brothers and sisters, but the realities of slavery eventually forced many of them apart, despite Rit's attempts to keep the family together. When Harriet was five years old, she was rented out as a nursemaid where she was whipped when the baby cried, leaving her with permanent emotional and physical scars.

Around age seven Harriet was rented out to a planter to set muskrat traps and was later rented out as a field hand. She later said she preferred physical plantation work to indoor domestic chores.

Harriet's desire for justice became apparent at age 12 when she spotted an overseer about to throw a heavy weight at a fugitive slave. Harriet stepped between the slave and the overseer—the weight struck her head.

Harriet's good deed left her with headaches and narcolepsy the rest of her life, causing her to fall into a deep sleep at random. She also started having vivid dreams and hallucinations which she often claimed were religious visions (she was a staunch Christian). Her infirmity made her unattractive to potential slave buyers and renters.

In 1840, Harriet's father was set free and Harriet learned that Rit's owner's last will had set Rit and her children, including Harriet, free. But Rit's new owner refused to recognize the will and kept Rit, Harriett and the rest of her children in bondage.

Around 1844, Harriet married John Tubman, a free black man, and changed her last name from Ross to Tubman. The marriage was not good, and John threatened to sell Harriet further south. Her husband's threat and the knowledge that two of her brothers—Ben and Henry—were about to be sold provoked Harriet to plan an escape. She refused to live in under the oppression of slavery and found the courage to liberate herself and those she loved.

On September 17, 1849, Harriet, Ben and Henry escaped their Maryland plantation. The brothers, however, changed their minds and went back. With the help of the Underground Railroad, Harriet persevered and traveled 90 miles north to Pennsylvania and freedom. She changed her name in 1849 when she escaped. She adopted the name Harriet after her mother and the last name Tubman after her first husband, John.

After her escape, Harriet Tubman became a "conductor" on the Underground Railroad, leading slaves to freedom before the Civil

War, all while carrying a bounty on her head. But she was also a nurse, a Union spy and a women's suffrage supporter. Tubman is one of the most recognized icons in American history and her legacy has inspired countless people from every race and background.

The Underground Railroad was a network of people, African American as well as white, offering shelter and aid to escaped slaves from the South. It developed as a convergence of several different clandestine efforts, operating from the late 18th century to the Civil War, at which point its efforts continued to undermine the Confederacy in a less-secretive fashion. In the early 1800s abolitionist Isaac T. Hopper and fellow-Quakers set up a network in Philadelphia. They are considered the first organized group to actively help escaped slaves on the run. At the same time, Quakers in North Carolina established abolitionist groups that laid the groundwork for routes and shelters for escapees.

The African Methodist Episcopal Church, established in 1816, was another proactive religious group helping fugitive slaves. The earliest mention of the Underground Railroad came in 1831 when slave Tice Davids escaped from Kentucky into Ohio and his owner blamed an "underground railroad" for helping Davids to freedom.

In 1839, a Washington newspaper reported an escaped slave named Jim had revealed, under torture, his plan to go north following an "underground railroad to Boston." Vigilance Committees—created to protect escaped slaves from bounty hunters in New York in 1835 and Philadelphia in 1838—soon expanded their activities to guide slaves on the run. By the 1840s, the term Underground Railroad was part of the American vernacular.

The 1850 Fugitive Slave Act allowed fugitive and free slaves in the north to be captured and enslaved. The Fugitive Slave Act or Fugitive Slave Law was passed by the United States Congress on September

18, 1850, as part of the Compromise of 1850 between Southern slave-holding interests and Northern Free-Soilers. The Act was one of the most controversial elements of the 1850 compromise and heightened Northern fears of a "slave power conspiracy". It required that all escaped slaves, upon capture, be returned to their masters and that officials and citizens of free states had to cooperate.

The Fugitive Slave Act made Harriet's job as an Underground Railroad conductor much harder and forced her to lead slaves further north to Canada, traveling at night, usually in the spring or fall when the days were shorter. She carried a gun for both her own protection and to "encourage" her charges who might be having second thoughts. She often drugged babies and young children to prevent slave catchers from hearing their cries.

There were many well-used routes stretching west through Ohio to Indiana and Iowa. Others headed north through Pennsylvania and into New England or through Detroit on their way to Canada. People known as "conductors" guided the fugitive slaves. Hiding places included private homes, churches and schoolhouses. These were called "stations," "safe houses," and "depots." The people operating them were called "stationmasters."

From 1851 to 1860 Harriet Tubman became the most famous conductor of the Underground Railroad. In that decade she made 19 trips. It's believed that Harriet personally led at least 70 slaves to freedom, including her elderly parents, relatives and friends and instructed dozens of others on how to escape on their own. In every trip she made, she risked her life. The passage of the Fugitive Slave Law as part of the Compromise of 1850 made her job more dangerous. She was a fugitive slave and she was helping others escape. Under the law anyone capturing her would be financially compensated. However, she was a religious person and found courage in her belief in God. She declared that God spoke to her and guided her in her expeditions.

Harriet Tubman met abolitionist William Lloyd Garrison who nicknamed her "Moses." Frederick Douglass was a strong supporter of her activities opening his house in Rochester, New York to passengers of the Underground Railroad. At one point in time, he hosted 11 fugitives on their way to Canada. Tubman also supported John Brown's activities recruiting supporters for the Harpers Ferry Raid. Brown called her "General Tubman."

When the Civil War broke out in 1861, Harriet found new ways to fight slavery. Her service was selfless. She was recruited to assist fugitive slaves at Fort Monroe and worked as a nurse, cook and laundress. Harriet used her knowledge of herbal medicines to help treat sick soldiers and fugitive slaves.

In 1863, Harriet became head of an espionage and scout network for the Union Army. She provided crucial intelligence to Union commanders about Confederate Army supply routes and troops; and she became the first woman in the Civil War to lead an assault, the Combahee River Raid in which 700 slaves were set free to form Black Union regiments.

Though just over five feet tall, she was a force to be reckoned with, although it took over three decades for the government to recognize her military contributions and award her financially.

After the Civil War, Harriet settled with family and friends on land she owned in Auburn, New York. In 1860, she married former slave and Civil War veteran Nelson Davis a man 22 years younger than her. A few years later. Harriet and Nelson adopted a baby girl named Gertie.

Harriet had an open-door policy for anyone in need. She supported her philanthropy efforts by selling her home-grown produce, raising pigs and accepting donations and loans from friends. She remained illiterate, yet toured parts of the northeast speaking on behalf of the women's suffrage movement and worked with noted suffrage leader Susan B. Anthony.

In 1896, Harriet purchased land adjacent to her home and opened the Harriet Tubman Home for Aged and Indigent Colored People. Tubman always helped those in need but her financial situation was dire.

It is believed that the head injury she suffered when she was a teenager triggered visions and dreams. Later in her life, when she was about 78 years old, she found herself constantly unable to fall asleep because of a buzz in her head; she underwent surgery in Massachusetts General Hospital. She refused to be given anesthetics and instead did as soldiers did during the civil war, chewed on a bullet. The head injury she suffered in her youth continued to plague her and she endured brain surgery to help relieve her symptoms. But her health continued to deteriorate and eventually forced her to move into her namesake rest home in 1911.

She was very frail and spent her final years in the Harriet Tubman Home for the aged. Harriet Tubman died of pneumonia on March 10, 1913 at age 93. She is buried at Fort Hill Cemetery in Auburn, New York.

CIVIL RIGHTS LEADERS AND ACTIVISTS
20TH CENTURY

Never hesitate to reach out to the community to give back. It's very important for all of us to look out for our youngsters and to protect the community they are growing up in. Many people protected me and looked out for wrongdoing in my community when I was growing up and they were a great support system.

The Heroes and Sheroes of the 20th Century featured here have been very familiar to me as I have heard their names and admired their deeds and courageous acts since I was a young child. In fact, they are part of my reason for wanting to serve the community and for my ongoing commitment to Make the Grade.

CORETTA SCOTT KING

Coretta Scott King (April 27, 1927 – January 30, 2006) was an American author, activist, civil rights leader, and the wife of **Martin Luther King, Jr**. Coretta Scott King helped lead the Civil Rights Movement in the 1960s. She was an active advocate for African-American equality. King met her husband while in college, and their participation escalated until they became central to the movement. In her early life, Coretta was an accomplished singer, and she often incorporated music into her civil rights work.

Coretta Scott was born in Marion, Alabama, the third of four children of Obadiah Scott (1899–1998) and Bernice McMurry Scott (1904–1996). She was born in her parents' home with her paternal great-grandmother Delia Scott, a former slave, presiding as midwife. Coretta's mother became known for her musical talent and singing voice.

As a child, Coretta's mother, Bernice, attended the local Crossroads School and only had a fourth-grade education. She worked as a school bus driver, a church pianist, and for her husband in his business ventures. Coretta's father was one of the first black people in their town to own a vehicle. Before starting his own businesses, he worked as a policeman. Along with his wife, he ran a clothing shop far from their home and later opened a general store. He also owned a lumber mill, which was burned down by white neighbors after Scott refused to lend his mill to a white male logger.

Coretta's maternal grandparents, Mollie and Martin van Buren McMurry, were both of African American and Irish descent. Mollie was born a slave and Martin, was born to a slave of Black Native American ancestry, and her white master. Coretta's paternal grandparents were Cora, who died in 1920 before Coretta's birth and Jefferson F. Scott, who was a farmer and a prominent figure in the rural black religious community; he was born to former slaves Willis and Delia Scott.

Coretta had an older sister, Edythe Scott Bagley (1924–2011), an older sister named Eunice who did not survive childhood, and a younger brother, Obadiah Leonard (1930–2012). During the Great Depression the Scott children picked cotton to help earn money. At age 12, Coretta Scott entered Lincoln School as a seventh grader.

Though lacking formal education, themselves, Coretta Scott's parents intended for all of their children to be educated. The Scott children attended a one-room elementary school 5 miles from their home and were later bussed to Lincoln Normal School, 9 miles from their home, which was the closest Black high school in Marion, Alabama. The bus was driven by Coretta's mother Bernice, who bussed all the local Black teenagers.

In her last two years there, Coretta became the leading soprano for the school's senior chorus. She also directed a choir at her home church in North Perry Country. Coretta Scott graduated valedictorian from Lincoln Normal School in 1945 where she played trumpet and piano, sang in the chorus, and participated in school musicals. She enrolled at Antioch College in Yellow Springs, Ohio during her senior year at Lincoln.

Antioch had envisioned itself as a laboratory in democracy but had no black students. Coretta's sister, Edythe became the first African American to attend Antioch on a completely integrated basis and was joined by two other Black female students in the fall of 1943. The Antioch Program for Interracial Education, which recruited non-white students, gave them full scholarships in an attempt to diversify the historically white campus. After being accepted to Antioch, Coretta applied for the Interracial Scholarship Fund for financial aid.

Coretta studied music with Walter Anderson, the first non-white chair of an academic department in a historically white college. She also became politically active and joined the nascent civil rights movement; the Antioch chapter of the National Association for the Advancement of Colored People (NAACP); and the college's Race Relations and Civil Liberties Committees.

The board denied Coretta's request to perform her second year of required practice teaching at Yellow Springs public schools. For her teaching certificate Coretta Scott appealed to the Antioch College administration, which was unwilling or unable to change the situation in the local school system, and instead employed her at the college's associated laboratory school for a second year.

Coretta transferred out of Antioch when she won a scholarship to the New England Conservatory of Music in Boston. It was while studying singing at that school with Marie Sundelius that she met Martin Luther

King, Jr. after mutual friend Mary Powell gave King her phone number. King called Coretta on the telephone and when the two met in person, she was surprised by how short he was. King would tell her that she had all the qualities that he was looking for in a wife, which Coretta dismissed since the two had only just met. When King asked to see her again, Coretta readily accepted his invitation to a weekend party.

She continued to see him on a regular basis in the early months of 1952. Two weeks after meeting Coretta, King wrote to his mother that he had met his wife. Their dates usually consisted of political and racial discussions, and in August of that year Coretta met King's parents Martin Luther King, Sr. and Alberta Williams King.

Despite envisioning a career for herself in the music industry, Coretta knew that would not be possible if she were to marry Martin Luther King, Jr. However, since King possessed many of the qualities she liked in a man, she found herself "becoming more involved with every passing moment." When asked by her sister what made Martin so "appealing" to her she responded, "I suppose it's because Martin reminds me so much of our father." At that moment, Coretta's sister knew Martin was "the one."

On Valentine's Day 1953, the couple announced their plans to marry, in the *Atlanta Daily World,* with a wedding date for June 8' 1953. In September 1954, after completing her degree in voice and piano at the New England Conservatory, Coretta moved with Martin to Montgomery, Alabama. Martin had accepted an invitation to be the pastor of Dexter Avenue Baptist Church. Before long, the couple found themselves in the middle of the Montgomery bus boycott, and Martin was elected leader of the protest movement. Coretta had a growing sense that she was involved in something of profound historic importance. She started to realize that they had been thrust at the forefront of a movement to liberate oppressed people, not only in Montgomery but also throughout our country, and this movement had worldwide implications.

Coretta felt blessed to have been called to be a part of such a noble and historic cause.

On September 1, 1954, Martin Luther King, Jr. became the full-time pastor of Dexter Avenue Baptist Church. It was a sacrifice for Coretta, who had to give up her dreams of becoming a classical singer. Her devotion to the cause while giving up on her own ambitions would become symbolic of the actions of African American women during the movement. The couple moved into the church's parsonage on South Jackson Street shortly after this. Coretta became a member of the choir and taught Sunday school, as well as participating in the Baptist Training Union and Missionary Society. She made her first appearance at the First Baptist Church on March 6, 1955, where she captivated her concert audience."

The Kings welcomed their first child Yolanda on November 17, 1955, who was named at Coretta's insistence and became the church's attention.

On Thursday, December 1, 1955, Rosa Parks refused to give up her seat for a white person on the bus she took on her regular ride home from the Montgomery Fair department store. The bus driver called the Montgomery police, who took her to the station and booked, fingerprinted, and incarcerated her. She was charged with violating the Alabama bus segregation laws. Bond was posted for Mrs. Parks, and she went home.

By Monday, a bus boycott was organized. The NAACP, Women's Political Council, Baptist Ministers Conference, and the city's African Methodist Episcopal (AME) Zionist ministers united with the community to help. After the successful beginning of the boycott, the Montgomery Improvement Association (MIA) came into being that afternoon, and Martin Luther King, Jr. accepted the presidency.

After her husband became involved in the Montgomery Bus Boycott, Coretta often received threats directed towards him. On December 23, a gunshot rang through the front door of the King home while Coretta, Martin and Yolanda were asleep. The three were not harmed. On Christmas Eve of 1955, Coretta took her daughter to her parents' house and Martin joined them the next day.

As MIA leader, King became the focus of white hatred. On January 30, 1956, the King home was bombed. Coretta and Dexter congregation member Roscoe Williams's wife Mary Lucy heard the "sound of a brick striking the concrete floor of the front porch." Coretta suggested that the two women get out of the front room and went into the guest room, as the house was disturbed by an explosion which caused the house to rock and fill the front room with smoke and shattered glass. The two went to the rear of the home, where Yolanda was sleeping, and Coretta called the First Baptist Church and reported the bombing to the woman who answered the phone. Martin returned to their home, and upon finding Coretta and his daughter unharmed, went outside.

King had been speaking at a mass meeting at the First Baptist Church. When he heard the news, he told the crowd what happened, and left the church.

Nearing his house, King saw Blacks brandishing guns and knives, and a barricade of white policemen. King went inside and pushed through the crowd in his house to the back room to make sure Coretta and his ten-week-old baby were okay. Back in the front room of the house, some white reporters were trying to leave to file their stories, but could not get out of the house, which was surrounded by armed, angry Blacks. King was able to turn them away with an impromptu speech.

A white man was reported by a lone witness to have walked halfway up to King's door and thrown something against the door before running back to his car and speeding off. "That night Coretta lost her fear of dying. She committed herself more deeply to the freedom struggle, as Martin had done four days previously, when jailed for the first time in his life." Coretta would later call it the first time she realized "how much I meant to Martin in terms of supporting him in what he was doing."

Coretta answered numerous phone calls threatening her husband's life. By the end of the boycott, Mrs. King and her husband had come to believe in nonviolent protests as a way of expression consistent with biblical teachings...Coretta took an active role in advocating for civil rights legislation.

The bombing inspired the MIA to file a federal suit directly attacking the laws establishing bus segregation. In the meanwhile, for thirteen months the 17,000 black people in Montgomery walked to work or obtained lifts from the small car-owning black population of the city. Eventually, the loss of revenue and a decision by the Supreme Court forced the Montgomery Bus Company to accept integration, and the boycott came to an end on December 20, 1956. The success of the boycott became apparent when King and several allies boarded a public bus in front of King's home on December 21, 1956.

On April 25, 1958, Coretta made an appearance at a concert at Peter High School Auditorium in Birmingham, Alabama. Coretta gave the audience "an emotional connection to the messages of social, economic, and spiritual transformation."

On September 3, 1958, Coretta accompanied her husband and Ralph Abernathy to a courtroom. Her husband was arrested outside the courtroom for "loitering" and "failing to obey an officer." A few weeks later, Coretta visited Martin's parents in Atlanta. At that time, she learned that he had been stabbed while signing copies of his book *Stride Toward Freedom* on September 20, 1958. Coretta rushed to see Martin and stayed with him for the remainder of his time in the hospital recovering.

On February 3, 1959, Coretta, Martin and Lawrence Reddick started a five-week tour of India. The three were invited to hundreds of engagements. During their trip, Coretta used her singing ability to enthuse crowds during stay. Martin and Coretta returned to the United States on March 10, 1959.

Martin Luther King was jailed on October 19, 1960, for picketing in a department store. After being released three days later, he was sent back to jail on October 22 for driving with an Alabama license while being a resident of Georgia and was sent to jail for four months of hard labor.

Coretta believed he would not make it out alive and telephoned her friend Harris Wofford who contacted Sargent Shriver in Chicago, where presidential candidate John F. Kennedy was campaigning. Shriver suggested that he telephone King and sometime afterward, Bobby Kennedy obtained King's release from prison. During John Kennedy's presidency, the Kings had come to respect him and understood his reluctance at times to get involved openly with civil rights.

In April 1962, Coretta served as delegate for the Women's Strike for Peace Conference in Geneva, Switzerland. Martin drove her to the hospital on March 28, 1963, where she gave birth to their fourth child, Bernice. After Coretta and her daughter were due to come home,

Martin rushed back to drive them himself. After Martin's arrest on April 12, 1963, Coretta tried to make direct contact with President Kennedy at the advisement of Reverend Wyatt Tee Walker, and succeeded in speaking with Robert F. Kennedy. The next day, President Kennedy reported to Coretta that the FBI had been sent into Birmingham the previous night and confirmed that her husband was fine.

Coretta and Martin learned of John F. Kennedy's assassination when reports initially indicated he had only been seriously wounded. Coretta joined her visibly shaken husband and watched Walter Cronkite announce the president's death.

Coretta worked hard to pass the Civil Rights Act of 1964. On March 26, 1965, Coretta's father joined her and Martin for a march that would later end in Montgomery. Her father called it "the greatest day in the whole history of America" after seeing chanting for his daughter's husband by both Caucasians and African Americans.

Coretta Scott King criticized the sexism of the Civil Rights Movement in January 1966 in *New Lady* magazine, saying in part, "Not enough attention has been focused on the roles played by women in the struggle. By and large, men have formed the leadership in the civil rights struggle but...women have been the backbone of the whole civil rights movement." Martin Luther King, Jr. himself limited Coretta's role in the movement, and expected her to be a housewife. Coretta participated in a "Women Strike for Peace" protest in January 1968, at the capital of Washington, D.C. with over five thousand women. In honor of the first woman elected to the House of Representatives, the group was called the Jeannette Rankin Brigade. Coretta co-chaired the Congress of Women conference with Pearl Willen and Mary Clarke.

Martin Luther King, Jr. was shot and killed in Memphis, Tennessee on April 4, 1968. Coretta learned of the shooting after being called by

Jesse Jackson when she returned from shopping with her eldest child Yolanda.

On April 5, 1968, Coretta arrived in Memphis to retrieve her husband's body and decided that the casket should be kept open during the funeral, with the hope that her children would realize upon seeing his body that he would not be coming home. On April 7, 1968, former Vice President Richard Nixon visited Mrs. King and recalled his first meeting with her husband in 1955. Nixon also went to Mrs. King's husband's funeral on April 9, 1968 but did not walk in the procession. Nixon believed participating in the procession would be "grandstanding."

On April 8, 1968, Mrs. King and her children headed a march with sanitation workers that her husband had planned to carry out before his death. With the end of the funeral service, Mrs. King led her children and mourners in a march from the church to Morehouse College, her late husband's alma mater.

Two days after her husband's death, King spoke at Ebenezer Baptist Church and made her first statement on his views since he had died. She said her husband told their children, "If a man had nothing that was worth dying for, then he was not fit to live." Not very long after the assassination, Coretta took his place at a peace rally in New York City. Using notes that he had written before his death, Coretta King constructed her own speech. She approached the African-American entertainer and activist Josephine Baker to take her husband's place as leader of the Civil Rights Movement, but Baker declined. Shortly after that, Mrs. King decided to take the helm of the movement herself.

On April 27, 1968, King spoke at an anti-war demonstration in Central Park in place of her husband. King made it clear that there was no reason "why a nation as rich as ours should be blighted by poverty, disease and illiteracy." King used notes taken from her husband's pockets upon his death, which included the "Ten Commandments on Vietnam."

Coretta Scott King eventually broadened her focus to include women's rights, LGBT rights, economic issues, world peace, and various other causes. She played a prominent role in the years after her husband's assassination when she took on the leadership of the struggle for racial equality herself and became active in the Women's Movement. In December 1968, she called for women to "unite and form a solid block of women power to fight the three great evils of racism, poverty and war", during a Solidarity Day speech.

In January 1969, King and Bernita Bennette left for a trip to India. Before arriving in the country, the two stopped in Verona, Italy and King was awarded the Universal Love Award. King became the first non-Italian to receive the award.

Every year after the assassination of her husband, Coretta attended a commemorative service at Ebenezer Baptist Church in Atlanta to mark his birthday on January 15. She founded the King Center and fought for years to make his birthday a national holiday. In 1972, she said that there should be at least one national holiday a year in tribute to an African-American man, "and, at this point, Martin is the best candidate we have."

During the 1980s, Coretta Scott King reaffirmed her long-standing opposition to apartheid, participating in a series of sit-in protests in Washington, D.C. that prompted nationwide demonstrations against South African racial policies.

On June 26, 1985, Coretta was arrested with her daughter Bernice and son Martin Luther King III while taking part in an anti-apartheid protest at the Embassy of South Africa in Washington, D.C. King had a 10-day trip to South Africa in September 1986, during which she met with Winnie Mandela, and called it "one of the greatest and most meaningful moments of my life." Upon her return to the United States, she urged Reagan to approve economic sanctions against South Africa.

Corretta Scott King was an early supporter in the struggle for gay and lesbian civil rights. In August 1983 in Washington, D.C., she urged the amendment of the Civil Rights Act to include gays and lesbians as a protected class. In 2003, she invited the National Gay and Lesbian Task Force to take part in observances of the 40th anniversary of the March on Washington and Martin Luther King's "I Have a Dream" speech. It was the first time that an LGBT rights group had been invited to a major event of the African American community.

The fight to make Dr. Martin Luther King Jr.'s birthday a holiday took 32 years, a lot of campaigning, and guest appearances including Stevie Wonder, Ted Kennedy, and the National Football League. Coretta's mission finally succeeded when, on November 2, 1983 Ronald Reagan signed legislation which established Martin Luther King, Jr. Day. The first federal King holiday was celebrated in 1986.

On January 17, 1992, President George H. W. Bush laid a wreath at the tomb of her husband and met with and was greeted by Mrs. King at the center. King praised Bush's support for the holiday and joined hands with him at the end of a ceremony and sang "We Shall Overcome."

By the end of her 77th year, Coretta began experiencing health problems. Hospitalized in April 2005, a month after speaking in Selma at the 40th anniversary of the Selma Voting Rights Movement, she was diagnosed with a heart condition and was discharged on her 78th and final birthday. Later, she suffered several small strokes. On August 16, 2005, she was hospitalized after suffering a stroke and a mild heart attack. She was released from Piedmont Hospital in Atlanta on September 22, 2005, after regaining some of her speech and continued physiotherapy at home. Due to continuing health problems, Mrs. King cancelled a number of speaking and traveling engagements throughout the remainder of 2005. On January 14, 2006, Coretta made her last public appearance in Atlanta at a dinner honoring her husband's memory.

On January 26, 2006, King checked into a rehabilitation center in Rosarito Beach, Mexico under a different name. Doctors did not learn her real identity until her medical records arrived the next day, and did not begin treatment due to her condition. Coretta Scott King died on the late evening of January 30, 2006, at the rehabilitation center in Rosarito Beach, Mexico, In the Oasis Hospital where she was undergoing holistic therapy for her stroke and advanced-stage ovarian cancer. The main cause of her death is believed to be respiratory failure due to complications from ovarian cancer.

Coretta King's eight-hour funeral at the New Birth Missionary Baptist Church in Lithonia, Georgia was held on February 7, 2006. Bernice King delivered her eulogy. Her funeral was attended by some 10,000 people, including four of five living US presidents: U.S. Presidents George W. Bush, Bill Clinton, George H.W. Bush and Jimmy Carter, and their wives, with the exception of former First Lady Barbara Bush who had a previous engagement. The Ford family was absent due to the illness of President Ford (who himself died later that year). Senator and future President Barack Obama, among other elected officials, attended the televised service.

President Jimmy Carter and Rev. Joseph Lowery delivered funeral orations.

Mrs. King was temporarily laid in a mausoleum on the grounds of the King Center until a permanent place next to her husband's remains could be built. On November 20, 2006, the new mausoleum containing the bodies of both Dr. and Mrs. King was unveiled in front of friends and family. The mausoleum is the third resting place of Martin Luther King, and the second of Mrs. King. Coretta Scott King was inducted into the Alabama Women's Hall of Fame and was the first African American to lie in the Georgia State Capitol. Coretta Scott King has been referred to as "First Lady of the Civil Rights Movement."

The Kings had four children; Yolanda, Martin III, Dexter and Bernice. All four children later followed in their parents' footsteps as civil rights activists.

Coretta was viewed during her lifetime and posthumously as having striven to preserve her husband's legacy. The King Center, which she created the year of his assassination, allowed her husband's tomb to be memorialized. King was buried with her husband after her death, on February 7, 2006. King "fought to preserve his legacy" and her construction of the King Center is said to have aided in her efforts.

AARON LLOYD DIXON

Political activist **Aaron Lloyd Dixon** (January 2, 1949) was born in Chicago, Illinois to Frances Sledge Dixon and Elmer James Dixon. The Dixons were leftist activists and valued the importance of fighting social injustice. Dixon moved to Seattle, Washington in 1958, when his father accepted a job as a technical illustrator for the United States Air Force. In 1961, at age eleven, Dixon walked alongside Dr. Martin Luther King Jr., in his march to end housing discrimination in Seattle. He attended Coleman Elementary School, Blaine Junior High School and in 1963, became one of the first African American youth to integrate predominantly white Queen Anne High School.

In 1967, Dixon attended Washington University and joined the local SNCC chapter. As a member of SNCC, Dixon met the black radical Larry Gossett, and co-founded the Seattle Area Black Student Union (SABSU). As members of the SABSU, Dixon, Gossett, and Dixon's younger brother, Elmer, promoted self-determination, self-respect and self-defense throughout Seattle's black community.

In 1968, after attending funeral services in Oakland, California for seventeen-year-old Bobby Hutton, a founding member of the Black Panther Party that was shot down by Oakland police, Dixon, Gossett, and others established the Seattle chapter of the Black Panther Party. As founding member and captain of the Seattle chapter of the Black Panther Party, Dixon helped launch the Free Breakfast for School Children Program, which fed over 10,000 children every day before school. Dixon was also instrumental in the opening of a free medical and legal clinic.

In 2002, Dixon founded the non-profit organization, Central House, to provide transitional housing for homeless young adults. Central House currently contains a youth leadership project that teaches youth to think positively, graduate high school and to control their destinies. In 2006, the Green Party of Washington nominated Dixon for the U.S. Senate. Following his campaign for U.S. Senate, Dixon organized the Center for Social Justice based out of the Seattle Central District. The Center for Social Justice organized an anti-war rally and march in January 2007.

SHIRLEY CHISOLM

Shirley Chisolm, born **Shirley Anita St. Hill Chisholm**, (November 30, 1924 - January 1, 2005) is an advocate for the rights of people of color and for women's rights. Shirley was born in Brooklyn, New York. In November 1968 she became the first black woman elected to the United States Congress.

Shirley was the eldest of four daughters of parents who were immigrants from Barbados. When she was three years old, Shirley was sent to live with her grandmother on a farm in Barbados, a former British colony in the West Indies. She received much of her primary education in the Barbadian school system, which stressed the traditional British teachings of reading, writing, and history.

When Chisholm was ten years old, she returned to New York during the height of the Great Depression (1929–39). Life was not easy for the Chisholms in New York, and Shirley's parents sacrificed much for their eight children.

Shirley attended New York public schools and was able to compete well in the mainly white classrooms. She attended Girls' High School in Bedford-Stuyvesant, a section of Brooklyn. She won tuition scholarships to several distinguished colleges but was unable to afford the room and board, so she decided to live at home and attend Brooklyn College.

While training to be a teacher, Shirley became active in several campus and community groups. She developed an interest in politics and learned the arts of organizing and fundraising. Soon, she developed a deep resentment toward the role of women in local politics, which, at the time, consisted mostly of staying in the background and playing a secondary role to their male equals. Through campus politics and her work with the National Association for the Advancement of Colored People (NAACP), Shirley found a way to voice her opinions about economic and social structures in a rapidly changing nation.

Shirley received her B.A. degree, graduating with honors from Brooklyn College of the City University of New York in 1946; and in 1952 she earned her M.A. degree from Columbia University while working as a nursery school teacher. Later, Shirley served as director of the Hamilton-Madison Child Care Center until the late 1950s, then as an educational consultant for New York City's Bureau of Child Welfare.

During her successful career as an educator, Shirley became involved in several organizations including the League of Women Voters and the Seventeenth Assembly District Democratic Club. She became politically active with the Democratic Party and quickly developed a reputation as a person who challenged the traditional roles of women,

African Americans, and the poor. In 1949, she married Conrad Chisholm, and the couple settled in Brooklyn.

After working several years as a teacher, Chisholm decided to run for the New York State Assembly. Her ideals were perfect for the times. In the mid-1960s the civil rights movement was in full swing. Across the nation, activists were working for equal civil rights for all Americans, regardless of race.

In 1964, Shirley began her political career as a member of the New York State legislature as an assemblyperson. During the time that she served in the assembly Chisholm sponsored fifty bills, but only eight of them passed. One of the successful bills she supported, helped poor students to go on to higher education. Another provided employment insurance coverage for personal and domestic employees. Still another bill reversed a law that caused female teachers in New York to lose their tenure (permanence of position) while they were out on maternity leave.

After four years as an assemblywoman, Shirley Chisholm was elected on the Democratic ticket to serve in the U.S. Congress. In 1969, she became the first Black woman to serve in the United States Congress and began the first of seven terms. Her opponent was the civil rights leader James Farmer. Shirley Chisolm's long career in the U.S. House of Representatives, lasted from the Ninety-first through the Ninety-seventh Congress (1969–1982).

After initially being assigned to the House Forestry Committee, Shirley shocked many by demanding reassignment. She was placed on the Veterans' Affairs Committee, eventually graduating to the Education and Labor Committee. She became one of the founding members of the Congressional Black Caucus in 1969.

Shirley Chisolm had served two terms, and in 1972 she ran in the New York Democratic primary for the highest office in the land, president of the United States of America, establishing another first for Black women. In addition to her interest in civil rights, she spoke out about the judicial system in the United States, police brutality, prison reform, gun control, drug abuse, and numerous other topics. Shirley did not win the Democratic nomination, but she did win an impressive 10 percent of the votes within the party. As a result of her candidacy, Chisholm was voted one of the ten most admired women in the world.

After her unsuccessful presidential campaign, Shirley continued to serve in the U.S. House of Representatives for another decade. As a member of the Black Caucus (a group of lawmakers who represent African Americans) she was able to watch black representation in the Congress grow and to welcome other black female congresswomen.

Shirley Chisholm's 1949 marriage to Conrad Chisholm ended in divorce in February 1977. Later that year she wed Arthur Hardwick Jr. In 1982, she announced her retirement from Congress.

After leaving Congress, Shirley was named to the Purington Chair at Mount Holyoke College in Massachusetts where she taught politics and women's studies for four years. Chisholm continued to be involved in politics by cofounding the National Political Congress of Black Women in 1984. She also worked for the presidential campaigns of Jesse Jackson in 1984 and 1988. In 1985 she became a visiting scholar at Spelman College in Atlanta, Georgia and in 1987 she retired from teaching altogether.

In the later years of her life, Chisholm became a sought-after speaker on the lecture circuit. In 1993 President Bill Clinton nominated Chisholm for the position of Ambassador to Jamaica. Because of declining health, she turned down the nomination.

Although Chisholm broke ground as the nation's first Black congresswoman and the first Black presidential candidate, she has said she would rather be remembered for continuing throughout her life to fight for rights for women and African Americans.

Shirley Chisholm died on January 1, 2005, at the age of 80, in Ormond Beach (near Daytona Beach), Florida. Nearly 11 years later, in November 2015, she was posthumously awarded the distinguished Presidential Medal of Freedom.

AL SHARPTON

Rev Al Sharpton, born **Alfred Charles Sharpton Jr**. (October 3, 1954) to parents to Ada (Richards) and Alfred Charles Sharpton Sr. in the Brownsville neighborhood of Brooklyn, New York. He is an American civil rights activist, Baptist minister, television/radio talk show host and a former White House adviser for President Barack Obama.

Sharpton began preaching at age four at Washington Temple Church of God & Christ in Brooklyn, where he was licensed by the legendary Bishop F. D. Washington at age nine to be a minister in that denomination. In 1963, Al and his mother moved from middle class Hollis, Queens, to the public housing projects in the Brownsville neighborhood of Brooklyn. Sharpton became an ordained Pentecostal minister at age 10.

He likewise started his civil rights career very young. At age 13, he was appointed, by Reverends Jesse Jackson and William Jones, the youth director of New York's Southern Christian Leadership Conference (SCLC) Operation Breadbasket (founded by Dr. Martin Luther King Jr.). In 1971, at age 16, Sharpton founded the National Youth Movement Inc. which organized young people around the country promoting voter registration, cultural awareness and job training programs, as well as social and economic justice for African Americans..

Al Sharpton was educated in public schools in New York. In 1972, he accepted the position of youth director for the presidential campaign of African-American Congresswoman Shirley Chisholm. That same year, he graduated from Tilden High School in Brooklyn, and briefly attended Brooklyn College, dropping out after two years in 1975. He was later presented with an honorary degree from A.P. Clay Bible College.

Between the years 1973 and 1980 Sharpton served as James Brown's tour manager. While touring with James Brown, he met future wife Kathy Jordan, who was a backup singer. Sharpton and Jordan married in 1980. The couple separated in 2004. Rev. Al and Kathy Jordan Sharpton have two daughters, Dominique and Ashley.

In 1991, Sharpton founded the National Action Network (NAN) a broad-based, progressive civil rights organization which he still heads. NAN promotes progressive policies, including affirmative action and reparations for African Americans for the enslavement of their ancestors. As the head of one of the most well-known civil rights organizations that has over forty chapters and affiliates across the United States, Rev. Sharpton has been applauded by both supporters and non-supporters for challenging the American political establishment to be inclusive to all people regardless of race, gender, class or beliefs.

From 1994 to 1998, Rev. Sharpton served as Director of the Ministers Division for the National Rainbow Push Coalition under Rev. Jesse Jackson while still serving as the head of NAN. Upon the death of Bishop Washington in the late 80s, Rev. Sharpton became a Baptist, and in 1994, he was re-baptized as a member of the Bethany Baptist Church by Rev. William Jones.

In the 1990s Sharpton entered the political arena, unsuccessfully seeking the Democratic Party nominations for mayor of New York City and U.S. senator from New York state. In 1999, when a young unarmed African immigrant was gunned down in the vestibule of his home by four New York City police officers, Sharpton led 1,200 people in the civil disobedience protest arrest. The throngs that followed him to jail in this protest included former mayors, congressman and religious and community leaders across racial, ethnic and political lines.

Rev. Sharpton's platforms against racial profiling and police brutality has reached an international audience, and his work on human rights issues has taken him to Sudan, Israel, Europe and further, where he has formed alliances with international peace activists across the world. But perhaps his most significant international visit was his sojourn to Vieques, Puerto Rico in 2001. Sharpton and three Latino elected officials from New York visited Vieques to protest the U.S. Naval bombing exercises on the island, a practice that has endured for over 60 years.

Sharpton and the other members of the "Vieques Four" led the protest at the U.S. Naval Base in Puerto Rico and were subsequently arrested, tried several weeks later and sentenced to 40 to 90 days – Sharpton received the longest sentence – in federal prison for their protests. While Sharpton was in jail, he fasted, losing eighty pounds.. Because of the stand that the "Vieques Four" took that summer, President

George W. Bush addressed the issue and ordered the Navy to end their exercises in 2003.

In 2004 Sharpton campaigned unsuccessfully for the Democratic nomination for the U.S. presidency. Sharpton subsequently began hosting a radio talk show, *Keepin' It Real*. He also appeared frequently as a television commentator, and in 2011 he became host of a news-and-opinion show, *PoliticsNation*, on the cable channel MSNBC.

Rev. Sharpton is a member of Bethany Baptist Church in his native Brooklyn neighborhood where the late William A. Jones, Jr., was the Pastor. Rev. Sharpton still preaches throughout the United States and abroad on most Sunday's, and averages eighty formal sermons a year.

MAXINE SMITH

Maxine (Atkins) Smith (October 31, 1929 — April 26, 2013) was born in Memphis, Tennessee. She was an academic, civil rights activist, and school board official.

Maxine Smith was considered the "Mother of the Civil Rights Movement in Memphis."

Smith's leadership in the National Association for the Advancement of Colored People (NAACP), and her involvement with educational planning at both the local and state levels in Tennessee, enabled her to support the American Civil Rights Movement and advance school desegregation.

She coordinated the desegregation of everything in Memphis from schools to lunch counters to theater seating, and libraries, as well as public accommodations and facilities. Maxine Smith was an unstoppable force during the Civil Rights Movement, not only in Memphis but across America.

Smith was the youngest of three children of Joseph and Georgia Rounds Atkins. In 1945, at age 15, she graduated from Booker T. Washington High School in Memphis. She earned a bachelor's degree in biology from Spelman College in Atlanta in 1949, and a master's degree in French from Middlebury College in Vermont. In 1955 she married Vasco A. Smith, Jr., a dentist, civil rights leader, and the first Black county commissioner in Memphis. Smith gave birth to a son in 1956.

Machine Smith became assistant professor of French at Prairie View A&M University in Prairie View, Texas, and then at Florida A&M University in Tallahassee, Florida. She then taught briefly at Le Moyne College in Syracuse, New York.

In 1957, Smith applied to pursue graduate studies at the University of Memphis but was denied admission because she was Black. This led her to become involved with the Memphis Branch of the NAACP. In 1962, Smith was named Executive Secretary of the branch, and continued in that role until her retirement in 1995.

In 1960, Smith assisted in desegregating Memphis public schools, and in 1961 Smith personally escorted the first 13 black children to their new desegregated schools. Through her leadership with the Memphis NAACP, Smith advocated for civil rights by organizing sit-ins, marches, lawsuits, voter registration drives, and student boycotts such as the "If You're Black, Take It Back" campaign to boycott downtown stores which had segregated water fountains and work forces.

In 1968, Smith served on the coordinating committee of the Memphis Sanitation Strike, an event which brought Martin Luther King, Jr. to the city, where he was assassinated.

In 1971, Smith was the first African-American elected to the Memphis Board of Education, a position she held until her retirement in 1995.

Smith advocated for the promotion of school principal W. W. Herenton to the role of school superintendent in 1978, the first African-American to hold that position in Memphis. Smith later supported Herenton's successful bid to become mayor of Memphis.

In 1991, Smith was elected president of the Memphis Board of Education, a role she served for two terms, retiring in 1995. In 1994, Tennessee Governor Ned McWherter appointed Smith to the Tennessee Board of Regents, the governing body for many public colleges and universities throughout the state.

Smith was presented with a Freedom Award by the National Civil Rights Museum in 2003 and awarded a Doctor of Humane Letters by her alma mater, Spelman College, in 2004. She was featured in the 2008 documentary about the Civil Rights Movement, "The Witness: From the Balcony of Room 306."

Maxine Smith suffered a number of health issues and underwent heart surgery in 2012. She died April 26, 2013 at age 83 and was buried at Elmwood Cemetery in Memphis.

DOROTHY PITMAN HUGHES

Gloria Steinem (left) Dorothy Pitman Hughes (right)

Dorothy Pitman Hughes (October 2, 1938) is a feminist, child-welfare advocate, Community activist, public speaker, author, pioneering African-American small business owner, and mother of three daughters. In 1990 Oprah Winfrey honored Hughes as one of America's "Great Moms."

Dorothy Ridley was born 1938 in Lumpkin, Georgia. Her father was beaten when she was ten years old and left for dead on the family's doorstep; the family believes it to be a crime committed by Ku Klux Klan members. Dorothy decided as a child in reaction to her family's experiences she would devote her life to improving the circumstances of people through activism.

Dorothy moved from Georgia to New York City in 1957 where she worked in entertainment as a singer through the 1960s. Her journey as a community activist began in the 60's when she gave up a budding singing career to become a full-time activist, on a mission to help people gain and maintain a better lifestyle, giving unselfishly to the needs of her community – wherever she has lived.

Dorothy began her activism by raising bail money for civil rights protesters. She organized the first shelter for battered women in New York City. Dorothy also owned and personally operated four child-care centers for infants to youth "after-school" programs in New York Communities, and co-founded the Agency for Child Development (ACD), noting that "too many women were being forced to leave their children home alone while they worked to feed their families." ACD remains active to this day, caring for over 175,000 children.

Dorothy Pitman Hughes and Gloria Steinem met in New York City because of their mutual work for women and child welfare. Dorothy and Gloria toured together speaking about race, class and gender throughout the 1970s. In 1971 Dorothy co-founded with Gloria Steinem the Women's Action Alliance, a pioneering national information center that specialized in nonsexist, multiracial children's education.

In 1971 Dorothy Pitman-Hughes, along with feminist and sociopolitical activist Gloria Steinem, was a co-founder of *Ms magazine*, an American liberal feminist magazine, which was published monthly and has enjoyed great popularity for decades. Dorothy and Gloria toured together to raise awareness of gender, race and class issues throughout the 1970s.

Hughes noted the unlikely nature of their friendship at the time, admitting the terror she felt of being seen in public with a white woman in her hometown of Lumpkin, Georgia when Steinem would visit. The two women spoke again in 2008 at Eckerd College where they reenacted their raised fist pose together.

Pitman Hughes has been a guest lecturer at Columbia University, taught a course called "The Dynamics of Change" at the College of New Rochelle, and a guest lecturer at City College, Manhattan.

In 1992, Dorothy co-founded the Charles Junction Historic Preservation Society in Jacksonville, Florida using the former Junction homestead to combat poverty through community gardening and food production.

In 1997 Dorothy Pitman-Hughes became the first African-American woman to own an office supply/copy center and to become a member of the Stationers Association of New York (SANY). The Harlem Office Supply and Copy Center was located on 125th Street in Harlem, New York from 1997 to 2007 In May 1997, Hughes, as CEO of Harlem Office Supply, Inc. began to offer HOS stock at $1.00 a share to individuals, corporations, partnerships and non-profit organizations focused on African-American children. She wrote about her experiences in *Wake Up and Smell the Dollars!* (2011), advocating small business ownership to other African Americans as a form of empowerment.

Dorothy Pitman Hughes was involved in the Upper Manhattan Empowerment Zone (UMEZ), a federal program instituted by the Clinton administration in 1994 designating $300 million of federal, state, and city money for the economic development of Harlem. Hughes was also part of the research team that created the Business Resource and Investment Service Center (BRISC), which focused on the development of small, locally owned businesses in Harlem.

Hughes later became a critic, stating that the programs brought large businesses like Old Navy and Disney into Harlem to create jobs; but they ultimately created more competition for locally owned businesses. "Some are convinced that empowering large corporations to provide low paying jobs for our residents will bring economic empowerment to the community.... [But] without African-American ownership, there is ultimately no local empowerment," stated Hughes, believing BRISC's resources were being unevenly distributed among small businesses in Harlem. Hughes later wrote *Just Saying... It Looks Like Ethnic Cleansing (The Gentrification of Harlem)* providing advice to African American business owners who might want to utilize similar government programs such as the JOBS Act, signed into law by U.S. President Barack Obama in 2012.

Dorothy Hughes relocated from New York to Jacksonville and for several years, she owned and operated the Gateway Bookstore in Jacksonville, Florida. Hughes now focuses her activism in the Northside community of Jacksonville, Florida and works with the Episcopal Children's Services to combat poverty by creating community food gardens, with support from friend and co-activist Gloria Steinem. She also recently joined forces with Reclaim Global Organization, founded by D. Kaye Smith to help women who were sexually abused as children to reclaim their identity and end the pain of sexual abuse. Presently, the organization boasts a membership of 28,000 people nationally. She continues to tour on occasion, speaking out about community issues and social injustices.

Now part of the National Portrait Gallery collection, Smithsonian Institution, Washington D.C., a special show of unity between Dorothy Hughes and Gloria Steinem was translated into an iconic black and white photograph of Hughes and Steinem. Taken by photographer Dan Wynn for Esquire Magazine and published in October 1971, Wynn captured Steinem and Hughes signaling their feminist solidarity by sharing the same large skirt and raising their fists in the raised-fist salute, first popularized by members of the Black Power movement.

Dorothy and Gloria's decades-long friendship will be etched forever in Gloria Steinem's biopic, "The Glorias: A Life on The Road." The film "follows Steinem's journey to become a crusader for equal rights and her groundbreaking work as a journalist and campaigner." Dorothy Pitman Hughes, who was a major part of that journey is portrayed by artist-activist Janelle Monae'.

"The greatness of people springs from their ability to grasp the grand conceptions of being. It is the absorption of a people, of a nation, of a rare, in large majestic and abiding things which lifts them up to the skies."
- Alexander Crummell

CHAPTER FIVE – SPIRITUALITY
FEATURING RELIGIOUS LEADERS

Your spiritual journey is individual and highly personal. It can't be organized or regulated. We all need to invest in our spiritual development. The bible says that we are made up of spirit, soul, and body. It would be beneficial to attend to all three.

The Fruit of the Holy Spirit is a biblical term that sums up nine attributes of a person or community living in accord with the Holy Spirit. According to Galatians 5:22: "But the fruit of the Spirit is love, joy, peace, patience, kindness, goodness, faithfulness, gentleness and self-control". The good book helps develop spiritual and personal growth.

These are some of the preachers who have spread the word and have made an impact in our society throughout history.

ALEXANDER CRUMMELL

Alexander Crummell (March 3, 1819 - September 10, 1898) was an important voice within the abolition movement and a leader of the Pan-African ideology. His legacy can be seen not in his personal achievements, but in the influence he exerted on other black nationalists and Pan-Africanists, such as Marcus Garvey, Paul Laurence Dunbar, and W. E. B. Du Bois. Du Bois paid tribute to Crummell with a memorable essay entitled "Of Alexander Crummell," collected in his 1903 book, "The Souls of Black Folk."

Crummell was born in New York City to Charity Hicks, a free woman of color, and Boston Crummell, a former slave. According to Crummell's own account, his paternal grandfather was an ethnic Temne born in Sierra Leone, who was captured into slavery when he was around 13 years old. Both parents were active abolitionists and allowed their home to be used to publish the first African-American newspaper, Freedom's Journal.

Crummell began his formal education in the African Free School No. 2 and at home with private tutors. He attended the Canal Street High School. After graduating, Crummell and his friend Garnet attended the

Noyes Academy in New Hampshire. However, a mob opposed to the new black first-year students attacked and destroyed the school. Crummell next enrolled in the Oneida Institute in central New York, established originally for the education of Native Americans. While there, Crummell decided to become an Episcopal priest. His prominence as a young intellectual earned him a spot as keynote speaker at the anti-slavery New York State Convention of Negroes when it met in Albany in 1840.

Denied admission to the General Theological Seminary in New York City because of his race, Crummell went on to study and receive holy orders; he was ordained in 1842 in Massachusetts. However, when he petitioned Bishop Onderdonk to help him build a larger congregation, he was told, "I will receive you into this diocese on one condition: No negro priest can sit in my church convention and no negro church must ask for representation there." Crummell is said to have paused for a moment, and then said: "I will never enter your diocese on such terms."

Crummell was a pioneering African-American minister, academic and African nationalist. He was ordained as an Episcopal priest in the United States. In 1847, Crummell traveled to England to raise money for his congregation at the Church of the Messiah, by preaching and lecturing about American slavery and abolitionism, and raised almost $2,000.

From 1849 to 1853, Crummell studied at Queens' College, Cambridge; and although he had to take his finals twice to receive his degree, he became the first officially Black student recorded in the university records as graduated. Abolitionists supported Crummell's three years of study at Cambridge University, where he developed concepts of Pan-Africanism.

Crummell continued to travel around Britain and speak out about slavery and the plight of Black people. During this period, Crummell formulated the concept of Pan-Africanism, which became his central belief for the advancement of the African race. Crummell believed that in order to achieve their potential, the African race as a whole, including those in the Americas, the West Indies, and Africa, needed to unify under the banner of race. To Crummell, racial solidarity could solve slavery, discrimination, and continued attacks on the African race. He decided to move to Africa to spread his message.

In 1853 Crummell moved to Liberia, where he worked to convert native Africans to Christianity and educate them, as well as to persuade American colonists of his ideas. He wanted to attract American Blacks to Africa on a colonial, civilizing mission. Crummell lived and worked for 20 years in Liberia and appealed to American Blacks to join him. While he successfully served as both a pastor and professor in Liberia, he could not create the society he envisioned. In 1873, fearing his life was in danger from the mulatto ascendancy, Crummell returned to the United States.

After returning to the United States, Crummell was called to St. Mary's Episcopal Mission in Washington, DC. In 1875, he and his congregation founded St. Luke's Episcopal Church, the first independent Black Episcopal church in the city. They built a new church on 15th Street, NW, beginning in 1876, and celebrated their first Thanksgiving there in 1879. Crummell served as rector there until his retirement in 1894. The church was designated a National Historic Landmark in 1976.

There he was called as pastor for St. Mary's Episcopal Mission in the Foggy Bottom area of Washington, DC, then an African-American neighborhood. In 1875, he and his congregation founded St. Luke's Episcopal Church, the first independent Black Episcopal church in the city. They raised the money to construct a new church on upper 15th Street, N.W., in the Columbia Heights area, beginning in 1876, and celebrated Thanksgiving in 1879 in it. Crummell served as rector at St. Luke's until his retirement in 1894. The church was designated a National Historic Landmark in 1976. Crummell taught at Howard University from 1895 to 1897.

Crummell never stopped working for the racial solidarity he had advocated for so long. Throughout his life, he worked for Black nationalism, self-help, and separate economic development. Crummell spent the last years of his life setting up the American Negro Academy, an organization to support African-American scholars, which opened in 1897. Alexander Crummell died in Red Bank, New Jersey, in 1898.

In 2002, the scholar Molefi Kete Asante listed Alexander Crummell on his list of 100 Greatest African Americans.

PATRICK FRANCIS HEALY

Patrick Francis Healy (February 27, 1834 – January 10, 1910) was a
Jesuit priest, educator, and the 29th President of Georgetown
University (1874–1882), known for expanding the school following
the American Civil War. Healy Hall was constructed during Healy's
tenure and is named after him. It was designated as a National Historic
Landmark in the late 20th century.

Although Healy was accepted as and identified as Irish-American
during his lifetime, in the 1950s and 1960s his mixed-race ancestry
became more widely known and acknowledged. He was recognized as
the first person of African-American descent to earn a PhD; the first
to become a Jesuit priest; and the first to be president of Georgetown
University, or any predominantly white college in the United States.

Patrick, as he was known, was born into slavery in 1834 in Macon,
Georgia, to the Irish-American plantation owner Michael Healy and
his African-American slave Mary Eliza. Mary Eliza was mixed-race
(mulatto), the daughter of a black slave and white slaveowner. Because

197

of the law established during colonial slavery in the United States that children took the legal status of the mother, by the principle of partus sequitur ventrum, Patrick and his siblings were legally considered slaves in Georgia, although their father was free, and they were three-quarters or more European in ancestry.

Their mother was mixed race and their father Irish, and identifying as Irish-American Catholics, Patrick Francis Healy and his siblings were among many mixed-race Americans of the 19th century who passed for European American.

Patrick was the third son of Mary Eliza and Michael Morris Healy, who had joined in a common-law marriage in 1829. After Patrick's father Michael bought his mother Mary Eliza, he fell in love with her and made her his common-law wife. The law prohibited their marriage, but they lived together all their lives. Discriminatory laws in Georgia prohibited the education of slaves and required legislative approval for each act of manumission, making these essentially impossible to gain.

Michael Healy arranged for all his children to leave Georgia and move to the North to obtain their educations and have opportunities in their lives. They were raised as Irish Catholics. Patrick's brothers and sisters were nearly all educated in Catholic schools and colleges. Many achieved notable firsts for Americans of mixed-race ancestry during the second half of the 19th century, and the Healy family of Georgia was remarkably successful.

Healy sent his older sons first to a Quaker school in Flushing, New York. Despite the Quakers' emphasis on equality, Patrick encountered some discrimination during his grade school years, chiefly because his father was a slaveholder, which by the late antebellum years the Quakers considered unforgivable. Patrick also met resistance in the school as an Irish Catholic. When Michael Healy heard of a new Jesuit college, the College of the Holy Cross in Worcester, Massachusetts, he sent his four oldest sons, including Patrick, to study there in 1844. (It had high school-level classes as well.) They were joined at Holy Cross by their younger brother Michael in 1849.

Following Patrick's graduation in 1850, he entered the Jesuit order (the first African American to do so) and continued his studies. The order sent him to Europe to study in 1858. His mixed-race ancestry had become an issue in the United States, where tensions were rising over slavery. He attended the Catholic University of Leuven in Belgium, earning his doctorate, becoming the first American of openly acknowledged part-African descent to do so. During this period, he was also ordained to the priesthood on September 3, 1864.

In 1866 Healy returned to the United States and taught philosophy at Georgetown University in Washington, DC. On July 31, 1874, he was selected as the school's twenty-ninth president. He was the first college president in the United States of African-American ancestry; at the time, he identified as Irish Catholic and was accepted as such.

Patrick Healy's influence on Georgetown was so far-reaching that he is often referred to as the school's "second founder," following Archbishop John Carroll. Healy helped transform the small nineteenth-century college into a major university for the twentieth century, likely influenced by his European education.

He modernized the curriculum by requiring courses in the sciences, particularly chemistry and physics. He expanded and upgraded the schools of law and medicine. He became one of the most renowned Jesuit priests of his time in that role. The most visible result of Healy's presidency was the construction of the university's flagship building designed by Paul J. Pelz, begun in 1877 and first used in 1881. The building was named in his honor as Healy Hall.

Healy left the College in 1882; he traveled extensively through the United States and Europe, often in the company of his brother James, a bishop in Maine. In 1908 he returned to the campus infirmary, where he died. He was buried on the grounds of the university in the Jesuit cemetery.

In 1969, the Alumni Association established the Patrick Healy Award to recognize individuals other than alumni who have "distinguished themselves by a lifetime of outstanding achievement and service to Georgetown, the community and his or her profession."

According to James O'Toole, who wrote about all the Healy family, it was not until the 1960s that the Healys' mixed-race ancestry was widely known. Patrick F. Healy was then recognized as the first African-American to earn a PhD, to become a Jesuit priest, and to become president of a predominantly white college.

His brother James Augustine Healy became Bishop of Portland, Maine. His brother Michael A. Healy joined the United States Revenue Cutter Service, becoming a celebrated sea captain, the sole representative of the U.S. government in the vast reaches of Alaska. His brother Sherwood Healy also became a priest and earned a doctorate at Saint-Sulpice in Paris. He became director of the seminary in Troy, New York, and rector of the Cathedral in Boston.

Three of the Healy sisters became nuns. Eliza, Sister Mary Magdalen, advanced to become a Mother Superior of the Villa Barlow Academy and convent in St. Albans, Vermont, run by her order based in Montreal, Canada. Martha left her order and moved to Boston. She married an Irish immigrant and had a son with him.

Aided by their father's wealth and their own educations, the Healy sons were accepted into U.S. Catholic society as Irish Americans. The daughters achieved education and status first in the Catholic Church in Canada, where people may have been less concerned about their mixed ancestry, especially given the many Catholic Métis in the Montreal area. The Coast Guard Captain Michael A. Healy married an Irish Catholic woman and had a family with her.

BISHOP T.D. JAKES

Bishop T. D. Jakes, born **Dexter Jakes Sr.** (June 9, 1957) is a pastor, author and filmmaker. For more than 40 years, Bishop T.D. Jakes has helped millions of people realize their purpose through his dynamic ministry. Recognized as "America's Best Preacher" by *Time Magazine*, as well as "One of the Nation's Most Influential & Mesmerizing Preachers" by *The New York Times*, Bishop Jakes remains a charismatic, yet humble man.

In 1996, with minimal resources, T.D. Jakes founded The Potter's House (TPH), a non-denominational, multicultural megachurch and global humanitarian organization, in Dallas, Texas. The church has since expanded to include more than 30,000 members, with more than 50 diverse ministries.

While TPH, located in southern Dallas, is the designated home to numerous members, Bishop Jakes has fulfilled the needs of those residing in the northern and western regions of the Dallas-Fort Worth metroplex, as well as out-of-state. TPH campuses are also present in Frisco and Fort Worth, Texas, as well as Denver, Colorado.

Jakes was born in South Charleston, West Virginia, and grew up in Vandalia, attending local Baptist churches. He spent his teenage years caring for his invalid father and working in local industries. Feeling a call to the ministry, he enrolled in West Virginia State University and began preaching part-time in local churches, but he soon dropped out of the university. He took a job at the local Union Carbide factory and continued preaching part-time. During this time, he met his future wife, Serita Jamison. The couple married in May 1982. In that same year Jakes became the pastor of the Greater Emanuel Temple of Faith, a small independent Pentecostal church in Montgomery, West Virginia, with just ten members. He moved the church twice: from Montgomery to Smithers and then to South Charleston, where the congregation grew from about 100 members to over 300. During this time, he began a radio ministry, The Master's Plan, which ran from 1982–1985.

Jakes also became acquainted with Bishop Sherman Watkins, founder of the Higher Ground Always Abounding Assembly (an association of over 200 Pentecostal churches). Watkins ordained Jakes as a minister of the Higher Ground Assembly and encouraged him to start a church in the Charleston, West Virginia, area. During this time, Jakes completed a B. A. and M.A. in 1990, and a Doctor of Ministry in Religious Studies from Friends International Christian University in 1995.

Jakes began to focus on the spiritual needs of the women in his church who had been abandoned and abused in their lives. He began a Sunday

School class for them, "Woman, Thou Art Loosed," in which he encouraged them to use their past pain as a foundation for new growth. He later started a similar class for men, which he called "Manpower." In 1993, Jakes self-published his first book, drawing on his experiences working with the women of his congregation. *Woman, Thou Art Loosed* would become Jakes's signature work and a national, religious bestseller.

He also began a new television ministry, Get Ready, which aired on Black Entertainment Television and the Trinity Broadcasting Network. Also, in 1993, Jakes moved his church to Cross Lanes, West Virginia. In 1994, he held the first of what would become a series of conferences for ministers and their spouses, "When Shepherds Bleed."[

In May 1996, Jakes moved his family and his ministry again, along with fifty other families involved in his work, to Dallas, Texas. There he purchased the former facilities of Eagle's Nest Church, a large Dallas church pastored by W.V. Grant. Renaming the church, The Potter's House, Jakes continued his work. The Potter's House, with a 5,000-seat auditorium and a 34-acre campus, had a congregation of 30,000.

Bishop T.D. Jakes, one of the world's most revered masterminds, leverages his pioneering vision and instinct to serve others in areas extending beyond the church. In order to help lead people to their destiny, you have to meet people where *they* are in life. It is with this earnest approach that Bishop Jakes has been able to reach millions of people from all socioeconomic backgrounds, races, nationalities, and creeds. Digital media, film, and television, among others, have been instrumental in helping Bishop Jakes meet the disparate needs of countless individuals.

Each year Bishop Jakes helps underserved communities through TPH ministries, including homeless outreach, GED/literacy programs, and AIDS outreach. Bishop Jakes also empowers communities through distinct national ministries, including Global Partner System (GPS), MegaCARE, and Texas Offenders Reentry Initiative (T.O.R.I.). With a steadfast love of people, TPH is consistently ranked amongst the nation's most influential churches each year.

Bishop Jakes also connects communities from across the globe through various multicultural conferences. For more than a decade, MegaFest continues to receive international recognition as the nation's largest faith and family festival. This phenomenal conference draws upwards of 100,000 attendees from as far as Singapore, China.

As a devoted husband to First Lady Serita Jakes, Bishop Jakes eagerly supports his beautiful wife of more than 35 years. Serita and T.D. have managed every business opportunity, as well as personal endeavors with their unwavering faith in God. The power couple has successfully raised five beautiful grown children, including Sarah Jakes, Cora Jakes-Coleman, Thomas Jakes, Jr., Jermaine Jakes, and Jamar Jakes.

REVEREND WYATT TEE WALKER

Wyatt Tee Walker (August 16, 1928 – January 23, 2018) was an African-American pastor, national civil rights leader, theologian, and cultural historian. Born in Brockton, MA., Reverend Dr. Wyatt Tee Walker was the son of Rev. John Wise Walker and Maude Pinn. He was the 8th of 9 children.

Wyatt attended elementary and high school in Merchantville, New Jersey. He earned a B.S. in chemistry and physics, as a double graduate, from Virginia Union University in Richmond in 1950. That same year he married Theresa Ann Walker. The couple had four children.

In 1953, Walker received his Master of Divinity from Virginia Union's Graduate School of Religion. He then went on to obtain his Doctorate of Ministry from the Rochester Theological Center in New York. Walker was considered a lifelong scholar through his graduate studies and research at several international universities.

After earning his degree, in 1953 Walker was called as pastor at historic Gillfield Baptist Church, the second oldest black church in Petersburg, Virginia and one of the oldest in the nation. He also served as president of the National Association for the Advancement of Colored People (NAACP) in that city and as director of the state's Congress of Racial Equality (CORE). Walker founded the Petersburg Improvement Association (PIA) which was patterned after the Montgomery Improvement Association (MIA).

His ministry began as the pastor of the historic Gillfield Baptist Church in Petersburg, VA (1952-1960), and he concurrently served Mt. Level Baptist Church in Dinwiddie, VA. His initial advocacy for civil rights began when he was arrested at the Petersburg library for attempting to check out a book in the "whites only" section. This sparked library protests around the country.

At King's invitation, Walker moved to Atlanta as the SCLC's first full-time executive director. During his leadership of 1960–1964, he brought the organization to "national power" in its efforts to bring about an end to legal segregation of African Americans. A strong manager, Walker (assisted by Dorothy Cotton and James Wood brought from the PIA) improved administration and fundraising, and coordinated the staff's far-ranging activities.

Walker led two major civil rights organizations in Virginia: he served as president for five years of the Petersburg branch of the National Association for the Advancement of Colored People (NAACP) and as state director of the Congress of Racial Equality (CORE), which he co-founded in 1958. In 1958, he also became a member of the Southern Christian Leadership Conference (SCLC), an organization headed by Dr. Martin Luther King, Jr.

While both were seminary students, Dr. Martin Luther King Jr. recognized Walker's abilities and organizing skills. Walker became increasingly close to Dr. Martin Luther King, Jr. in the Civil Rights Movement. In 1958 King chose Walker for the board of SCLC. Walker eventually was selected as Executive Director of the Southern Christian Leadership Conference (SCLC) based in Atlanta, King's chief of staff and a key strategist for the civil rights movement of the 1960's.

Walker spent the next two years building the organization in Virginia by capitalizing on his network of relationships with clergy throughout the state from his activities with NAACP and CORE. He also continued demonstrations and actions intended to highlight, challenge and end segregation.

Walker helped found the Petersburg Improvement Association (PIA), modeled after the Montgomery Improvement Association (MIA) in Alabama. It developed strategies against segregation, including publicizing its activities. By May 1960 the PIA had 3,000 members. By conducting sit-ins in 1960 at the Trailways bus terminal, Walker and PIA members gained agreement by the president of the Bus Terminal Restaurants to desegregate lunch counters in Petersburg and several other Virginia cities. This was achieved the year before the Freedom Riders arrived in 1961.

Walker's civil rights participation reached beyond his administrative duties. On May 25, 1961, Walker was arrested in Birmingham, Alabama for participating in a Freedom Ride. Two years later, he helped organize the 1963 March on Washington.

Dr. Walker held the position until 1964. He built the SCLC into a national organization with chapters throughout the country. He wrote the blueprint for the 1963 campaign that desegregated Birmingham. It is noteworthy that the Letter from a Birmingham Jail was written from Dr. King's cell on scraps of paper. Dr. Walker collected King's notes upon his visits and then helped translate the manifesto for publication.

He was a key organizer of the March on Washington. At the request of Mrs. Coretta King, he also organized and arranged Dr. King's funeral.

On September 1, 1967, Walker relocated to New York City to become pastor of Canaan Baptist Church of Christ in Harlem. Under his dynamic leadership, Canaan's congregation grew from 800 to 3,000. He commanded a major pulpit in the struggle for tolerance and social justice. He also continued to compose sacred music. He connected his studies of other traditions to the use of music in the Black church and social movements. Walker helped teach people about the relationship between movements around the world. During the years in which Africans sought independence, Walker hosted numerous leaders from the continent, including Nelson Mandela of South Africa, who were active in struggles against colonialism and apartheid.

During the 1970s Walker served as Urban Affairs Specialist to Gov. Nelson A. Rockefeller, helping advise in a volatile social environment. In 1975 he completed his doctorate at Colgate Rochester Divinity School. In his graduate studies and research, Walker also studied at the University of Ife in Nigeria and the University of Ghana. During these years in Harlem, he wrote and published books on the relation of music and social movements, and community development.

Dr. Walker was also increasingly active in the anti-apartheid movement, which had a strong base in the African-American community. In 1978 he founded the International Freedom Mobilization to draw attention to the abuses of apartheid in South Africa. He served on the National Committee on the American Committee on Africa (ACOA) (since 2001 called Africa Action). In the 1980s he served on the ACOA Board, including as president.

In 1988, during the height of the anti-apartheid struggle Walker helped co-found the Religious Action Network (RAN) of the ACOA, together with Canon Frederick B. Williams of the Church of the Intercession in Harlem.

In 1993, Walker received national recognition when *Ebony* magazine named him one of America's "15 Greatest Black Preachers." Walker also used the church's leadership in local economic and community development, writing about their efforts in *The Harvard Paper: The African-American Church and Economic Development* (1994). He was chair of the Central Harlem Local Development Corporation, to generate affordable housing units in Harlem to fill a critical need. Under his leadership, Dr. Walker sponsored seven housing properties, including three senior housing developments.

Because of Walker's leading role in the Civil Rights Movement, the Schomburg Center for Research in Black Culture at the New York Public Library collected his papers from the period of 1963–1982. They include both personal and official correspondence, papers and lectures on a wide variety of topics, and are available for research.

In 1999, he joined with businessman-philanthropist Steve Klinsky to found the first ever charter school in New York State, now named the Sisulu-Walker Charter School of Harlem in honor of Walter Sisulu (Nelson Mandela's ally) and Dr. Walker. This school was one of just three New York charter schools to open in the law's first year of 1999 and is the only one from that year to survive. The school is community-run and has substantially outperformed the traditional public schools in Harlem's District 5, where most of the school's students live.

After 37 years as senior pastor, Walker retired in 2004 with the title of *pastor emeritus* of Canaan Baptist Church. He spent his final years in Virginia and taught at the Samuel DeWitt Proctor School of Theology at his *alma mater* Virginia Union University in Richmond.

Walker continued to support charter school reform from his home in Virginia. In 2008 he was inducted into the Civil Rights "Walk of Fame" in Atlanta, Georgia. On January 18, 2009, during the inauguration events in Washington, D.C. for President Barack Obama, Walker received the "Keepers of the Flame" award at the African-American Church Inaugural Ball. In 2016, he was awarded the Lifetime Achievement Award from the National Charter School Alliance.

Reverend Dr. Wyatt Tee. Walker passed away in Chester, Virginia on January 23, 2018. He was 88 years old.

BISHOP MICHAEL BRUCE CURRY

Michael Bruce Curry (March 13, 1953) is the first African American to serve as presiding bishop in The Episcopal Church. Previously the bishop of the Diocese of North Carolina, on November 1, 2015 Curry was installed as the 27th Presiding Bishop and Primate of the Episcopal Church.

He is also the Chief Pastor and serves as President and Chief Executive Officer, and as Chair of the Executive Council of the Episcopal Church. He was elected to a nine-year term and confirmed at the 78th General Convention of the Episcopal Church in Salt Lake City, UT, on June 27, 2015.

The descendant of enslaved Africans brought to North America by way of the trans-Atlantic slave routes, Presiding Bishop Curry was born in Chicago, Illinois. His father, mother and grandmother grounded him in Christian beliefs and practices through their example and their teachings. His parents were Dorothy and the Rev. Kenneth Curry, who had been Baptists but became Episcopalians when they were allowed to drink from the same chalice as whites in racially segregated Ohio.

Presiding Bishop Curry's father was an Episcopal priest and his mother was a devout Episcopalian. She died at a young age, and Presiding Bishop Curry, along with his sister, was raised by his father and his grandmother.

Michael attended public schools in Buffalo, NY, and, even at a young age, he learned about social activism through his father's leadership and his own dedication to righting a broken world. He was graduated with high honors from Hobart College in Geneva, New York, in 1975.

He received a Master of Divinity degree in 1978 from Yale University Divinity School in New Haven, Connecticut in association with Berkeley Divinity School. He has furthered his education with continued study at The College of Preachers, Princeton Theological Seminary, Wake Forest University, the Ecumenical Institute at St. Mary's Seminary, and the Institute of Islamic, Christian and Jewish Studies. In addition, Bishop Curry has received honorary degrees from Episcopal Divinity School; Sewanee: The University of the South; Virginia Theological Seminary; and Yale.

Presiding Bishop Curry was ordained to the diaconate in June 1978, at St. Paul's Cathedral, Buffalo, New York, by the Rt. Rev. Harold B. Robinson, and to the priesthood in December 1978, at St. Stephen's, Winston-Salem, North Carolina, by the Rt. Rev. John M. Burgess. He began his ministry as deacon-in-charge at St. Stephen's, Winston-Salem, in 1978 and was rector from 1979-1982. He next accepted a call as rector at St. Simon of Cyrene, Lincoln Heights, Ohio, serving from 1982-1988. In 1988 he was called to become rector of St. James', Baltimore, Maryland, where he served until his election as the 11th Bishop of the Episcopal Diocese of North Carolina on February 11, 2000.

When he was consecrated at Duke Chapel in Durham on June 17, 2000, he became the first African-American diocesan bishop of the

Episcopal Church in the American South. Nearly 40 bishops participated in the service, including Robert Hodges Johnson, J. Gary Gloster, and Barbara C. Harris as consecrators.

As a diocesan bishop, he served on the board of directors of the Alliance for Christian Media and chaired the board of Episcopal Relief and Development. Presiding Bishop Curry instituted a network of canons, deacons, and youth ministry professionals dedicated to supporting the ministry that happens in local congregations. He refocused the Diocese on the Episcopal Church's Millennium Development Goals through a $400,000 campaign to buy malaria nets that saved over 100,000 lives.

In January 2016, Primates in the Anglican Communion gathered at Canterbury Cathedral, mother church of the global Anglican Communion, at the invitation of the Most Rev. Justin Welby, Archbishop of Canterbury. It was the first such meeting attended by Curry as presiding bishop. Human sexuality and the Episcopal Church's July 2015 approval of same-sex marriage rites were prominent topics of discussion. In the aftermath of the sanctions, Curry maintained his public support for same-sex marriage.

As part of the final communique from the gathering, the Anglican primates announced that the Archbishop of Canterbury would appoint a "task group" aimed at healing the rift and rebuilding of mutual trust amidst deep differences. The Archbishop of Canterbury named Curry as one of the 10 members of that "task group" in May 2016.

In October 2016, Curry represented the Anglican Communion as part of a delegation of Anglican primates to the Vatican led by the Archbishop of Canterbury. The leaders joined together in an ecumenical Vespers service led jointly by the Archbishop of Canterbury and the Roman Pontiff, followed by a private meeting between Pope Francis and the Anglican primates.

Bishop Curry was invited by Prince Harry and Meghan Markle to deliver the sermon at their wedding. The wedding took place on May 19, 2018, at St George's Chapel, Windsor Castle in England. Curry's 14-minute sermon attracted considerable comment and reactions were mixed. The sermon emphasized the redemptive potential of love and used fire as a metaphor for its power and significance. The address was wide-ranging in its sources quoting from Martin Luther King Jr., the traditional African-American spiritual "There Is a Balm in Gilead", New Testament Epistles, and the French Jesuit priest and scientist, Pierre Teilhard de Chardin.

Bishop Curry also officiated at the funeral of George H.W. Bush in the Washington National Cathedral on December 5, 2018. Less than a week later he delivered a sermon-like address at "The Spirit of Apollo" program organized by the National Air and Space Museum. The program was held at Washington National Cathedral and commemorated the fiftieth anniversary of the Apollo 8 mission to the moon.

Presiding Bishop Curry is married to the former Sharon Clement, and they have two adult daughters, Rachel and Elizabeth.

> *"Never be limited by other people's limited imaginations. If you adopt their attitudes, then the possibility won't exist because you'll have already shut it out...You can hear other people's wisdom, but you've got to re-evaluate the world for yourself."*
> **-Mae Jemison**

CHAPTER SIX – HEALTH & SCIENCE
FEATURING MEDICAL PROFESSIONALS AND SCIENTISTS

There are countless men and women who have made great contributions to American society throughout the 20th century, advancing health and science. The Innovations and advancements of medical professionals and scientists often goes unnoticed or untold. Charles Drew's work in blood transfusions, for example, saved thousands of lives during World War II and is still used in medicine today. Daniel Hale Williams was the first person to successfully complete open-heart surgery. Dorothy Lavinia Brown was the first female surgeon of African-American ancestry from the Southeastern United States. Mae Carol Jemison became the first African American woman to travel in space...and the list goes on.

DR. DANIEL HALE WILLIAMS

Daniel Hale Williams (January 18, 1856 – August 4, 1931) was an African-American general surgeon, who, on July 10, 1893 performed heart surgery. His patient survived for the next twenty years. Referred to as "the first successful heart surgery" by Encyclopedia Britannica, the surgery took place at Provident Hospital.

Williams repaired the torn pericardium of a knife wound patient, James Cornish. Cornish, who was stabbed directly through the left fifth costal cartilage, had been admitted the previous night. Williams decided to operate the next morning in response to continued bleeding, cough and "pronounced" symptoms of shock. He performed this surgery, without the benefit of penicillin or blood transfusion, at Provident Hospital, Chicago. It was not reported until 1897. He undertook a second procedure to drain fluid. About fifty days after the initial procedure, Cornish left the hospital.

At the time that Williams graduated from medical school, Black doctors were not allowed to work in Chicago hospitals. As a result, in 1891, Williams had founded the Provident Hospital and training school for nurses in Chicago. This was established mostly for the benefit of African-American residents, to increase their accessibility to health care. Provident Hospital, the first non-segregated hospital in the United States, and also founded an associated nursing school for African Americans. In 1913, he was elected as the only African-American charter member of the American College of Surgeons.

In 1893, during the administration of President Grover Cleveland, Williams was appointed surgeon-in-chief of Freedman's Hospital in Washington, D.C., a post he held until 1898. Williams was a Professor of Clinical Surgery at Meharry Medical College in Nashville, Tennessee and was an attending surgeon at Cook County Hospital in Chicago. He worked to create more hospitals that admitted African Americans. In 1895 he co-founded the National Medical Association for African American doctors, and in 1913 he became a charter member and the only African-American doctor in the American College of Surgeons.

Daniel Hale Williams was born in 1856 and raised in the city of Hollidaysburg, Pennsylvania. His father, Daniel Hale Williams, Jr. was the son of a black barber and a Scots-Irish woman. His mother was African American and likely also mixed race.

The fifth child born, Williams lived with his parents, a brother and five sisters. His family eventually moved to Annapolis, Maryland. Shortly after, when Williams was nine, his father died of tuberculosis. Williams' mother realized she could not manage the entire family and sent some of the children to live with relatives. Williams was apprenticed to a shoemaker in Baltimore, Maryland but ran away to join his mother, who had moved to Rockford, Illinois. He later moved to Edgerton, Wisconsin, where he joined his sister and opened his own barber shop. After moving to nearby Janesville, Wisconsin, Williams became fascinated by the work of a local physician and decided to follow his path.

He began working as an apprentice to Dr. Henry W. Palmer, studying with him for two years. In 1880 Williams entered Chicago Medical College, now known as Northwestern University Medical School. After graduation from Northwestern in 1883, he opened his own medical office in Chicago, Illinois.

Williams was married in 1898 to Alice Johnson, natural daughter of American sculptor, Moses Jacob Ezekiel, and a mixed-race maid. Williams died of a stroke in Idlewild, Michigan on August 4, 1931. His wife, Alice Johnson, had died in 1924.

In the 1890s several attempts were made to improve cardiac surgery. On September 6, 1891 the first successful pericardial sac repair operation in the United States of America was performed by Henry C. Dalton of Saint Louis, Missouri. The first successful surgery on the heart itself was performed by Norwegian surgeon Axel Cappelen on September 4, 1895 at Rikshospitalet in Kristiania, now Oslo. The first successful surgery of the heart, performed without any complications, was by Dr. Ludwig Rehn of Frankfurt, Germany, who repaired a stab wound to the right ventricle on September 7, 1896.

Despite these improvements, heart-related surgery was not widely accepted in the field of medical science until during World War II. Surgeons were forced to improve their methods of surgery in order to repair severe war wounds. Although they did not receive early recognition for their pioneering work, Dalton and Williams were later recognized for their roles in cardiac surgery.

Williams received honorary degrees from Howard and Wilberforce Universities, was named a charter member of the American College of Surgeons and was a member of the Chicago Surgical Society.

A Pennsylvania State Historical Marker was placed at U.S. Route 22 eastbound (Blair St., 300 block), Hollidaysburg, Pennsylvania, to commemorate his accomplishments and mark his boyhood home.

DR. DOROTHY LAVINIA BROWN

Dorothy Lavinia Brown (January 7, 1919 – June 13, 2004), also known as "Dr. D." was an African-American surgeon, legislator, and teacher. She was the first female surgeon of African-American ancestry from the Southeastern United States. She was also the first African American to serve in the Tennessee General Assembly having been elected to the Tennessee House of Representatives.

Brown was born in Philadelphia, Pennsylvania, and was placed in an orphanage in Troy, New York at five months old by her mother, Edna Brown, where she lived until the age of 12. While at the orphanage, she underwent a tonsillectomy operation, an experience that led to her interest in the field of medicine. Although her mother tried to persuade the young Dorothy to live with her, Brown kept running away from home, only to return to the Troy orphanage. Upon reaching the age of fifteen, Brown ran away to enroll at the Troy High School. She worked as a mother's helper in the house of Mrs. W. F. Jarrett, in Albany, New

York. Assisted by a principal of the school, she was introduced to Samuel Wesley and Lola Redmon, a couple who became her foster parents. When she was fifteen she worked at a self-service laundry.

After finishing high school, while working as a domestic helper, Brown attended Bennett College in Greensboro, North Carolina, receiving assistance from the Women's Division of Christian Service of a Methodist Church in Troy in order to gain a scholarship. Following college, she worked at the Rochester Army Ordnance Department in Rochester, New York for two years. In 1941, she obtained her Bachelor of Arts degree, and became an inspector for a defense plant in Troy. In 1944, Brown began studying medicine at Meharry Medical College in Nashville, finishing her internship at the Harlem Hospital in New York City. After graduating in 1948, she became a resident at Hubbard Hospital of Meharry in 1949, despite opposition to female surgeons and having convinced the then chief surgeon, Matthew Walker, Sr., M.D., Brown completed her residency in 1954.

Brown was the chief surgeon at the now-defunct Riverside Hospital in Nashville from 1957 to 1983. In 1966, she became the first African-American female to be elected to the Tennessee General Assembly (known also as the Tennessee State Legislature), a position she held for two years. She almost succeeded in having abortions legalized in cases of rape or incest, and in expanding the already existing legally permitted abortions in cases when the "mother's life was in danger". During her career as a politician, Brown also became involved in the passing of the Negro History Act, which required public schools in Tennessee to "conduct special programs during Negro History Week to recognize accomplishments made by African Americans."

In 1968, Brown tried to obtain a seat in the Tennessee Senate, but lost in part due to her support for abortion laws. In 1968, following her departure from politics, Brown returned to becoming a full-time physician at the Riverside Hospital. Brown also acted as an attending surgeon at the George W. Hubbard and General Hospitals, as director of education for the clinical rotation program of the Riverside and Meharry Hospitals. She was also a surgery professor at the Meharry Medical College and consulted for the National Institutes of Health in the National Heart, Lung and Blood Advisory Council.

In 1959, Brown became the third woman to become a Fellow of the American College of Surgeons, the first African-American woman to be elected. In 1971, the Dorothy L. Brown Women's Residence at Meharry Medical College, Nashville, was named after her. She also received honorary doctorate degrees from the Russell Sage College in Troy, New York, and also from Bennett College in Greensboro, North Carolina. In particular, she received her honorary degrees in the Humanities from Bennett College and Cumberland University.

Brown was a member of the board of trustees at Bennett College and of the Delta Sigma Theta sorority. She participated as a speaker on panels that discussed scientific, religious, medical, and political issues. Brown was also awarded the Horatio Alger Award in 1994 and the Carnegie Foundation's humanitarian award in 1993.

Dr. Dorothy Brown died in Nashville, Tennessee, in 2004 from congestive heart failure.

DR. MAE JEMISON

Mae Carol Jemison (born October 17, 1956) is an American engineer, physician and NASA astronaut. She became the first African American woman to travel in space when she went into orbit aboard the Space Shuttle Endeavour on September 12, 1992. After medical school and a brief general practice, Jemison served in the Peace Corps from 1985 until 1987, when she was selected by NASA to join the astronaut corps. She resigned from NASA in 1993 to found a company researching the application of technology to daily life. She has appeared on television several times, including as an actress in an episode of Star Trek: The Next Generation. She is a dancer and holds nine honorary doctorates in science, engineering, letters, and the humanities. She is the current principal of the 100 Year Starship organization.

Mae Carol Jemison was born in Decatur, Alabama, on October 17, 1956, the youngest child of Charlie Jemison and Dorothy Green. Her father was a maintenance supervisor for a charity organization, and her mother worked most of her career as an elementary school teacher of English and math at the Beethoven School in Chicago.

The family moved to Chicago, Illinois, when Jemison was three years old, to take advantage of the better educational and employment opportunities there. In her childhood, Jemison learned to make connections to science by studying nature. Once when a splinter infected her thumb as a little girl, Jemison's mother turned it into a learning experience. She ended up doing a whole project about pus. Jemison's parents were very supportive of her interest in science, while her teachers were not. At the time of the Apollo airing, Jemison was irritated that there were no women astronauts. She was inspired by Martin Luther King Jr.; to her King's dream was not an elusive fantasy but a call to action.

Jemison began dancing at the age of 11 — African dancing, ballet, jazz, modern — even Japanese dancing. She wanted to become a professional dancer. Jemison's dancing skills got her into the lineup of West Side Story as a background dancer. She loved the sciences and the arts and saw the theatre as an outlet for her passion, so she decided to pursue the dream. During her senior year in college, she was trying to decide whether to go to New York to medical school or become a professional dancer.

Jemison graduated from Chicago's Morgan Park High School in 1973 and entered Stanford University at the age of 16. She graduated from Stanford in 1977, receiving a B.S. in chemical engineering and fulfilling the requirements for a B.A. in African and Afro-American Studies.

Jemison obtained her Doctor of Medicine degree in 1981 at Cornell Medical College. She interned at Los Angeles County-USC Medical Center, and in 1982, she worked as a general practitioner. During medical school, Jemison traveled to Cuba, Kenya and Thailand, to provide primary medical care to people living there. During her years at Cornell Medical College, Jemison took lessons in modern dance at the Alvin Ailey school. She later built a dance studio in her home and choreographed and produced several shows of modern jazz and African dance.

After completing her medical training, Jemison joined the staff of the Peace Corps and served as a Peace Corps Medical Officer from 1983 to 1985, responsible for the health of Peace Corps Volunteers serving in Liberia and Sierra Leone. Jemison's work in the Peace Corps included supervising the pharmacy, laboratory, medical staff as well as providing medical care, writing self-care manuals, and developing and implementing guidelines for health and safety issues. Jemison also worked with the Center for Disease Control (CDC) helping with research for various vaccines.

Once while serving as a doctor for the Peace Corps, a volunteer became seriously ill, and a doctor diagnosed malaria. The volunteer's condition progressively worsened, and Jemison was sure it was meningitis with life-threatening complications that could not be treated in Sierra Leone. Jemison called for an Air Force hospital plane based in Germany for a military medical evacuation at a cost of $80,000. The embassy questioned whether Jemison had the authority to give such an order, but she told them she did not need anyone's permission for a medical decision. By the time the plane reached Germany with Jemison and the volunteer on board, she had been up with the patient for 56 hours. The patient survived.

After the flight of Sally Ride in 1983, Jemison felt the astronaut program had opened up, so she applied. Jemison's inspiration for joining NASA was African-American actress Nichelle Nichols, who portrayed Lieutenant Uhura on Star Trek. Jemison's involvement with NASA was delayed after the Space Shuttle Challenger disaster in 1986, but after reapplying in 1987, she received the news of her acceptance into the astronaut program.

Her work with NASA before her shuttle launch included launch support activities at the Kennedy Space Center in Florida and verification of Shuttle computer software in the Shuttle Avionics Integration Laboratory (SAIL) Jemison was in the first class of astronauts selected after the Challenger accident back in 1986, ... she actually worked the launch of the first flight after the Challenger accident.

On Sept. 12, 1992, Mae Jemison became the first African American woman in space when the space shuttle Endeavour carried her and six other astronauts on 126 orbits around the Earth. Jemison flew her only space mission from September 12 to 20, 1992, as a Mission Specialist on STS-47, a cooperative mission between the United States and Japan, as well as the 50th shuttle mission. She was a co-investigator of two bone cell research experiments, one of 43 investigations that were done on STS-47. Jemison also conducted experiments on weightlessness and motion sickness on herself and six other crew members.

The shuttle landed at Kennedy Space Center in Florida on Sept. 20. Over the course of her only space voyage, Jemison logged 190 hours, 30 minutes, and 23 seconds in space.

STS-47 was a cooperative mission between the United States and Japan that included 44 Japanese and United States life science and materials processing experiments. Jemison logged 190 hours, 30 minutes, 23 seconds in space. One of the experiments she supervised on the mission was to induce female frogs to ovulate, fertilize the eggs and then see how tadpoles developed in zero gravity.

Jemison resigned from NASA in March 1993. She left NASA because she was very interested in how social sciences interact with technologies. Plus, she was not driven to be the "first black woman to go into space." She went on to teach at Dartmouth College.

Jemison is a Professor-at-Large at Cornell University and was a professor of Environmental Studies at Dartmouth College from 1995 to 2002. She continues to advocate strongly in favor of science education and getting minority students interested in science. She sees science and technology as being very much a part of society, and African-Americans as having been deeply involved in U.S. science and technology from the beginning. She has been a member of various scientific organizations, such as the American Medical Association, the American Chemical Society, the Association for Space Explorers and the American Association for the Advancement of Science. Additionally, she served on the board of directors of the World Sickle Cell Foundation from 1990 to 1992.

In 1993 Jemison founded her own company, the Jemison Group, which seeks to encourage a love of science in students and bring advanced technology to schools around the world; as well as researches, markets, and develops science and technology for daily life. Jemison founded the Dorothy Jemison Foundation for Excellence and named the foundation in honor of her mother.

In 1999, Jemison founded BioSentient Corp and has been working to develop a portable device that allows mobile monitoring of the involuntary nervous system. BioSentient has obtained the license to commercialize NASA's space-age technology known as Autogenic Feedback Training Exercise (AFTE), a patented technique that uses biofeedback and autogenic therapy to allow patients to monitor and control their physiology as a possible treatment for anxiety and stress-related disorders.

Jemison participated with First Lady, Michelle Obama, in a forum for promising girls in the Washington, D.C. public schools in March 2009. In 2012, Jemison made the winning bid for the DARPA 100 Year Starship project through the Dorothy Jemison Foundation for

Excellence. The project works to make human space travel beyond the solar system a reality within the next century. The Dorothy Jemison Foundation for Excellence was awarded a $500,000 grant for further work.

In 2016, Jemison partnered with Bayer Corporation to promote and advance science literacy in schools, emphasizing hands-on experimentation. Jemison is Bayer Corporation USA's national science literacy ambassador. She is the space operations advisor for the upcoming National Geographic global miniseries MARS. Jemison is a member of the U.S. National Academy of Medicine and on the board of Kimberly-Clark Corporation, Valspar corporations, Texas Medical Center, and the National Board of Professional Teaching Standards. She was the Founding Chair of the Texas State Product Development and Small Business Incubator Board, Chair of the Texas State Biotechnology and Life Sciences Industry Cluster and the Greater Houston Partnership Disaster Planning and Recovery Task Force. Jemison is an inductee of the National Women's Hall of Fame, the National Medical Association Hall of Fame and Texas Science Hall of Fame as well as a recipient of the National Organization for Women's Intrepid Award, the Kilby Science Award and National Association of Corporate Director's Directorship 100 most influential people in the boardroom and corporate governance in 2014, among many honors.

DR. PERCY LAVON JULIAN

Percy Lavon Julian, Ph.D. (April 11, 1899 – April 19, 1975) was an African American research chemist and a pioneer in the chemical synthesis of medicinal drugs from plants. He was the first to synthesize the natural product physostigmine, and a pioneer in the industrial large-scale chemical synthesis of the human hormones, progesterone and testosterone from plant sterols such as stigmasterol and sitosterol. His work laid the foundation for the steroid drug industry's production of cortisone, other corticosteroids, and birth control pills.

He later started his own company to synthesize steroid intermediates from the wild Mexican yam. His work helped greatly reduce the cost of steroid intermediates to large multinational pharmaceutical companies, helping to significantly expand the use of several important drugs.

Julian received more than 130 chemical patents. He was one of the first African Americans to receive a doctorate in chemistry. He was the first African-American chemist inducted into the National Academy of Sciences, and the second African-American scientist inducted (behind David Blackwell) from any field.

Percy Lavon Julian was born in Montgomery, Alabama, as the first child of six born to James Sumner Julian and Elizabeth Lena Julian, (Adams). Both of his parents were graduates of what was to be Alabama State University. His father, James, whose own father had been a slave, was employed as a clerk in the Railway Service of the United States Post Office, while his mother, Elizabeth, worked as a schoolteacher.

Percy Julian grew up in the time of racist Jim Crow culture and legal regime in the southern United States. Among his childhood memories was finding a lynched man hanged from a tree while walking in the woods near his home. At a time when access to an education beyond the eighth grade was extremely rare for African-Americans, Julian's parents steered all of their children toward higher education.

Julian attended DePauw University in Greencastle, Indiana. The college accepted few African-American students. The segregated nature of the town forced social humiliations. Julian was not allowed to live in the college dormitories and first stayed in an off-campus boarding home, which refused to serve him meals. It took him days before Julian found an establishment where he could eat. Julian graduated from DePauw in 1920 as a Phi Beta Kappa and valedictorian.

After graduating from DePauw, Julian wanted to obtain his doctorate in chemistry, but learned it would be difficult for an African-American to do so. Instead he obtained a position as a chemistry instructor at Fisk University. In 1923 he received an Austin Fellowship in Chemistry, which allowed him to attend Harvard University to obtain his M.S. However, worried that white students would resent being taught by an African-American, Harvard withdrew Julian's teaching assistantship, making it impossible for him to complete his Ph.D. at Harvard.

In 1929, while an instructor at Howard University, Julian received a Rockefeller Foundation fellowship to continue his graduate work at the University of Vienna, where he earned his Ph.D. in 1931. Julian was one of the first African Americans to receive a Ph.D. in chemistry, after St. Elmo Brady and Dr. Edward M.A. Chandler.

After returning from Vienna, Julian taught for one year at Howard University. At Howard, in part due to his position as a department head, Julian became caught up in university politics, setting off an embarrassing chain of events, which forced him to resign. Julian lost his position and everything he had worked for. In 1932 Julian's former mentor, William Martin Blanchard, professor of chemistry at DePauw offered Julian a position to teach organic chemistry at DePauw University. Julian then helped Josef Pikl, a fellow student at the University of Vienna, to come to the United States to work with him at DePauw. In 1934, Butenandt and Fernholz, in Germany, had shown that stigmasterol, isolated from soybean oil, could be converted to progesterone by synthetic organic chemistry.

Around the same time, in 1935 Julian and Pikl completed the total synthesis of physostigmine and confirmed the structural formula assigned to it. Robert Robinson of Oxford University in the U.K. had been the first to publish a synthesis of physostigmine, but Julian noticed that the melting point of Robinson's end product was wrong, indicating that he had not created it.

When Julian completed his synthesis, the melting point matched the correct one for natural physostigmine from the calabar bean. Julian also extracted stigmasterol, which took its name from *Physostigma venenosum*, the west African calabar bean that he hoped could serve as raw material for synthesis of human steroidal hormones.

On December 24, 1935 Julian married Anna Roselle (Ph.D. in Sociology, 1937, University of Pennsylvania). They had two children:

Percy Lavon Julian, Jr. (August 31, 1940 – February 24, 2008), who became a noted civil rights lawyer in Madison, Wisconsin; and Faith Roselle Julian (1944–), who still resides in their Oak Park home and often makes inspirational speeches about her father and his contributions to science.

In 1936 Julian was denied a professorship at DePauw for racial reasons. DuPont had offered a job to fellow chemist Josef Pikl but declined to hire Julian, despite his superlative qualifications as an organic chemist, apologizing that they were "unaware he was a Negro". Julian next applied for a job at the Institute of Paper Chemistry (IPC) in Appleton, Wisconsin. However, Appleton was a sundown town, forbidding African Americans from staying overnight, stating directly: "No Negro should be bed or boarded overnight in Appleton."

Meanwhile, Julian had written to the Glidden Company, a supplier of soybean oil products, to request a five-gallon sample of the oil to use as his starting point for the synthesis of human steroidal sex hormones. After receiving the request, W. J. O'Brien, a vice-president at Glidden, made a telephone call to Julian, offering him the position of director of research at Glidden's Soya Products Division in Chicago. He fluent in German, and Glidden had just purchased a modern continuous countercurrent solvent extraction plant from Germany for the extraction of vegetable oil from soybeans for paints and other uses.

Julian supervised the assembly of the plant at Glidden when he arrived in 1936. He then designed and supervised construction of the world's first plant for the production of industrial-grade, isolated soy protein from oil-free soybean meal.

During World War II, Julian's isolated soy protein was used in the development of Aer-O-Foam for the U.S. Navy's which was used to smother oil and gasoline fires aboard ships and was particularly useful on aircraft carriers. It saved the lives of thousands of sailors and airmen. Citing this achievement, in 1947 the NAACP awarded Julian the Spingarn Medal, its highest honor.

Julian's research at Glidden changed direction in 1940 when he began work on synthesizing progesterone, estrogen, and testosterone from the plant sterols stigmasterol and sitosterol, isolated from soybean oil by a foam technique he invented and patented. At that time clinicians were discovering many uses for the newly discovered hormones. His work made possible the production of these hormones on a larger industrial scale, with the potential of reducing the cost of treating hormonal deficiencies. Julian and his co-workers obtained patents for Glidden on key processes for the preparation of progesterone and testosterone from soybean plant sterols.

On April 13, 1949, rheumatologist Philip Hench at the Mayo Clinic announced the dramatic effectiveness of cortisone in treating rheumatoid arthritis. On September 30, 1949, Julian announced an improvement in the process of producing cortisone.

Around 1950, Julian moved his family to the Chicago suburb of Oak Park, becoming the first African-American family to reside there. Although some residents welcomed them into the community, there was also opposition. Before they even moved in, on Thanksgiving Day, 1950, their home was fire-bombed. Later, after they moved in, the house was attacked with dynamite on June 12, 1951. The attacks galvanized the community, and a community group was formed to support the Julians. Julian and his son often kept watch over the family's property by sitting in a tree with a shotgun.

In 1953, Glidden decided to leave the steroid business, which had been relatively unprofitable over the years, despite Julian's innovative work. On December 1, 1953, Julian left Glidden after 18 years, to found his own research company, Julian Laboratories, Inc., taking over the small, concrete-block building of Suburban Chemical Company in Franklin Park, Illinois. On December 2, 1953, Pfizer acquired exclusive licenses of Glidden patents for the synthesis of Substance S.

Julian brought many of his best chemists from Glidden to Julian Laboratories, including African-Americans and women.

He won a contract to provide Upjohn with $2 million worth of progesterone (equivalent to $16 million today). To compete against Syntex, he would have to use the same Mexican yam, but he could not get a permit from the government to harvest the yams, so he set up an operation in Guatemala. After several years of operations, Julian sold the company in 1961 for $2.3 million. The U.S. and Mexico facilities were purchased by Smith Kline, and Julian's chemical plant in Guatemala was purchased by Upjohn.

In 1964, Julian founded Julian Associates and Julian Research Institute, which he managed for the rest of his life.

DR. RICK ANTONIUS KITTLES

Rick Antonius Kittles (1976) was born in Sylvania, Georgia in an area his family had inhabited for several generations, but he grew up in Central Islip, New York, on Long Island outside of New York City. As a child, he was always the only black kid in the class, was curious about human origins and differences, and wondered why everybody in school looked different. He obviously remained curious and ultimately earned a B.S. degree in biology from the Rochester Institute of Technology (1989) and a Ph.D. in biology from George Washington University in Washington, D.C.

Rick Kittles, Ph.D., is professor and founding director of the Division of Health Equities within the Department of Population Sciences at City of Hope. Dr. Kittles is well-known for his research of prostate cancer and health disparities among African-Americans. His research has focused on understanding the complex issues surrounding race, genetic ancestry and health disparities. He is also associate director of health equities in the comprehensive cancer center.

In 1990 Kittles began his career as a teacher in several New York and Washington, D.C. area high schools. From approximately 1995 until 1999, as a researcher with the New York African Burial Ground Project (NYABGP), a federally funded project in New York City, in which Howard University researchers, led by anthropologist Michael Blakey, exhumed the remains of 408 African Americans from an 18th-century graveyard. Kittles gathered DNA samples from the remains and compared them with samples from a DNA database to determine from where in Africa the individuals buried in the graveyard had come.

As he was completing his doctoral degree at George Washington University in 1998, Kittles was hired as an assistant professor of microbiology at Washington's Howard University and was named director of the African American Hereditary Prostate Cancer (AAHPC) Study Network at the university's National Human Genome Center.

Kittles also co-directed the molecular genetics unit of Howard University's National Human Genome Center. He served in these positions until 2004. Beginning in 2004, he served as an associate professor in the Department of Molecular Virology, Immunology & Medical Genetics at the Tzagournis Medical Research Facility of Ohio State University in Columbus, Ohio.

As a professor at Ohio State University, Dr. Kittles became one of the hottest young scientific researchers in the country in the early 2000s. When he was hired by Ohio State in 2004, the *Columbus Dispatch* reported that he would bring to the university more than $1 million in research grants in addition to his teaching expertise. He was a nationally recognized investigator whose specialties encompassed such vital topics as prostate cancer and the role of genetics in disease.

Over the last 20 years, he has been at the forefront of the development of ancestry-informative genetic markers, and how genetic ancestry can be quantified and utilized in genomic studies on disease risk and outcomes. His work has shown the impact of genetic variation across populations in pharmacogenomics, biomarker discovery and disease gene mapping.

Although a major focus of Dr. Kittles' work over the past years has been on measuring and utilizing West African admixture in studies of genetic disease among African-Americans, presently he is expanding his research focus to further include Latino and Native American populations to further enhance the robustness of the experimental design of his research studies.

Kittles is currently the leader of the Washington, D.C.-based African Ancestry Inc., a genetic testing service for determining individuals' African ancestry, which he co-founded with Gina Paige in February 2003. His company, African Ancestry, Inc., used his expertise in genetic testing to put African Americans, from celebrities to ordinary genealogy buffs, in touch with their roots in a way that Americans of European descent took for granted but that a displaced and enslaved people had mostly only dreamed of. Kittles offered his customers a glimpse into their specific African ancestries, pinpointing an actual African ethnic group to which one or two of the customer's ancestors had belonged. The path that led to the founding of African Ancestry was complicated and not without controversy, but Kittles found that his research often fed into the deep interest in African-American genealogy that had been awakened by the publication of Alex Haley's book *Roots* in the 1970s.

Kittles also serves as an associate professor in the Department of Medicine and the Division of Epidemiology and Biostatistics at the University of Illinois, Chicago.

Kittles was featured in the BBC Two films *Motherland: A Genetic Journey* and *Motherland – Moving On* (released in 2003 and 2004, respectively), as well as in part 4 of the 2006 PBS series *African American Lives* (hosted by Henry Louis Gates). On October 7, 2007, he was featured on the American TV newsmagazine *60 Minutes*. In February 2008 he appeared in part 4 of *African American Lives 2*.

He has published on genetic variation and prostate cancer genetics of African Americans. In addition, he discovered, through a DNA analysis, he descends mainly of people of Dakar, Senegal, and Nigeria's Hausa people.

In 2010, Dr. Kittles was named in *Ebony* magazine's "The Ebony Power 100." *Ebony* selected the nation's top 100 African-American "power players" in sports, academia, religion, business, environment, science and tech, entertainment, arts and letters, fashion, politics, media, activism and health. In March of 2012, Dr. Kittles presented the Keynote Address to the United Nations General Assembly, "International Day of Remembrance of Victims of Slavery and the Transatlantic Slave Trade." Recently, he was named by *The Huffington Post* as one of "50 Iconic Black Trailblazers Who Represent Every State in America."

DR. RONALD MCNAIR

Ronald Erwin McNair, Ph. D. (October 21, 1950 – January 28, 1986) was an American physicist and NASA astronaut. He died during the launch of the Space Shuttle Challenger on mission STS-51-L, in which he was serving as one of three mission specialists. He is survived by his wife, Cheryl, and two children.

Born October 21, 1950, in Lake City, South Carolina, his parents were Pearl M. and Carl C. McNair. He had two brothers, Carl S. and Eric A. McNair. In the summer of 1959, he refused to leave the segregated Lake City Public Library without being allowed to check out his books. After the police and his mother were called, he was allowed to borrow books from the library, which is now named after him. A children's book, Ron's Big Mission, offers a fictionalized account of this event.

McNair graduated as valedictorian of Carver High School in 1967.

In 1971, he received a Bachelor of Science degree in Engineering Physics, magna cum laude, from North Carolina A&T State University in Greensboro, North Carolina. McNair was a member of Omega Psi Phi Fraternity. In 1976, he received a Ph.D. degree in Physics from the Massachusetts Institute of Technology under the guidance of Michael Feld, becoming nationally recognized for his work in the field of laser physics.

He received four honorary doctorates, a score of fellowships and commendations and achieved a 6th degree black belt in taekwondo. After graduation from MIT, he became a staff physicist at the Hughes Research Lab in Malibu, California. McNair was a member of the Bahá'í Faith.

In 1978, McNair was selected as one of thirty-five applicants from a pool of ten thousand for the NASA astronaut program. He flew on STS-41-B aboard Challenger from February 3 to February 11, 1984, as a mission specialist becoming the second African American and the first Bahá'í to fly in space. Following this mission, McNair was selected for STS-51-L, which launched on January 28, 1986, and was subsequently killed when Challenger disintegrated nine miles above the Atlantic Ocean just 73 seconds after liftoff.

Before his last fateful space mission, he had worked with the composer Jean-Michel Jarre on a piece of music for Jarre's then-upcoming album Rendez-Vous. It was intended that he would record his saxophone solo on board the Challenger, which would have made McNair's solo the first original piece of music to have been recorded in space. However, the recording was never made as the flight ended in disaster and the deaths of its entire crew. The last of the Rendez-Vous pieces, "Last Rendez-Vous", had the additional name "Ron's Piece". Ron McNair was supposed to take part in the concert through a live feed.

McNair was posthumously awarded the Congressional Space Medal of Honor in 2004, along with all crew members lost in the Challenger and Columbia disasters. The crater McNair on the Moon is named in his honor. The McNair Building at MIT, his alma mater, houses the Kavli Institute for Astrophysics and Space Research. Ronald McNair Boulevard in Lake City, South Carolina, is named in his honor and lies near other streets named for astronauts who perished in the Challenger crash.

The U.S. Department of Education offers the TRIO Ronald E. McNair Post-Baccalaureate Achievement Program for students with low income, first generation students, and/or underrepresented students in graduate education for doctorate education. Several K-12 schools have also been named after McNair. The Ronald E. McNair Space Theater inside the Davis Planetarium in downtown Jackson, Mississippi, is named in his honor.

The Naval ROTC building on the campus of Southern University and A&M College in Baton Rouge, Louisiana is named in his honor. The McNair Post-baccalaureate Achievement Program, which operates at 179 campuses in the U.S. (April 7), awards research money and internships to first-generation and otherwise underrepresented students in preparation for graduate work.

DR. CHARLES DREW

Dr. Charles Richard Drew (June 3, 1904 – April 1, 1950) broke barriers in a racially divided America to become one of the most important scientists of the 20th century. His pioneering research and systematic developments in the use and preservation of blood plasma during World War II not only saved thousands of lives but innovated the nation's blood banking process and standardized procedures for long-term blood preservation and storage techniques adapted by the American Red Cross.

Charles Richard Drew was an American physician, surgeon, and medical researcher. He researched in the field of blood transfusions, developing improved techniques for blood storage, and applied his expert knowledge to developing large-scale blood banks early in World War II. This allowed medics to save thousands of lives of the Allied forces.

As the most prominent African American in the field, Drew protested against the practice of racial segregation in the donation of blood, as it lacked scientific foundation, and resigned his position with American Red Cross, which maintained the policy until 1950.

Drew was born into an African-American middle-class family in Washington, D.C. His father, Richard, was a carpet layer and his mother, Nora Burrell, was a teacher.[Drew and his siblings grew up in D.C.'s Foggy Bottom neighborhood and he graduated from Dunbar High School in 1922. He won an athletics scholarship to Amherst College in Massachusetts, where he graduated in 1926.

Beyond sports, Drew didn't have a clear direction until a biology professor piqued his interest in medicine. Drew completed his bachelor's degree at Amherst in 1926 but didn't have enough money to pursue his dream of attending medical school.

After college, he worked for two years (1926–1928) as a professor of chemistry and biology, the first Athletic Director, and the football coach for Morgan College, now Morgan State University, in Baltimore to earn the money to pay for medical school. In 1928, Drew applied to medical schools and enrolled at McGill University in Montreal, Canada. There, he distinguished himself, winning the annual scholarship prize in neuroanatomy, the J. Francis Williams Prize in medicine after beating the top 5 students in an exam competition; becoming elected to the medical honor society as a member of Alpha Omega Alpha; as well as staffing the McGill Medical Journal.

Drew's interest in transfusion medicine began during his internship and surgical residency at Montreal Hospital (1933-1935) working with bacteriology professor John Beattie on ways to treat shock with fluid replacement, and they examined problems and issues regarding blood transfusions. In 1933, Drew earned both Doctor of Medicine and Master of Surgery degrees, graduating second in a class of 137. He did his internship and residency at the Royal Victoria Hospital and the Montreal General Hospital.

A few years later, Drew did graduate work at Columbia University, where he earned his Doctor of Medical Science degree, becoming the first African American to do so.

After his father's death, Drew returned to the United States. Drew aspired to continue training in transfusion therapy at the Mayo Clinic, but racial prejudices at major American medical centers barred black scholars from their practices. He would instead join the faculty at Howard University College of Medicine, starting as a pathology instructor in 1935, and then the following year, progressing to surgical instructor and chief surgical resident at Freedmen's Hospital in Washington, DC, in addition to his work at the university.

In 1938, Drew received a Rockefeller Fellowship to study at Columbia University and train with eminent surgeon Allen Whipple at the Presbyterian Hospital in New York City. Instead of following the traditional path of residents to gain experience in surgical pathology and bacteriology, surgical laboratory research, outpatient clinic, operating rooms and surgical wards, Whipple assigned Drew to work under John Scudder, who was granted funding to set up an experimental blood bank. This would prevent Drew from privileges afforded to his white peers, especially direct access to patients; instead, he continued his exploration of blood-related matters with John Scudder.

Drew developed a method for processing and preserving blood plasma, or blood without cells. Plasma lasts much longer than whole blood, making it possible to be stored or "banked" for longer periods of time. He discovered that the plasma could be dried and then reconstituted when needed. Scudder considered his protege "naturally great" and a "brilliant pupil" and Whipple would later be won over by

Drew's talent, supporting both his surgical training and doctoral research. Drew's research served as the basis of his doctorate thesis, "Banked Blood: A Study in Blood Preservation." Drew received his doctorate degree in 1940, becoming the first African-American to earn this degree from Columbia University.

In 1939, Drew married Minnie Lenore Robbins, a professor of home economics at Spelman College whom he had met earlier that year. The couple had three daughters and a son.

In late 1940, before the U.S. entered World War II and just after earning his doctorate, Drew was recruited by John Scudder to help set up and administer an early prototype program for blood storage and preservation. He was to collect, test, and transport large quantities of blood plasma for distribution in the United Kingdom. Drew went to New York City as the medical director of the United States' Blood for Britain project, where he organized the collection and processing of blood plasma from several New York hospitals, and the shipments of these life-saving materials overseas to treat causalities in the war. The Blood for Britain project was a project to aid British soldiers and civilians by giving U.S. blood to the United Kingdom.

Drew created a central location for the blood collection process where donors could go to give blood. He made sure all blood plasma was tested before it was shipped out. He ensured that only skilled personnel handled blood plasma to avoid the possibility of contamination. The Blood for Britain program operated successfully for five months, with total collections of almost 15,000 people donating blood, and with over 5,500 vials of blood plasma. As a result, the Blood Transfusion Betterment Association applauded Drew for his work. Drew also started what would be later known as bloodmobiles, which were trucks containing refrigerators of stored blood; this allowed for greater mobility in terms of transportation as well as prospective donations.

In 1941, Drew spearheaded another blood bank effort, this time for the American Red Cross. He worked on developing a blood bank to be used for U.S. military personnel. But not long into his tenure there, Drew became frustrated with the military's request for segregating the blood donated by African Americans. At first, the military did not want to use blood from African Americans, but they later said it could only be used for African-American soldiers. Drew was outraged by this racist policy and resigned his post after only a few months.

After creating two of the first blood banks, Drew returned to Howard University in 1941. He served as a professor there, heading up the university's department of surgery. He also became the chief surgeon at Freedmen's Hospital. Later that year, he became the first African-American examiner for the American Board of Surgery.

In 1944, the National Association for the Advancement of Colored People honored Drew with its 1943 Spingarn Medal for "the highest and noblest achievement" by an African American "during the preceding year or years." The award was given in recognition of Drew's blood plasma collection and distribution efforts.

For the final years of his life, Drew remained an active and highly regarded medical professional. He continued to serve as the chief surgeon at Freedmen's Hospital and a professor at Howard University.

Beginning in 1939, Drew had been traveling to Tuskegee, Alabama to attend the annual free clinic at the John A. Andrew Memorial Hospital. For the 1950 Tuskegee clinic, Drew drove along with three other black physicians. Drew was driving around 8 a.m. on April 1. Still fatigued from spending the night before in the operating theater, he lost control of the vehicle near Burlington, North Carolina. After careening into a field, the car somersaulted three times. The three other physicians suffered minor injuries. Drew was trapped with serious wounds; his foot had become wedged beneath the brake pedal. When reached by emergency technicians, he was in shock and barely alive due to severe leg injuries.

Drew was taken to Alamance General Hospital in Burlington, North Carolina. He was pronounced dead a half hour after he first received medical attention. Drew's funeral was held on April 5, 1950, at the Nineteenth Street Baptist Church in Washington, D.C.

DR. BEN CARSON

Renowned neurosurgeon **Ben Carson** was born in Detroit, Michigan, on September 18, 1951. His mother, though under-educated herself, pushed her sons to read and believe in themselves. Carson went from being a poor student to receiving academic honors and eventually attending medical school. As a doctor, he became director of pediatric neurosurgery at Johns Hopkins Hospital at age 33 and earned fame for his groundbreaking work separating conjoined twins.

Benjamin Solomon Carson was born in Detroit, Michigan, on September 18, 1951, the second son of Sonya and Robert Solomon Carson. Sonya married Baptist minister and factory worker Robert Carson when she was 13 but after having two children, she discovered her husband was a bigamist. They divorced when Ben was 8 and his brother, Curtis was 10. In spite of their difficulties, Sonya taught her boys that anything was possible. Ben had thoughts of a career in medicine, after his family would have to wait for hours to get medical care at the hospital. As doctors and nurses went about their routines, he was dreaming that one day they would be calling for a "Dr. Carson."

A fifth-grade science teacher was one of the first to encourage Ben's interests in lab work after he was the only student able to identify an obsidian rock sample brought to school. Despite some racial challenges, Ben began to excel and in the eighth grade, he received a certificate of achievement for being at the top of his class. At Southwestern High School in inner-city Detroit, Carson's science teachers recognized his intellectual abilities and mentored him further. Other educators helped him to stay focused when outside influences pulled him off course. Despite his academic successes, Ben had a raging temper that translated into violent behavior as a child. Terrified by his own actions, he started praying, asking God to help him find a way to deal with his temper, finding salvation in the Book of Proverbs. Carson began to realize that much of his anger stemmed from constantly putting himself in the center of events happening around him. Carson graduated with honors from Southwestern, having also become a senior commander in the school's ROTC program. He earned a full scholarship to Yale, receiving a B.A. degree in psychology in 1973.

Ben Carson enrolled in the School of Medicine at the University of Michigan, choosing to become a neurosurgeon. In 1975, he married Lacena "Candy" Rustin, whom he met at Yale. Carson earned his medical degree, and the young couple moved to Baltimore, Maryland, where he became an intern at Johns Hopkins University in 1977. His excellent eye-hand coordination and three-dimensional reasoning skills made him a superior surgeon early on. By 1982, he was chief resident in neurosurgery at Hopkins.

In 1983, Carson received an important invitation. Sir Charles Gairdner Hospital in Perth, Australia, needed a neurosurgeon and invited Carson to take the position. Resistant at first to move so far away from home, he eventually accepted the offer. It proved to be an important one. Australia at the time was lacking doctors with highly sophisticated training in neurosurgery. Carson gained several years' worth of experience while he was at Gairdner Hospital and honed his skills tremendously.

Carson returned to Johns Hopkins in 1984 and, by 1985, he became director of pediatric neurosurgery at the age of 33; at the time, the youngest U.S. physician to hold such a position. In 1987, Carson attracted international attention by performing a surgery to separate 7-month-old occipital craniopagus twins in Germany. Patrick and Benjamin Binder were born joined at the head. Their parents contacted Carson, who went to Germany to consult with the family and the boys' doctors. Because the boys were joined at the back of the head, and because they had separate brains, he felt the operation could be performed successfully.

On September 4, 1987, after months of rehearsals, Carson and a huge team of doctors, nurses and support staff joined forces for what would be a 22-hour procedure. Part of the challenge in radical neurosurgery is to prevent severe bleeding and trauma to the patients. In the highly complex operation, Carson had applied both hypothermic and circulatory arrest. Although the twins did suffer some brain damage and post-operation bleeding, both survived the separation, allowing Carson's surgery to be considered by the medical establishment the first successful procedure of its kind.

In 1994, Carson and his team went to South Africa to separate the Makwaeba twins. The operation was unsuccessful, as both girls died from complications of the surgery. Carson was devastated, but vowed

251

to press on, as he knew such procedures could be successful. In 1997, Carson and his team went to Zambia in South Central Africa to separate infant boys Luka and Joseph Banda. This operation was especially difficult because the boys were joined at the tops of their heads, facing in opposite directions, making it the first time a surgery of this type had been performed. After a 28-hour operation, that was supported by previously rendered 3-D mapping, both boys survived and neither suffered brain damage.

Over time, Ben Carson's operations began to gain media attention. At first, what people saw was the soft-spoken surgeon explaining complicated procedures in simple terms. But in time, Carson's own story became public—a troubled youth growing up in the inner city to a poor family eventually finding success. Soon, Carson began traveling to schools, businesses and hospitals across the country telling his story and imparting his philosophy of life. Out of this dedication to education and helping young people, Carson and his wife founded the Carson Scholars Fund in 1994. The foundation grants scholarships to students and promotes reading in the younger grades.

In 2003, Ben Carson faced what was perhaps his biggest challenge: separating adult conjoined twins. Ladan and Laleh Bijani were Iranian women who were joined at the head. For 29 years, they had literally lived together in every conceivable way. Like normal twins, they shared experiences and outlooks, including earning law degrees, but as they got older and developed their own individual aspirations, they knew they could never lead independent lives unless they separated. As they told Carson at one point, "We would rather die than spend another day together."

This type of medical procedure had never been attempted on conjoined adults because of the dangerous outcomes. By this time, Carson had been conducting brain surgery for nearly 20 years and had performed several craniopagus separations.

Carson and a team of more than 100 surgeons, specialists and assistants traveled to Singapore in Southeast Asia. On July 6, 2003, Carson and his team began the nearly 52-hour operation. They again relied on a 3-D imaging technique that Carson had utilized to prepare for the Banda twins' operation. The computerized images allowed the medical team to conduct a virtual surgery before the operation. During the procedure, they followed digital reconstructions of the twins' brains.

The surgery revealed more difficulties outside of the girls' ages; their brains not only shared a major vein but had fused together. The separation was completed during the afternoon on July 8. But it was soon apparent that the girls were in deep critical condition. At 2:30 p.m., Ladan died on the operating table. Her sister Laleh died a short time later. The loss was devastating to all, especially Carson, who stated that the girls' bravery to pursue the operation had contributed to neurosurgery in ways that would live far beyond them.

In 2002, Carson was forced to cut back on his breakneck pace after developing prostate cancer. He took an active role in his own case, reviewing X-rays and consulting with the team of surgeons who operated on him. Carson fully recovered from the operation cancer-free. The brush with death caused him to adjust his life to spend more time with his wife and their three children, Murray, Benjamin Jr. and Rhoeyce.

In 2000, the Library of Congress selected Carson as one of its "Living Legends." The following year, CNN and *Time* magazine named Carson as one of the nation's 20 foremost physicians and scientists. In 2006, he received the Spingarn Medal, the highest honor bestowed by the NAACP. In February 2008, President George W. Bush awarded

Carson the Ford's Theatre Lincoln Medal and the Presidential Medal of Freedom. And in 2009, actor Cuba Gooding Jr. portrayed Carson in the TNT television production *Gifted Hands*.

Dr. Ben Carson retired from medicine in 2013, and two years later he entered politics, making a bid to become the Republican candidate for U.S. president. After struggling in the primary elections, Carson dropped out of the race in March 2016, and then became a vocal supporter of Republican nominee and former rival Donald Trump. After Trump was elected president, he nominated Carson to become the secretary of the Department of Housing and Urban Development.

> *"I want you to understand that your first duty is to humanity. I want others to look at us and see that we care not just about ourselves but about others."*
> **- Madame C. J. Walker**

CHAPTER SEVEN - FINANCIAL LITERACY
FEATURING BUSINESS MOGULS

I had great mentors in Hal Jackson and Percy Sutton. Percy was an Intelligence Officer with the Tuskegee Airmen, an attorney, a politician, cofounder of Inner-City Broadcasting Corporation and my dear friend. One of the things he used to tell me was, "I keep about 5 or 6 or 7 businesses because if 1 or 2 or 3 or even 4 fail I'm still in business." *That's a serious quote.* To this day, I rely on Percy's wisdom to guide me through many of my financial decisions; and I've learned so much from Hal Jackson who was brilliant in the business of radio and television.

It's never too early to start preparing for your future; but for many of us, too often it's too late. Throughout the various stages of your life, there should be a thought process and an evaluation about what you have, what you want and what you need. Money is the common thread but it's not the end all. How you get it, how you maintain it, how you keep it and how you increase it is not about guessing, it's about planning. To journey through life the best way possible, I advise you to ask questions, read books, attend seminars, talk to a financial advisor, hire an accountant, know your limitations and follow the rules. Follow your dreams. Find out what you want to do in life, and you will Make the Grade.

255

PERCY SUTTON

Percy Sutton (November 24, 1920 to December 26, 2009), attorney, politician, civil rights activist, and businessman, was born in San Antonio, Texas.

Percy Ellis Sutton was the youngest of 15 children born to Samuel Johnson Sutton and Lillian Sutton. Samuel was an early civil rights activist who farmed, sold real estate and owned a mattress factory, a funeral home and a skating rink—all in addition to being a full-time principal at the all-black Phyllis Wheatley High School. Lillian was also a full-time educator.

The couple raised their family on a farm in Prairie View, Texas. All the children were given chores on the farm, in addition to their studies. Percy was responsible for milking the cows, often accompanying his father on trips to deliver milk to the poor. He also helped his father in his strides toward equality, helping to educate others about racism. His efforts made him the target of a policeman and, at the age of 13, he was beaten by members of the local law enforcement for passing out NAACP brochures in an all-white neighborhood. Instead of discouraging him, this incident would later fuel his desire to earn equality for all races.

Thanks to his parents' emphasis on hard work and education, Percy and all of his siblings went on to earn college degrees. As each of the older siblings established themselves professionally, they would help their younger siblings financially so that they could afford school. Although Percy attended three different prestigious universities—Prairie View Agricultural and Mechanical College, the Tuskegee Institute and the Hampton Institute—he didn't complete his college degree. Instead, he traveled to New York at the beginning of World War II to enlist in the U.S. Army.

While serving in the armed forces, Percy Sutton became an intelligence officer with the famous all-Black Tuskegee Airmen, earning several combat honors. After completing his service time, Sutton was discharged honorably as a captain. After leaving the military, Sutton was determined to finish his education. He enrolled in Columbia University's law program with the help of the G.I. bill and his previous college grades.

Sutton eventually transferred to Brooklyn Law School in order to support himself financially. In addition to his rigorous class schedule, he was employed at the post office from 4 p.m. until midnight, then worked as a subway conductor until 8:30 a.m. He then attended his law classes at 9:30 a.m. Sutton continued this hectic schedule until graduation. Shortly after law school, Sutton—who mistakenly believed he'd failed the bar exam— returned to the military during the Korean War, enlisting in the U.S. Air Force. He later learned he had passed the test required to practice law, but he was already on his way to serve in the Korean War.

In 1950 Sutton earned a law degree from Brooklyn College Law School, and after his honorable discharge at the end of the conflict in 1953 he opened a law firm in New York City's Harlem district. During the peak of the civil rights movement, Sutton became a nationally recognized civil rights attorney representing political activists such as Malcolm X. . He represented Malcolm X until the civil rights leader's assassination in 1965. After Malcolm's death, Sutton made the leader's funeral arrangements, and also worked to represent Malcolm's widow, Betty Shabazz.

Sutton was a Freedom Rider, civil rights activist and prominent African-American lawyer. He also entered the political scene in the 1960s. He became a leader in the Harlem Clubhouse, a political group that controlled Democratic politics in Harlem. Soon after joining, he formed a powerful alliance with other Black politicians including future New York City mayor David Dinkins, Congressman Charles Rangel, and Basil Paterson who eventually served as the first Black Secretary of State for New York and whose son, David Paterson, became the state's first Black governor in 2008.

Sutton served in the New York State Assembly from 1964 to 1966. In 1966, when Manhattan borough president Constance Baker Motley received a federal judgeship, the City Council chose Sutton as her replacement. He served the remaining three years of her term. and was re-elected to two more terms after that, in 1969 and 1973. Sutton won that seat in a landslide with 80% of the vote. He became the highest-ranking African-American elected official in New York City in 1966, when he won election as president of the city's Manhattan borough, serving until 1977. As Borough President, Sutton pushed for the economic development of Harlem and his office promoted Harlem tourism.

In 1971, while still serving as borough president, Sutton began investing in media companies including *The New York Amsterdam News*, New York's largest Black newspaper. He also co-founded Inner City Broadcasting Corporation which bought the New York based AM radio station WLIB. His acquisitions made him the first Black owner of a radio station in New York City. In 1974, Sutton and his investors added WBLS-FM to their holdings, as well as more than 18 radio stations and cable franchises.

Percy Sutton left the Assembly in 1977 to campaign for the Democratic nomination for Mayor of New York City. He entered a crowded field which included Congressman Ed Koch, New York Secretary of State Mario Cuomo, incumbent Mayor Abraham Beame, former Congresswoman Bella Abzug, and Congressman Herman Badillo. Koch won the nomination and mayoral race.

By 1980, WBLS had the largest listening audience of any radio station in the nation. In 1981, Sutton made headlines when he and his investment partners purchased the crumbling Apollo Theater in Harlem and revitalized the once bankrupt facility. The legendary theater reopened in 1985, and boasted more than $20 million in renovations, including a cable television studio that was used to produce the variety show *It's Showtime at the Apollo*.

In 1987 Sutton was awarded the National Association for the Advancement of Colored People's (NAACP) Spingarn Medal for his work in media. In 2007, the U.S. Congress passed legislation to name the post office on 125th Street in Harlem after Percy Sutton.

Sutton retired in 1991, and in 1992 a nonprofit foundation took over the Apollo after Sutton could no longer afford to maintain the building. It continues to run as a concert hall and national landmark. Although he wasn't officially working in politics anymore, President Bill Clinton tapped Sutton, along with several other politicians, to attend meetings with the Group of Seven Nations in 1995.

Percy Sutton died, at the age of 89, on December 26, 2009 in New York City. He was survived by his wife, Leatrice O'Farrel Sutton, and his children, Pierre and Cheryl Lynn.

HAL JACKSON

Hal Jackson, born **Harold Baron Jackson** (November 3, 1914 – May 23, 2012) was an American disc jockey, radio personality, a legendary broadcaster, radio station owner, and philanthropist who broke a number of color barriers in American radio broadcasting.

Harold "Hal" Jackson was born in Charleston, South Carolina to Eugene and Laura Jackson. Eugene Jackson owned a successful tailor shop in Charleston allowing the family to live in a comfortable home in an affluent Black neighborhood. When Hal Jackson was nine, both of his parents unexpectedly passed away within several months of one another. Jackson lived with relatives in New York and Washington, D.C. until he reached the age of 13 when he independently moved into a District of Columbia boarding house.

Jackson attended Dunbar High School in D.C. and supported himself by working as a shoeshine boy. While in school, he excelled in sports and during his free time worked as an usher for Washington Senators baseball games. After high school Jackson attended Howard University where he worked as a sports announcer for Howard's home baseball games, local Negro league baseball games and basketball games.

Jackson began his broadcasting career in 1939 with the nightly interview program, *The Bronze Review*, on Washington, D.C. based radio station WINX. The show was an instant hit and was soon aired on four stations in three cities. Jackson's success did not come without a struggle. Initially WINX did not want to give Jackson a show because he would have been the first African American entertainer on the station and management feared losing part of their radio audience and sponsors. To counter their fears, Jackson found sponsors in Washington's African American business community and hired Elrich and Merrick, a prominent local white advertising agency, to buy airtime on his show.

During his career, Jackson worked on a variety of shows on a host of stations, including: a rhythm and blues show, a sports show, and his signature variety show, *The House that Jack Built*. In 1949 Jackson moved to New York City and became the first radio personality to broadcast three daily shows on three different New York stations. Four million listeners tuned in nightly to hear his mix of music and conversations with jazz and show business celebrities. He used his fame to spread awareness and show support for the emerging Civil Rights Movement. In the mid-1950s Jackson interviewed Dr. Martin Luther King Jr. and aired his speeches on his programs.

Throughout the 1960s Jackson continued to work in stations along the East Coast. Jackson continued to break down the racial barrier in entertainment. In 1971, Jackson and Percy Sutton, a former Manhattan borough president, co-founded the Inner City Broadcasting

Corporation (ICBC), which acquired WLIB — becoming the first African-American owned-and-operated station in New York. The following year, ICBC acquired WLIB-FM, changing its call letters to WBLS ("the total BLack experience in Sound").

In 1971 he produced the Miss Black Teenage America contest in Atlanta, Georgia. The competition, now known as the Hal Jackson's Talented Teen contest, was an alternative to the Miss America contest, and allowed girls of color to compete. Over the next two decades the contests provided more than $250,000 in scholarship money to those competitors.

In 1990, Hal Jackson was the first minority inducted into the National Association of Broadcaster's Hall of Fame. In 1995, he became the first African-American inducted into the National Radio Hall of Fame. In 2001 the Broadcast and Cable Hall of Fame inducted Mr. Jackson. For over 11 years he hosted a radio program rated #1 by Arbitron in its time slot on 107.5 WBLS in New York, the Hal Jackson Sunday Morning Classics.

In 1995 Jackson became the first African American to be inducted into the Radio Hall of Fame. He was given a Pioneer Award by the Rhythm and Blues Foundation in 2003. In October 2010 he was named a "Giant in Broadcasting" by the Library of American Broadcasting. Jackson was also inducted into the *Guinness Book of World Records* as being the oldest broadcaster, with a record 73 year-career.

Jackson continued to host Sunday Classics on WBLS every Sunday, with Clay Berry and Deborah Bolling Jackson (Debi B.), his wife of 25 years. He passed away of natural causes on May 23, 2012 in New York City at the age of 96. Hal often signed off the air with the motto; reminding listeners, "It's nice to be important, but it's more important to be nice."

MADAME C. J. WALKER

Madam C. J. Walker, born **Sarah Breedlove** (December 23, 1867 – May 25, 1919) was an African-American entrepreneur, philanthropist, and a political and social activist. Eulogized as one of the first female self-made millionaires in the United States, she became one of the wealthiest self-made women in America and one of the most successful women and African-American business owners ever.

Sarah Breedlove was born on December 23, 1867, near Delta, Louisiana, to Owen and Minerva (Anderson) Breedlove. Sarah was one of six children, which included an older sister, Louvenia, and four brothers: Alexander, James, Solomon, and Owen Jr. Breedlove's parents and her older siblings were enslaved on Robert W. Burney's Madison Parish plantation, but Sarah was the first child in her family born into freedom after the Emancipation Proclamation was signed. Her mother died, possibly from cholera, in 1872; her father remarried, but he died within a few years. Orphaned at the age of seven, Sarah moved to Vicksburg, Mississippi, at the age of ten and worked as a domestic. Prior to her first marriage, she lived with her older sister, Louvenia, and brother-in-law, Jesse Powell. She had only three months of formal education, which she learned during Sunday school literacy lessons at the church she attended during her earlier years.

In 1882, at the age of fourteen, Sarah married Moses McWilliams, possibly to escape mistreatment from her brother-in-law. Sarah and Moses had one daughter, Lelia McWilliams, born on June 6, 1885. When Moses died in 1887, Sarah was twenty; Lelia was two years old. Sarah remarried in 1894, but left her second husband, John Davis, around 1903 and moved to Denver, Colorado, in 1905.

In January 1906, Sarah married Charles Joseph Walker, a newspaper advertising salesman she had known in Missouri. Through this marriage, she became known as Madam C. J. Walker. The couple divorced in 1912; Charles died in 1926. Lelia McWilliams adopted her stepfather's surname and became known as A'lelia Walker.

In 1888 Sarah and her daughter moved to Saint Louis, Missouri, where three of her brothers lived. Sarah found work as a laundress, barely earning more than a dollar a day, but she was determined to make enough money to provide her daughter with a formal education. During the 1880s, Breedlove lived in a community where ragtime music was developed—she sang at the St. Paul African Methodist Episcopal Church and started to yearn for an educated life as she watched the community of women at her church.

As was common among black women of her era, Sarah experienced severe dandruff and other scalp ailments, including baldness, due to skin disorders and the application of harsh products such as lye that were included in soaps to cleanse hair and wash clothes. Other contributing factors to her hair loss included poor diet, illnesses, and infrequent bathing and hair washing during a time when most Americans lacked indoor plumbing, central heating and electricity.

Initially, Sarah learned about hair care from her brothers, who were barbers in Saint Louis. Around the time of the Louisiana Purchase Exposition (World's Fair at St. Louis in 1904), she became a commission agent selling products for Annie Turnbo Malone, an African American hair-care entrepreneur, millionaire, and owner of the Poro Company. While working for Malone, who would later become Walker's largest rival in the hair-care industry, Sarah began to take her knowledge of hair learned from selling Annie Malone's hair products to develop her own product line.

In July 1905, when she was thirty-seven years old, Sarah and her daughter moved to Denver, Colorado, where she continued to sell products for Malone and develop her own hair-care business. A controversy developed between Annie Malone and Sarah because it was Malone's hair growing formula that Sarah was using to market as her own. Following her marriage to Charles Walker in 1906, she became known as Madam C. J. Walker and marketed herself as an independent hairdresser and retailer of cosmetic creams. ("Madam" was adopted from women pioneers of the French beauty industry.) Her husband, who was also her business partner, provided advice on advertising and promotion; Sarah sold her products door to door, teaching other black women how to groom and style their hair.

In 1906 Walker put her daughter in charge of the mail order operation in Denver while she and her husband traveled throughout the southern and eastern United States to expand the business. In 1908 Walker and her husband relocated to Pittsburgh, Pennsylvania, where they opened a beauty parlor and established Lelia College to train "hair culturists". After closing the business in Denver in 1907, A'lelia ran the day-to-day operations from Pittsburgh, while Walker established a new base in Indianapolis in 1910. A'lelia also persuaded her mother to establish an office and beauty salon in New York City's Harlem neighborhood in 1913.

In 1910 Walker relocated her business to Indianapolis, where she established the headquarters for the Madame C. J. Walker Manufacturing Company. She initially purchased a house and factory at 640 North West Street. Walker later built a factory, hair salon, and beauty school to train her sales agents, and added a laboratory to help with research. She also assembled a competent staff that included Freeman Ransom, Robert Lee Brokenburr, Alice Kelly, and Marjorie Stewart Joyner, among others, to assist in managing the growing company. Many of her company's employees, including those in key management and staff positions, were women.

To increase her company's sales force, Walker trained other women to become "beauty culturists" using "The Walker System", her method of grooming that was designed to promote hair growth and to condition the scalp through the use of her products Walker's system included a shampoo, a pomade stated to help hair grow, strenuous brushing, and applying iron combs to hair. This method claimed to make lackluster and brittle hair become soft and luxurious. Walker's product line had several competitors. Similar products were produced in Europe and manufactured by other companies in the United States, which included her major rivals, Annie Turnbo Malone's Poro System from which she derived her original formula and later, Sarah Spencer Washington's Apex System.

Between 1911 and 1919, during the height of her career, Walker and her company employed several thousand women as sales agents for its products. By 1917 the company claimed to have trained nearly 20,000 women. Dressed in a characteristic uniform of white shirts and black skirts and carrying black satchels, they visited houses around the

United States and in the Caribbean offering Walker's hair pomade and other products packaged in tin containers carrying her image. Walker understood the power of advertising and brand awareness. Heavy advertising, primarily in African American newspapers and magazines, in addition to Walker's frequent travels to promote her products, helped make Walker and her products well known in the United States. Walker's name became even more widely known by the 1920s, after her death, as her company's business market expanded beyond the United States to Cuba, Jamaica, Haiti, Panama, and Costa Rica.

Walker made her fortune by developing and marketing a line of beauty and hair products for black women through Madame C. J. Walker Manufacturing Company, the successful business she founded. Walker was also known for her philanthropy and activism. She made financial donations to numerous organizations and became a patron of the arts. Villa Lewaro, Walker's lavish estate in Irvington-on-Hudson, New York, served as a social gathering place for the African-American community.

In addition to training in sales and grooming, Walker showed other black women how to budget, build their own businesses, and she encouraged them to become financially independent. In 1917, inspired by the model of the National Association of Colored Women, Walker began organizing her sales agents into state and local clubs. The result was the establishment of the National Beauty Culturists and Benevolent Association of Madam C. J. Walker Agents (predecessor to the Madam C. J. Walker Beauty Culturists Union of America). Its first annual conference convened in Philadelphia during the summer of 1917 with 200 attendees. The conference is believed to have been among the first national gatherings of women entrepreneurs to discuss business and commerce. During the convention Walker gave prizes to women who had sold the most products and brought in the most new sales agents. She also rewarded those who made the largest contributions to charities in their communities.

About 1913 Walker's daughter, A'lelia, moved to a new townhouse in Harlem, and in 1916 Walker joined her in New York, leaving the day-to-day operation of her company to her management team in Indianapolis. In 1917 Walker commissioned Vertner Tandy, the first licensed black architect in New York City and a founding member of Alpha fraternity, to design her house in Irvington-on-Hudson, New York. Walker intended for Villa Lewaro, which cost $250,000 to build, to become a gathering place for community leaders and to inspire other African Americans to pursue their dreams She moved into the house in May 1918 and hosted an opening event to honor Emmett Jay Scott, at that time the Assistant Secretary for Negro Affairs of the U.S. Department of War.

Profits from her business significantly impacted Walker's contributions to her political and philanthropic interests. In 1918 the National Association of Colored Women's Clubs(NACWC) honored Walker for making the largest individual contribution to help preserve Frederick Douglass's Anacostia house. Before her death in 1919, Walker pledged $5,000 (the equivalent of about $65,000 in 2012) to the NAACP's anti-lynching fund. At the time it was the largest gift from an individual that the NAACP had ever received. Walker bequeathed nearly $100,000 to orphanages, institutions, and individuals; her will directed two-thirds of future net profits of her estate to charity.

Walker died on May 25, 1919, from kidney failure and complications of hypertension at the age of fifty-one. Walker's remains are interred in Woodlawn Cemetery in The Bronx, New York City.

At the time of her death Walker was considered to be the wealthiest African American woman in America. She was eulogized as the first female self-made millionaire in America, and Walker's estate was worth an estimated $600,000 (about $8 million in present-day dollars). Upon her death. Her daughter, A'lelia Walker, became the president of the Madame C. J. Walker Manufacturing Company.

OPRAH WINFREY

Oprah Winfrey, (born January 29, 1954, Kosciusko, Mississippi, U.S.) is an American television personality, actress, and entrepreneur whose syndicated daily talk show was among the most popular of the genre. She became one of the richest and most influential women in the United States.

Winfrey was born into poverty to a teenage single mother. She spent the first years of her life in rural Mississippi with her grandmother, Hattie Mae Lee. At age six, Oprah was sent to live with her mother, Vernita Lee, in Wisconsin where she worked as a housemaid. Oprah recalled Vernita's roommate was a light-skinned black woman who took an instant dislike to her because of her dark complexion; and she was forced to sleep on a porch while her light-skinned half-sister slept indoors. She has stated that she was molested during her childhood and early teens and became pregnant at 14; her son was born prematurely and died in infancy.

In her early teens she was sent to Nashville, Tennessee to live with Vernon Winfrey the man she calls her father. Vernon , who was a barber, proved to be a positive influence in Oprah's life. She landed a job in radio while still in high school. At age 19 Winfrey became a news anchor for the local CBS television station. Oprah's often emotional, extemporaneous delivery eventually led to her transfer to the daytime talk show arena, and after boosting a third-rated local Chicago talk show to first place, she launched her own production company and became internationally syndicated.

Following her graduation from Tennessee State University in 1976, she was made a reporter and co-anchor for the ABC news affiliate in Baltimore, Maryland. She found herself constrained by the objectivity required of news reporting, and in 1977 she became co-host of the Baltimore morning show *People Are Talking*.

Winfrey excelled in the casual and personal talk-show format, and in 1984 she moved to Chicago to host the faltering talk show *AM Chicago*. Winfrey's honest and engaging personality quickly turned the program into a success, and in 1985 it was renamed *The Oprah Winfrey Show*. Syndicated nationally in 1986, the program became the highest-rated television talk show in the United States and earned several Emmy Awards.

In 1985 Winfrey appeared in Steven Spielberg's adaptation of Alice Walker's 1982 novel *The Color Purple*. Her critically acclaimed performance led to other roles, including a performance in the television miniseries *The Women of Brewster Place* (1989). Winfrey formed her own television production company, Harpo Productions, Inc., in 1986, and a film production company, Harpo Films, in 1990.

The Harpo companies began buying film rights to literary works, including Connie May Fowler's *Before Women Had Wings*, which appeared in 1997 with Winfrey as both star and producer, and Toni Morrison's *Beloved*, which appeared in 1998, also with Winfrey in a starring role.

In 1998 Winfrey expanded her media entertainment empire when she cofounded Oxygen Media, which launched a cable television network for women. Winfrey further expanded her presence in the publishing industry with the highly successful launch of *O, the Oprah Magazine* in 2000 and *O at Home* in 2004. *O at Home* folded in 2008.

Winfrey lent her voice to several animated films, including *Charlotte's Web* (2006) and *The Princess and the Frog* (2009). In 2006 the Oprah & Friends channel debuted on satellite radio. Winfrey is engaged in numerous philanthropic activities, including the creation of Oprah's Angel Network, which sponsors charitable initiatives worldwide. In 2007 she opened a $40 million school for disadvantaged girls in South Africa. She became an outspoken crusader against child abuse and received many honors and awards from civic, philanthropic, and entertainment organizations.

Oprah brokered a partnership with Discovery Communications in 2008, through which the Oprah Winfrey Network (OWN) replaced the Discovery Health Channel in January 2011. In 2009 Winfrey announced that her television talk show would end in 2011; it was speculated that she would focus on OWN.

In 2010 she was named a Kennedy Center honoree, and the following year she received the Jean Hersholt Humanitarian Award from the Academy of Motion Picture Arts and Sciences. The last episode of *The Oprah Winfrey Show* aired in May 2011, and *Oprah's Next Chapter*, a weekly prime-time interview program on OWN, debuted in January 2012.

Oprah appeared in *Lee Daniels' The Butler* (2013). In 2013 Winfrey was awarded the Presidential Medal of Freedom. She won the Cecil B. DeMille Award (a Golden Globe for lifetime achievement). In 2014 *Selma* (2014), a film about Martin Luther King, Jr., that Winfrey produced and also appeared in, was nominated for an Academy Award for best picture.

In 2017 it was announced that Discovery was acquiring a majority share in OWN, though Winfrey would remain involved in the channel. That year she also became a special correspondent for the newsmagazine *60 Minutes*, which aired on CBS.

She subsequently starred in the HBO TV movie *The Immortal Life of Henrietta Lacks* (2017), portraying the daughter of a woman whose cancerous cells were, unbeknownst to her and her family, used in research that led to numerous scientific advances. Winfrey then appeared as Mrs. Which in the 2018 film adaptation of Madeleine L'Engle's acclaimed 1962 sci-fi novel, *A Wrinkle in Time.*

Oprah Winfrey has transitioned her hit talk show into a media, entertainment and business empire bringing her estimated net worth to $2.7 billion. She has donated $425 million throughout her career, including over $100 million to the Oprah Winfrey Leadership Academy for Girls in South Africa.

As a board member and brand ambassador for Weight Watchers since 2015, she has seen her shares grow from $43.5 million to more than $400 million. In 2018 Winfrey signed a multi-year content partnership deal with Apple that includes programs for Apple's original content lineup.

She received the Cecil B. DeMille Award for lifetime achievement at the Golden Globes in 2018; and her impassioned speech—in which she called for racial and gender equality—was widely seen as one of the ceremony's most memorable moments, inspiring a viral plea for a presidential run.

DAYMOND JOHN

Daymond John, born **Daymond Garfield John** (February 23, 1969) is an American businessman, investor, television personality, author, and motivational speaker. He is best known as the founder, president, and CEO of FUBU, and appears as an investor on the ABC reality television series *Shark Tank*. Based in New York City, John is the founder of The Shark Group.

Daymond John was born in Brooklyn, New York but grew up in the Queens neighborhood of Hollis. He is the son of Garfield John and Margot John. He attended Bayside High School and began working at the age of 10, when his parents divorced. In high school, he participated in a program that allowed him to work a full-time job and attend school on an alternating weekly basis, which he credits with instilling an entrepreneurial spirit.

After graduating high school, Daymond started a commuter van service. He grew up during the 1980s in the heart of hip-hop culture;

and eventually, he stumbled on the idea of making clothes for fans of rap music.

In 1992, when he was 23 years old, Daymond started FUBU (For Us By Us) and began selling hats outside of a local mall. He launched FUBU in his mother's house in Hollis, Queens. When he first had the idea for a clothing company for young men, his mother taught him how to sew and supported him by allowing her house to be taken over to grow the business.

Wool ski hats with their tops tied off with fishing line were popular, and Daymond noticed them being sold for $20, which he considered overpriced. He went home and sewed around 90 hats with his next-door neighbor. They sold their homemade hats for $10 each and made $800 in a single day.

After the hats, they began selling screen-printed T-shirts. To break into the market, they sold on consignment and at large events around the Northeast. To make ends meet, Daymond held a full-time job at Red Lobster, working on the FUBU business in between shifts.

Sensing potential, Daymond and his mother mortgaged their house for $100,000 to generate start-up capital. He recruited longtime friends into the business, and began sewing the FUBU logo onto hockey jerseys, sweatshirts, and T-shirts. They loaned about 10 of the hockey jerseys out to rappers for their music videos for two years and got product placements in about 30 videos.

They were perceived as a large clothing brand, despite being a relatively small company and stores started requesting their brand. In 1993, he convinced LL Cool J, an old neighborhood friend, to wear a FUBU T-shirt for a promotional campaign. Later, while filming a 30-second advertising spot for The Gap, LL Cool J wore a FUBU hat in the commercial and incorporated the line "for us, by us" in his rapping.

Between 1992 and 1994, John received $300,000 in orders and also an offer for participating in Macy's (M) at a Las Vegas fashion trade show, MAGIC. They had to take out a second mortgage of his mother's house in order to fulfill the orders. After being turned down by 27 banks for a loan, his mother used the last of their money to take out an advertisement in the NY Times As a result of the ad, FUBU made a deal with Samsung Textiles, allowing them to complete their orders. Three years later, FUBU was bringing in $350 million in sales.

In 2009, Daymond received a call from Mark Burnett asking him to join the cast of ABC's new realty business show *Shark Tank*, which gives entrepreneurs the opportunity to pitch their businesses to investors, or "Sharks" in the hopes of receiving an investment. Initially, Daymond declined the two proposals from the series, but he is now a seasoned team member.

Daymond invested in Bubba's-Q Boneless Ribs on Season 5 of *Shark Tank* and has helped grow the company from $154,000 in sales to $16 million in 3 years. In 2017, Bubba's-Q Boneless Ribs partnered up with Carl's Jr. to create the limited-edition Baby Back Rib Burger.

On Season 6 of *Shark Tank*, John made a unique deal with 15-year-old Moziah "Mo" Bridges, who is the owner of Mo's Bows. Daymond decided not to invest in Mo's Bows, but instead to mentor the young entrepreneur. Recently, Mo's Bows agreed to a seven-figure licensing partnership with the NBA to create bow ties that use the teams' logos.

After Daymond invested in Bombas Socks on Season 6 of *Shark Tank,* total sales for the company increased from $450,000 in the first nine months to $12 million. For every pair of socks sold, Bombas donates a pair to someone in need and, as of August 2017, they have donated over 4 million pairs of socks.

John is the CEO and founder of The Shark Group, a brand management and consulting firm. The Shark Group office is located in Manhattan, New York.

FUBU has earned over $6 billion in global sales. The company is featured at the Smithsonian's National Museum of African-American History and Culture.

PART TWO

MORE NOTABLE PEOPLE WHO HAVE DONE EXTRAORDINARY THINGS TO MAKE THE GRADE

MORE EDUCATORS
WHO MAKE THE GRADE.......

Armand Lanusse (1810 - March 16, 1868[1]) was an Afro-Creole educator and poet who lived in New Orleans his entire life.

Benjamin Banneker (November 9, 1731 – October 9, 1806) was a free African American almanac author, surveyor, naturalist, and farmer.

Benjamin W. Arnett (1838–1906) was an African-American educator, minister, bishop and elected official.

Charles Henry Turner (February 3, 1867 – February 14, 1923) was an American research biologist, educator, zoologist, and comparative psychologist born in Cincinnati, Ohio.

Charlotte Hawkins Brown (June 11, 1883 – January 11, 1961) was an American author, educator, and founder of the Palmer Memorial Institute in Sedalia, North Carolina.

Daniel Alexander Payne (February 24, 1811 - November 2, 1893) born to free Black parents London and Martha Payne in Charleston, South Carolina, was a Bishop in the African Methodist Episcopal (A.M.E.) Church, President of Wilberforce University, abolitionist, educator, and historian.

David Levering Lewis (born May 25, 1936) is an American Historian; he is the Julius Silver University Professor, and the Professor of History at New York University.

Esau Jenkins (July 3, 1910 – October 30, 1972) was a South Carolina Afro-American Human Rights leader, businessman, and community organizer.

James Edward Maceo West (born February 10, 1931 in Farmville, Prince Edward County, Virginia) is an African American inventor and acoustician, who holds over 250 foreign and U.S. patents for the production and design of microphones and techniques for creating polymer foil electrets.

Fanny Jackson Coppin (January 8, 1837 – January 21, 1913) was an African-American educator and missionary and a lifelong advocate for female higher education.

Gloria Blackwell, also known as **Gloria Rackley** (March 11, 1927 – December 7, 2010), was an African-American civil rights activist and educator.

James E. Shepard (November 3, 1875 – October 6, 1947) was an American pharmacist, civil servant and educator, the founder of what became the North Carolina Central University in Durham, North Carolina.

James West (February 10, 1931) was born in Prince Edward County, Virginia, and studied physics at Temple University. West authored 200 patents and more than 60 technical and scientific publications and he, with Gerhard Sessler, developed the foil electret microphone, which became the industry standard.

Jeanne Laveta Noble (July 18, 1926 – October 17, 2002)[1] was an African-American educator who served on education commissions for three U.S.

John Wesley Gilbert (July 6, 1864 – November 18, 1923 was the first African-American archaeologist, the first graduate of Paine College, the first African-American professor of that school, and the first African-American to receive a master's degree from Brown University

Jeanne Laveta Noble (July 18, 1926 – October 17, 2002) was an African-American educator who served on education commissions for three U.S. presidents. Noble was the first to analyze and publish the experiences of female African Americans in college.

Katherine Butler Jones was born on March 19,1936 and grew up at 409 Edgecombe Avenue in Harlem's Sugar Hill neighborhood. In 1966, she founded the Newton Public Schools' Metropolitan Council for Educational Opportunities (METCO) Program, which still enrolls students of color from Boston in Newton schools.

Kelly Miller (July 18, 1863 – December 29, 1939) was an African-American mathematician, sociologist, essayist, newspaper columnist, author, and an important figure in the intellectual life of black America for close to half a century. He was known as "The Bard of the Potomac".

Maxine (Atkins) Smith (October 31, 1929 — April 26, 2013) born in Memphis, Tennessee, United States, was an academic, civil rights activist, and school board official. Smith's leadership in the National Association for the Advancement of Colored People (NAACP) enabled her to support the American Civil Rights Movement and advance school desegregation.

Nannie Helen Burroughs, (May 2, 1879 – May 20, 1961) was an African-American educator, orator, religious leader, civil rights activist, feminist and businesswoman in the United States.

Septima Poinsette Clark (May 3, 1898 – December 15, 1987) was an American educator and civil rights activist. Clark developed the literacy and citizenship workshops that played an important role in the drive for voting rights and civil rights for African Americans in the

Civil Rights Movement. Martin Luther King, Jr. commonly referred to Clark as "The Mother of the Movement."

Virginia Estelle Randolph (August 6, 1870 – March 16, 1958)[1] was an African-American educator in Henrico County, Virginia. She was named the United States' first "Jeanes Supervising Industrial Teacher" by her Superintendent of Schools, Jackson T. Davis.

MORE CIVIL RIGHTS LEADERS
AND ACTIVISTS WHO MAKE THE GRADE ....

A.Philip Randolph, (April 15, 1889 - May 16, 1979) was born Asa Philip Randolph in Crescent City, Florida and died in New York City. He was a trade unionist and civil-rights leader who was dedicated and persistent in the struggle for justice and parity for the African American community.

Angela Davis, born Angela Yvonne Davis (January 26, 1944) is an American political activist, academic, and author. She emerged as a prominent counterculture activist in the 1960s working with the Communist Party USA, of which she was a member until 1991, and was briefly involved in the Black Panther Party during the Civil Rights Movement.

Bayard Rustin (March 17, 1912 – August 24, 1987) was an American leader in social movements for civil rights, socialism, nonviolence, and gay rights. An early member of the Communist Party, Rustin worked with A. Philip Randolph on the March on Washington Movement in 1941 to press for an end to discrimination in employment. Rustin later organized Freedom Rides and helped to organize the Southern Christian Leadership Conference to strengthen Martin Luther King Jr.'s leadership, teaching King about nonviolence and later serving as an organizer for the March on Washington for Jobs and Freedom. After the passage of the civil rights legislation of 1964–65, Rustin became the head of the AFL–CIO's A. Philip Randolph Institute, At the time of his death in 1987, he was on a humanitarian mission in Haiti. On November 20, 2013, President Barack Obama posthumously awarded Rustin the Presidential Medal of Freedom

Benjamin Ward (August 10, 1926 – June 10, 2002) who began his career as a traffic officer in white gloves on First Avenue, moved through a succession of state and city law-enforcement posts and eventually became the first African American New York City Police Commissioner.

Bobby Seale, named **Robert Seale** (October 22, 1936) was born in Dallas, Texas. He was an African-American political activist, the founder, along with Huey Newton of the Black Panther Party, as well as the organization's national chairman. Seale was one of a generation of young African-American radicals who broke away from the traditionally nonviolent Civil Rights Movement to preach a doctrine of militant black empowerment.

Dorothy (Irene) Height, (March 24, 1912 - April 20, 2010) was born in Richmond, Virginia and died in Washington, D.C. Dorothy was an American civil rights and women's rights activist, and a widely respected and influential leader of organizations focused primarily on improving the circumstances of and opportunities for African American women.

Elijah Muhammad, whose original name was **Elijah Poole**, (October 7, 1897 - February 25, 1975), was born in Sandersville, Georgia and died in Chicago, Illinois. He was the leader of the black separatist religious movement known as the Nation of Islam in the United States.

Ella Baker (December 13, 1903 - Dec. 13, 1986). She was born in Norfolk, Virginia and grew up in North Carolina. Ella had enormous influence on the Civil Rights Movement of the 1950s and 1960s. In 1956, she organized *In Friendship*, a group that raised money for the Montgomery Bus Boycott. She influenced MLK and taught Rosa

Parks how to resist peacefully. Baker continued to organize students involved in political activism through the 1970s. In recognition of her work she was awarded a doctorate of letters in May 1985 from the City College of New York.

Frances Ellen Watkins Harper (September 24, 1825 – February 22, 1911) was an African-American abolitionist, suffragist, poet, teacher, public speaker, and writer. She was active in social reform and was a member of the Woman's Christian Temperance Union, which advocated the federal government taking a role in progressive reform. She is considered "the mother of African-American journalism."

Frederick Lee "Fred" Shuttlesworth born **Fred Lee Robinson** (March 18, 1922 – October 5, 2011), was a U.S. civil rights activist who led the fight against segregation and other forms of racism as a minister in Birmingham, Alabama. He was a co-founder of the Southern Christian Leadership Conference, initiated and was instrumental in the 1963 Birmingham Campaign, and continued to work against racism and for alleviation of the problems of the homeless in Cincinnati, Ohio, where he took up a pastorate in 1961. He returned to Birmingham after his retirement in 2007. He helped Martin Luther King Jr. during the Civil Rights Movement.

Hazel Dukes, born **Hazel Nell Dukes** (March 17, 1932), An important civil rights activist of the 1960s and 1970s and government official, Hazel Nell Dukes is a leading figure in the National Association for the Advancement of Colored People (NAACP) and served as the organization's national president between 1989 and 1992. Dukes built a career in various social service agencies, but she was most successful working for the New York City Off-Track Betting Corporation (NYCOTB). She worked for the corporation for 25 years before being made its president by New York City Mayor David Dinkins in 1990.

Ida B. Wells-Barnett, (July 16, 1862 - March 25, 1931) born **Ida Bell Wells** in Holly Springs, Mississippi and died in Chicago, Illinois. She was an African American journalist who led an anti-lynching crusade in the United States in the 1890s. She later was active in promoting justice for African Americans.

James Weldon Johnson (June 17, 1871 – June 26, 1938) was an American author, educator, lawyer, diplomat, songwriter, and civil rights activist. Johnson is best remembered for his leadership of the National Association for the Advancement of Colored People (NAACP), where he started working in 1917. In 1920, he was the first African American to be chosen as executive secretary of the organization, effectively the operating officer. He served in that position from 1920 to 1930. Johnson established his reputation as a writer, and was known during the Harlem Renaissance for his poems, novels, and anthologies, collecting both poems and spirituals of black culture.

Julian Bond, born **Horace Julian Bond** (January 14, 1940 – August 15, 2015) was an American social activist and leader in the Civil Rights Movement, politician, professor and writer. While a student at Morehouse College in Atlanta, Georgia, during the early 1960s, he helped to establish the Student Nonviolent Coordinating Committee (SNCC). Bond was elected to four terms in the Georgia House of Representatives and later to six terms in the Georgia State Senate, serving a combined twenty years in both legislative chambers. From 1998 to 2010, he was chairman of the National Association for the Advancement of Colored People (NAACP) and the first president of the Southern Poverty Law Center.

John Lewis, born **John Robert Lewis** (February 21, 1940) is an American politician and civil rights leader. He is the U.S. Representative for Georgia's 5th congressional district, serving in his

17th term in the House, having served since 1987, and is the senior member of the Georgia congressional delegation. His district includes three-quarters of Atlanta. Lewis, who as chairman of the Student Nonviolent Coordinating Committee (SNCC) was one of the "Big Six" leaders of groups who organized the 1963 March on Washington, played many key roles in the Civil Rights Movement and its actions to end legalized racial segregation in the United States. He is a member of the Democratic Party leadership in the U.S. House of Representatives and has served as a Chief Deputy Whip since 1991 and Senior Chief Deputy Whip since 2003.

Kamala Devi Harris (October 20, 1964) is an American attorney and politician and a member of the Democratic Party. She has been the junior United States Senator for California since 2017, and she previously served as the 32nd Attorney General of California from 2011 to 2017, and as District Attorney of San Francisco from 2004 to 2011. On January 21, 2019, she officially announced her campaign to run for the Democratic nomination for President of the United States in the 2020 United States presidential election.

Kim Royster became the highest-ranking black woman in the New York Police Department's history. Royster was promoted to deputy chief by former Commissioner Ray Kelly in October 2013. Royster is one of the fewer than 10 female chiefs in the 35,000-person department and its first black female to be promoted to assistant chief. Royster has more than 30 years of experience with the department. She has been credited for being at the forefront of the NYPD gun buyback program, which is responsible for taking more than 8,000 weapons off the streets.

Kwame Ture born **Stokely Carmichael**, (June 29, 1941 – November 15, 1998) was a prominent organizer in the Civil Rights Movement in the United States and the global Pan-African movement. Born in

Trinidad, he grew up in the United States from the age of 11 and became an activist while attending Howard University. He eventually developed the Black Power movement, first while leading the Student Nonviolent Coordinating Committee (SNCC), later serving as the "Honorary Prime Minister" of the Black Panther Party (BPP), and lastly as a leader of the All-African People's Revolutionary Party (A-APRP).

Lenora Fulani born **Lenora Branch** (April 25, 1950) is an American psychologist, psychotherapist, and political activist, best known for her presidential campaign and development of youth programs serving minority communities in the New York City area. In the1988 United States presidential election, heading the New Alliance Party ticket, she became the first woman and the first African American to achieve ballot access in all fifty states. She received more votes for President in a U.S. general election than any other woman in history until Jill Stein of the Green Party of the United States in 2012. Fulani's political concerns include racial equality, gay rights and, for the past decade, political reform, specifically to encourage third parties.

Mahatma Ghandi, born **Mohandas Karamchand Gandhi** (October 2, 1869 – January 30, 1948) was an Indian activist who was the leader of the Indian independence movement against British rule. Employing nonviolent civil disobedience, Gandhi led India to independence and inspired movements for civil rights and freedom across the world. Born and raised in a Hindu merchant caste family in coastal Gujarat, India, and trained in law at the Inner Temple, London, Gandhi first employed nonviolent civil disobedience as an expatriate lawyer in South Africa, in the resident Indian community's struggle for civil rights. After his return to India in 1915, he set about organizing peasants, farmers, and urban labourers to protest against excessive land-tax and discrimination. Gandhi influenced important leaders and political movements. Leaders of the civil rights movement in the

United States, including Martin Luther King Jr., James Lawson, and James Bevel, drew from the writings of Gandhi in the development of their own theories about nonviolence. Anti-apartheid activist and former President of South Africa, Nelson Mandela, was inspired by Gandhi.

Malala Yousafzai (*Malālah Yūsafzay*: (July 12, 1997) is a Pakistani activist for female education and the youngest Nobel Prize laureate. She is known for human rights advocacy, especially the education of women and children in her native Swat Valley in Khyber Pakhtunkhwa, northwest Pakistan, where the local Taliban had at times banned girls from attending school. Yousafzai was born to a Pashtun family in Mingora, Khyber Pakhtunkhwa, Pakistan. Her family came to run a chain of schools in the region. In early 2009, when she was 11–12, she wrote a blog under a pseudonym for the BBC Urdu detailing her life during the Taliban occupation of Swat. She rose in prominence, giving interviews in print and on television, and she was nominated for the International Children's Peace Prize by activist Desmond Tutu. On October 9, 2012, while on a bus in the Swat District, after taking an exam, Yousafzai and two other girls were shot by a Taliban gunman in an assassination attempt in retaliation for her activism. Following her recovery, Yousafzai became a prominent activist for the right to education. The 2013, 2014 and 2015 issues of *Time* magazine featured her as one of the most influential people globally.

Malcolm X (May 19, 1925 - February 21, 1965) was named **Malcolm Little**. He was born in Omaha, Nebraska, the fourth of seven children of Grenada-born Louise Helen Little (Norton) and Georgia-born Earl Little. Malcolm X was an American Muslim minister and human rights activist. He has been called one of the greatest and most influential African Americans in history. At a speaking engagement in the Manhattan's Audubon Ballroom, three gunmen rushed Malcolm onstage. They shot him 15 times at close range. The 39-year-old was pronounced dead on arrival at New York's Columbia Presbyterian Hospital.

Marcus Mosiah Garvey Jr. (August 17, 1887 – June 10, 1940) was a Jamaican-born political leader, publisher, journalist, entrepreneur, and orator. He *was a staunch proponent of the Black nationalism and Pan-Africanism movements, founder of the Universal Negro Improvement Association and African Communities League (UNIA-ACL), and founder of the Black Star Line, which promoted the return of the African diaspora to their ancestral lands.* Garvey died in London on June 10, 1940, at the age of 52, after having suffered two strokes.

Martin Luther King Jr. (January 15, 1929 – April 4, 1968) was an American Baptist minister and activist who became the most visible spokesperson and leader in the civil rights movement from 1954 until his assassination in 1968. Born in Atlanta, King is best known for advancing civil rights through nonviolence and civil disobedience tactics. He was inspired by his Christian beliefs and the nonviolent activism of Mahatma Gandhi. On October 14, 1964, King won the Nobel Peace Prize for combating racial inequality through nonviolent resistance. In 1977, the Presidential Medal of Freedom was posthumously awarded to King by President Jimmy Carter.

Mary Jackson, born **Mary Winston Jackson** (April 9, 1921 – February 11, 2005) was an African American mathematician and aerospace engineer at the National Advisory Committee for Aeronautics (NACA), which in 1958 was succeeded by the National Aeronautics and Space Administration (NASA). She worked at Langley Research Center in Hampton, Virginia, for most of her career. She started as a "human computer" at the segregated West Area Computing division. She took advanced engineering classes and, in

1958, became NASA's first black female engineer. After 34 years at NASA, Jackson had earned the most senior engineering title available. She accepted a demotion to become a manager of both the Federal Women's Program, in the NASA Office of Equal Opportunity Programs, and of the Affirmative Action Program.

Medgar Wiley Evers (July 2, 1925 – June 12, 1963) was an African American civil rights activist in Mississippi, the state's field secretary of the NAACP, and World War II veteran, having served in the United States Army. He worked to overturn segregation at the University of Mississippi, to end segregation of public facilities, and to expand opportunities for African Americans, including enforcement of voting rights. He was assassinated by a white supremacist and Klansman.

Meghan, Duchess of Sussex, born **Rachel Meghan Markle**; (August 4, 1981), is a retired American actress who became a member of the British royal family upon her marriage to Prince Harry. Markle was born and raised in Los Angeles, California, and has a mixed ethnic heritage. During her studies at Northwestern University, she began playing small roles in American television series and films. From 2011 to 2017, she played Rachel Zane, on the American legal drama series *Suits*. An outspoken feminist, Markle has addressed issues of gender inequality, and her lifestyle website *The Tig* featured a column profiling influential women. She represented international charity organizations in the 2010s. From 2011 until their divorce in 2013, Markle was married to actor and producer Trevor Engelson. In 2017, she announced her engagement to Prince Harry, grandson of Queen Elizabeth II, and moved to London. She retired from acting, closed her social media accounts, and started undertaking public engagements as part of the British royal family. She became the Duchess of Sussex upon her marriage to Prince Harry in May 2018.

Nelson Rolihlahla Mandela (July 18, 1918 – December 5, 2013) was a South African anti-apartheid revolutionary, political leader, and philanthropist who served as President of South Africa from 1994 to 1999. He was the country's first black head of state and the first elected in a fully representative democratic election. His government focused on dismantling the legacy of apartheid by tackling institutionalized racism and fostering racial reconciliation. Ideologically an African nationalist and socialist, he served as President of the African National Congress (ANC) party from 1991 to 1997.

Rosa Parks (February 4, 1913 – October 24, 2005) born **Rosa Louise McCauley Parks** was an American activist in the civil rights movement best known for her pivotal role in the Montgomery Bus Boycott. The United States Congress has called her "the first lady of civil rights" and "the mother of the freedom movement."

Roy Wilkins, (August 30, 1901 - September 8, 1981) was born in St. Louis, Missouri and died in New York City. After graduation from the University of Minnesota, Minneapolis (1923), Wilkins became a reporter and later managing editor of the *Kansas City Call,* a newspaper serving the black community. Wilkins was an African American civil-rights leader who served as the executive director of the National Association for the Advancement of Colored People (NAACP) and was often referred to as the senior statesman of the U.S. Civil Rights Movement. Wilkins edited the NAACP's official publication, *The Crisis,* between 1934 and 1949, after W.E.B. DuBois left the position.

Sonya Maria Sotomayor (June 25, 1954) made history on August 6, 2009, when the U.S. Senate confirmed her nomination to the U.S. Supreme Court. Sonia Maria Sotomayor was born in New York City in the borough of the Bronx. She was valedictorian of her class at Blessed Sacrament, and at Cardinal Spellman High School. She applied to Princeton, where she was accepted and awarded a full scholarship, graduated *summa cum laude* and won the University's Moses Taylor Pyne Prize, the highest honor Princeton awards its undergraduates. She was offered a scholarship to Yale Law School, graduated and passed the bar in 1980. She became a U.S. District Court Judge in 1992 and in 1997, President Bill Clinton nominated Sotomayor for the U.S Court of Appeals for the Second Circuit and a bipartisan majority confirmed her appointment in 1998. In her 11 years as an appeals court judge, Sotomayor heard more than 3,000 cases, and wrote nearly 400 opinions. Shortly after his inauguration, President Barack Obama nominated her to the Supreme Court of the United States, to fill the vacancy left by the retirement of Justice David Souter. She was the third woman, and the first person of Latin American descent to join the Court in its 220-year history. At the time of her appointment, she was the only Justice on the Court with experience as a trial judge and had more federal judicial experience than any Justice in the previous 100 years.

Vernon Eulion Jordan Jr. (born August 15, 1935) is an American business executive and civil rights activist in the United States. A leading figure in the Civil Rights Movement, he was chosen by President Bill Clinton as a close adviser. Jordan has become known as an influential figure in American politics.

W.E.B. Du Bois, (February 23, 1868 - August 27, 1963) whose full name was **William Edward Burghardt Du Bois,** was born in Great Barrington, Massachusetts and died in Accra, Ghana. DuBois was an American sociologist, historian, author, editor, and activist who was the most important black protest leader in the United States during the first half of the 20th century. He shared in the creation of the National Association for the Advancement of Colored People (NAACP) in 1909 and edited *The Crisis*, its magazine, from 1910 to 1934. His collection of essays *The Souls of Black Folk* (1903) is a landmark of African American literature.

Walter Francis White (July 1, 1893 - March 21, 1955) was born in Atlanta, Georgia. Before he became president of the United States, William Henry Harrison fathered several children with one of his slaves. One of these children was Walter White's grandmother. Though he had blonde hair and blue eyes, Walter embraced his African-American heritage, and fought to end the discrimination that surrounded African Americans. As a member of the NAACP, White investigated lynchings and worked to end segregation. He was the organization's executive secretary from 1931 to 1955, when, at age 61, he died in New York City.

William Lloyd Garrison, (December 10, 1805 - May 24, 1879) was born in Newburyport, Massachusetts and died in New York, New York. Garrison was the son of a seaman who deserted his family and grew up during the abolition movement, which he joined at age 25. In 1828, he was editor of the *National Philanthropist* (Boston) and the *Journal of the Times* (Bennington, Vermont) in 1828–29. Garrison became a controversial figure who saw the U.S. Constitution as inherently flawed because of its equivocation on slavery. He was outspoken and uncompromising in his stance against slavery and boldly demanded the immediate emancipation of slaves. As an American journalistic crusader, Garrison published a newspaper, *The Liberator* (1831–65), and helped lead the successful abolitionist campaign against slavery in the United States.

MORE RELIGIOUS LEADERS
WHO MAKE THE GRADE ....

A.R. Bernard, born **Alphonso R. Bernard, Sr.** (August 10, 1953) is the pastor of the Christian Cultural Center Megachurch in Brooklyn, New York. In November 1979, A. R. Bernard, Sr. left a 10-year career with a major New York banking institution and together with his wife, Karen, went into full-time ministry. What started as a small storefront church in Williamsburg, Brooklyn has grown into a 37,000+ member church that sits on an 11½-acre campus in Brooklyn, New York. He is founder and CEO of the Christian Cultural Center.

Adam Clayton Powell Jr. (November 29, 1908 – April 4, 1972) was a Baptist pastor and an American politician, who represented Harlem, New York City, in the United States House of Representatives (1945–71). He was the first person of African-American descent to be elected from New York to Congress

C. L. Franklin, born **Clarence LaVaughn Walker** (January 22, 1915 – July 27, 1984) was an American Baptist minister and civil rights activist. Known as the man with the "Million-Dollar Voice", Franklin served as the pastor of New Bethel Baptist Church in Detroit, Michigan, from 1946 until his retirement in 1979. Franklin was also the father of American singer–songwriter Aretha Franklin.

Calvin O. Butts, born **Calvin O. Butts III** (July 19, 1949) is the Pastor of the Abyssinian Baptist Church in the City of New York, President of the State University of New York College at Old Westbury, and Chairman and founder of the Abyssinian Development

Corporation, which is an engine for $500 million in housing and commercial development in Harlem.

Charles Stith, (August 29, 1949) born **Charles Richard Stith**, a diplomat, minister, professor, and urban reformer, presently serves as the Director of the African Presidential Archives and Research Center at Boston University in Massachusetts. In 1998, President Bill Clinton named him Ambassador to Tanzania.

Conrad Bennette Tillard, Sr. (September 15, 1964) born in St. Louis, Missouri is an American clergyman (faith leader), and civil right leader in the African-American consciousness movement tradition. Reverend Tillard is an author, educator, youth advocate, community activist, and public speaker.

Cordy Tindell Vivian, known as **C. T. Vivian** (born July 28, 1924), is a distinguished minister, author, and organizer. A leader in the Civil Rights Movement and friend to Martin Luther King, Jr., he participated in Freedom Rides and sit-ins across our country. Vivian also helped found numerous civil rights organizations, including Vision, the National Anti-Klan Network, and the Center for Democratic Renewal. In 2012, he returned to serve as interim President of the Southern Christian Leadership Conference. Vivian resides in Atlanta, Georgia and most recently founded the C. T. Vivian Leadership Institute, Inc. He is a member of the Alpha Phi Alpha fraternity. On August 8, 2013, President Barack Obama named Vivian as a recipient of the Presidential Medal of Freedom.

Creflo Augustus Dollar Jr. (born January 28, 1962) is an American televangelist, pastor, and the founder of the non-denominational World Changers Church International based in College Park, Georgia, a suburb of Atlanta.

Dennis Dillon is one of New York City's most influential black leaders. Reverend Dillon is pastor of the Brooklyn Christian Center and publisher of *Christian Times.*

Eugene Franklin Rivers, III (April 9, 1950) was born in Boston, Massachusetts. Reverend Eugene Rivers is a youth activist and pastor of the Azusa Christian Community Center in Dorchester, co-founder of the Boston TenPoint Coalition and co-chair of the National TenPoint Leadership Foundation, both working on issues of urban violence that impacts African Americans.

Floyd Harold Flake (January 30, 1945) is the senior pastor of the 23,000 member Greater Allen African Methodist Episcopal Cathedral in Jamaica, Queens, New York, and former president of Wilberforce University. He is a former member of the United States House of Representatives, serving from 1987 to 1997.

Gardner Calvin Taylor (June 18, 1918 – April 5, 2015) was an American Baptist preacher. He was admired for his eloquence as well as his understanding of Christian faith and theology. He became known as "the dean of American preaching.

Gilbert Earl Patterson (September 22, 1939 – March 20, 2007) was an American Pentecostal-Holiness leader and minister who served as the international Presiding Bishop and Chief Apostle of the Church of God in Christ (COGIC), Inc. Bishop Patterson was the second youngest person to ever be elected Presiding Bishop of COGIC at the age 60 in 2000,

Herbert Daughtry (January 13, 1931) is the national presiding minister of the House of the Lord Pentecostal Church. In 1982, Daughtry founded the African People's Christian Organization, which sought to create an African Christian nation by highlighting both African origins and biblical teachings. Later, Daughtry became a special assistant to Reverend Jesse Jackson during his presidential campaign; and in 2003, he led a delegation of multi-faith protesters to Iraq, in a last-ditch effort to preserve peace in that nation.

Hezekiah Walker (December 24, 1962) is a popular American gospel music artist and pastor of prominent Brooklyn New York megachurch, Love Fellowship Tabernacle. Bishop Walker has released several albums on Benson Records and Verity Records as Hezekiah Walker & The Love Fellowship Crusade Choir.

James Alexander Forbes, Jr. (born 1935) is the Senior Minister *Emeritus* of the Riverside Church, an interdenominational (American Baptist and United Church of Christ) church on the Upper West Side of Manhattan, New York City. He was the first African American minister to lead this multicultural congregation and served it for 18 years.

Jeremiah Alvesta Wright Jr. (born September 22, 1941) is pastor emeritus of Trinity United Church of Christ in Chicago, a congregation he led for 36 years, during which its membership grew to over 8,000 parishioners. Wright, who was Barack Obama's former pastor, gained national attention when he was uninvited from giving a public invocation at Obama's February 10, presidential announcement.

Jesse Louis Jackson Sr. (October 8, 1941) is an American civil rights activist, Baptist minister, and politician. He was a candidate for the Democratic presidential nomination in 1984 and 1988 and served as a shadow U.S. Senator for the District of Columbia from 1991 to 1997.He is also the founder of the organizations that merged to form Rainbow/PUSH.

Joseph Echols Lowery (October 6, 1921) is an American minister in the United Methodist Church and leader in the Civil Rights Movement. He later became the third president of the Southern Christian

Leadership Conference, after Martin Luther King Jr. and his immediate successor, Ralph Abernathy, and participated in most of the major activities of the Civil Rights Movement of the 1960s.

Joseph Ward Simmons (November 14, 1964), better known by the stage name **Run, Rev. Run** or **DJ Run**, is a musician, rapper and actor. Simmons is one of the founding members of the influential hip hop group Run–D.M.C. He is also a practicing minister, known as **Reverend Run.**

Kirbyjon H. Caldwell is pastor of Windsor Village United Methodist Church, a 14,000-member megachurch at Windsor Village in Houston, Texas. He was one of President George W. Bush's spiritual advisors.

Louis Farrakhan, formerly known as **Louis X**, born **Louis Eugene Walcott** (May 11, 1933), is the leader of the religious group Nation of Islam (NOI). Previously, he served as the minister of mosques in Boston and Harlem and had been appointed National Representative of the Nation of Islam by former NOI leader Elijah Muhammad. After Warith Deen Muhammad disbanded the NOI, Farrakhan started rebuilding the NOI. In 1981 he renamed his organization from Final Call to the Nation of Islam, reviving the group and establishing its headquarters at Mosque Maryam. In October 1995, he organized and led the Million Man March in Washington, D.C. Due to health issues, he reduced his responsibilities with the NOI in 2007. However, Farrakhan has continued to deliver sermons and speak at NOI events. In 2015, he led the 20th Anniversary of the Million Man March: Justice or Else.

Mother Teresa, born **Anjezë Gonxhe Bojaxhiu** (August 1910 – 5 September 1997), was known in the Roman Catholic Church as **Saint Teresa of Calcutta**[She was an Albanian-Indian]Roman Catholic nun and missionary from Skopje (now the capital of Macedonia, then part of the Kosovo Vilayet of the Ottoman Empire. After living in Macedonia for eighteen years she moved to Ireland and then to India, where she lived for most of her life. Pope Francis canonized her at a ceremony on September 4, 2016 in St. Peter's Square in Vatican City. Tens of thousands of people witnessed the ceremony, including 15 government delegations and 1,500 homeless people from across Italy. It was televised live on the Vatican channel and streamed online; Skopje, Teresa's hometown, announced a week-long celebration of her canonization. In India, a special mass was celebrated by the Missionaries of Charity in Kolkata. On September 5, 2017, St. Teresa Cathedral, the first Roman Catholic cathedral named in Teresa's honor, was consecrated in Kosovo. The Cathedral is also Kosovo's first Roman Catholic cathedral.

Otis Moss Jr. (born February 26, 1935) is an American pastor, theologian, speaker, author, and activist. Moss is well-known for his involvement in the Civil Rights Movement and his friendship with both Martin Luther King Jr. and Martin Luther King Sr.

Vashti Murphy McKenzie (born May 28, 1947) is a Bishop of the African Methodist Episcopal Church. McKenzie is the first female elected as Bishop in the denomination's history.

Warren Stewart, Sr. is the Senior Pastor of the First Institutional Baptist Church (FIBC) of Phoenix, Arizona and has served there since July 1, 1977. Dr. Stewart served as the first General Chairperson for ARIZONANS FOR A MARTIN LUTHER KING, JR. STATE HOLIDAY which contributed significantly to the legislative passage of Arizona's Martin Luther King, Jr. holiday on September 21, 1989. Dr. Stewart also organized and led VICTORY TOGETHER, INC., a broad-based coalition that campaigned for a Martin Luther King, Jr./Civil Rights Day in Arizona which was won by a historic vote of the people in the general election on November 3, 1992. Dr. Stewart was appointed Executive Secretary of the Home Mission Board of the National Baptist Convention, USA, Inc., in November 1994 and served through January 2005, and also continued serving as Chair of that Board through January 2010. In 2004, FIBC established FIBCO Family Services, Inc., Samaritan House for Homeless Families, Ujima House for Unwed Teenage Mothers and their Infants, as well as sponsors the Broadway House low-income housing complex and several residential homes for the seriously mentally ill, all of which provide social services to thousands monthly.

William G. Sinkford (1946–) serves as the senior minister for the First Unitarian Church in Portland, Oregon. Reverend Sinkford is more widely known for being the seventh president of the Unitarian Universalist Association of Congregations (UUA), a position he held from 2001 to 2009. His installation as UUA president made him the first African American to lead that organization.

MORE BUSINESS MOGULS
WHO MAKE THE GRADE ....

Andrew McCollum is the American co-founder of Facebook as well as an angel investor and has a net worth of $20 million. McCollum attended Harvard University where he met co-founder Mark Zuckerberg and worked for Facebook from 2004 to 2006. One of the original five Harvard students who helped build the largest social network in the world McCollum became friends with Mark Zuckerberg through the many computer science classes they took together in Harvard and was one of the first people Zuckerberg told about his idea for Facebook before it launched on Feb. 4, 2004. For more than a year after that, McCollum worked as part of the small founding team in Boston and later Palo Alto, California. Like Zuckerberg and cofounder Dustin Moskovitz, McCollum left Harvard to work full-time on the startup. For the better part of the next decade, McCollum kept a low profile on and off campus. He graduated from Harvard in 2007 with a degree in computer science and a master's degree in education. He's mentioned a handful of times in media articles, mostly as a guy in the background. The other four original Harvard students are listed as cofounders on Facebook.

B. Smith, born Barbara Elaine Smith (August 24, 1949) is an American restaurateur, model, author, and television host. Smith owned multiple restaurants called "B. Smith". The first opened in 1986, on Eighth Avenue at 47th Street in New York City, and several years later moved around the corner to Restaurant Row on 46th Street; followed by another one in Sag Harbor, Long Island, New York. She also owned a restaurant in the historic Beaux-Arts Union Station in

Washington, D.C. in September 2013; it was reported that restaurant would close. In June 2014, Smith revealed that she had been diagnosed with early-onset Alzheimer's disease, stating that she came out with the information to counter the stigma associated with the disease. In 2014, the Sag Harbor restaurant was shuttered, followed by the Manhattan location in January 2015. Smith was the first black model to be on the cover of *Mademoiselle* magazine in 1976.

Christopher Isaac "Biz" Stone (March 10, 1974) is an American entrepreneur who co-founded Twitter, among other Internet-based services. His first startup was Xanga in 1999. Stone co-founded his latest venture, Jelly, with Ben Finkel. Jelly was launched in 2014 and is described as a new kind of search engine with the core assumption that for every question there is a person with the answer. Stone is Jelly's CEO. On May 16, 2017, Biz Stone announced he is returning to Twitter Inc. in an unannounced role.

Dr. Dre, born **Andre Romelle Young** (born February 18, 1965), is an American rapper, record producer, and entrepreneur. He is the founder and CEO of Aftermath Entertainment and Beats Electronics, and was previously co-owner of Death Row Records. He has produced albums for and overseen the careers of many rappers, including 2Pac, The D.O.C., Snoop Dogg, Eminem, Xzibit, Knoc-turn'al, 50 Cent, The Game, and Kendrick Lamar. He is credited as a key figure in the crafting and popularization of West Coast G-funk, a rap style characterized as synthesizer-based with slow, heavy beats. As of 2018, he is the third richest figure in hip hop, with a net worth of $770 million.

Earvin "Magic" Johnson Jr. (August 14, 1959) is an American retired professional basketball player and current president of basketball operations of the Los Angeles Lakers of the National Basketball Association (NBA). Among his many business ventures,

Johnson runs Magic Johnson Enterprises, a conglomerate company that has a net worth of $700 million; its subsidiaries include Magic Johnson Productions, a promotional company; Magic Johnson Theaters, a nationwide chain of movie theaters; and Magic Johnson Entertainment, a film studio.

Eduardo Luiz Saverin (March 19, 1982) is a Brazilian-born entrepreneur and angel investor. Saverin is one of the co-founders of Facebook. In 2012, he owned 53 million Facebook shares (approximately 2% of all outstanding shares), valued at approximately $2 billion at the time. He also invested in early-stage startups such as Qwiki and Jumio. Saverin renounced his U.S. citizenship in September 2011, and therefore avoided an estimated $700 million in capital gains taxes; this generated some media attention and controversy. Saverin stated that he renounced his citizenship because of his "interest in working and living in Singapore" where he has been since 2009 and denied that he left the U.S. to avoid paying taxes.

Evan Clark Williams (March 31, 1972) is an American computer programmer and Internet entrepreneur who has founded several Internet companies. Williams was previously chairman and CEO of Twitter, one of the top ten websites on the Internet. He also founded Blogger and Medium. Among Obvious Corporation projects was Twitter, a popular, free social networking and micro-blogging service. Twitter was spun out into a new company in April 2007, with Williams as co-founder, board member, and investor. In October 2008, Williams became CEO of Twitter, displacing Jack Dorsey, who became chairman of the board. By February 2009, Compete.com ranked Twitter the third most-used social network. In October 2010, Williams stepped down from the CEO position, explaining that he would be "completely focused on product strategy," and appointed Dick Costolo as his replacement. Following the announcement of Twitter's initial public offering (IPO) in 2013, the company was valued at between $14 billion and $20 billion. One media report anticipated that Williams, with a 30 to 35 percent stake in the company, would see his personal wealth grow from $2 billion to $8 billion in the wake of Twitter's stock flotation. As of February 2013, Twitter had 200 million registered users and as of August 2015, was ranked twelfth in the world. On April 6, 2017, an article announced Williams would sell 30 percent of his stock in Twitter, for "personal reasons."

Iman, born **Zara Mohamed Abdulmajid** (July 25, 1955) is a Somali fashion model, actress and entrepreneur. A pioneer in cosmetics for women of color, she is also noted for her philanthropic work. She is the widow of English rock musician David Bowie, whom she married in 1992.

Jack Patrick Dorsey (November 19, 1976) is an American computer programmer and Internet entrepreneur who is co-founder and CEO of Twitter, and founder and CEO of Square, a mobile payments company. When he first saw implementations of instant messaging, Dorsey wondered whether the software's user status output could be shared easily among friends. He approached Odeo, which at the time happened to be interested in text messaging. Dorsey and Biz Stone decided that SMS text suited the status-message idea, and built a prototype of Twitter in about two weeks. The idea attracted many users at Odeo and investment from Evan Williams, who had left Google after selling Pyra Labs and Blogger.

Lawrence Edward Page (March 26, 1973) is an American computer scientist and Internet entrepreneur who co-founded Google with Sergey Brin. Page is the chief executive officer of Alphabet Inc. (Google's parent company). After stepping aside as Google CEO in August 2001, in favor of Eric Schmidt, he re-assumed the role in April 2011. He announced his intention to step aside a second time in July 2015, to become CEO of Alphabet, under which Google's assets would be reorganized. Under Page, Alphabet is seeking to deliver major advancements in a variety of industries. As of December 2018, Page was the 8th-richest person in the world, with a net worth of $51.3 billion. Page is the inventor of PageRank, Google's best-known search ranking algorithm. Page received the Marconi Prize in 2004 with Brin.

Maggie Lena Walker (July 15, 1864 – December 15, 1934) was an African-American teacher and businesswoman. Walker was the first African American female bank president to charter a bank in the United States.

Mark Elliot Zuckerberg, (May 14, 1984) is an American technology entrepreneur and philanthropist. He is known for co-founding and leading Facebook as its chairman and chief executive officer. Born in White Plains, New York, Zuckerberg attended Harvard University, where he launched Facebook from his dormitory room on February 4, 2004, with college roommates Eduardo Saverin, Andrew McCollum, Dustin Moskovitz, and Chris Hughes. Originally launched to select college campuses, the site expanded rapidly and eventually beyond colleges, reaching one billion users by 2012. Zuckerberg took the company public in May 2012 with majority shares. In December 2016, Zuckerberg was ranked 10th on *Forbes* list of The World's Most Powerful People. His net worth is estimated to be $55 billion as of November 30, 2018, declining over the last year with Facebook stock as a whole. He is also one of the youngest billionaires in the world: as of 2018, he is the only person in the Forbes Top 10 Billionaires list who is under the age of 50, and the only one in the Top 20 Billionaires list who is under the age of 40.

Noah Glass is an American software developer, best known for his early work launching Twitter and Odeo, a podcasting company that closed in 2007. In 2006, while with Odeo, Glass had helped to create and develop the seed idea for what would eventually become known as Twitter. Not only was Glass the prime motivating force leading to its eventual development, he is acknowledged as being responsible for coining the name "Twitter", which began as the abbreviated version, "Twttr," and was later changed to "Twitter." Glass is given credit as being a co-founder of Twitter, having helped realize the idea, and designing some of its core features.

Sean John Combs (born November 4, 1969), also known by his various stage names **Puff Daddy**, **P. Diddy**, **Diddy**, **Puffy**, and **Brother Love**, is an American rapper, singer, songwriter, actor, record producer, and entrepreneur. He worked as a talent director at Uptown Records before founding his own record label, Bad Boy Entertainment, in 1993. Combs has won three Grammy Awards and two MTV Video Music Awards, and is the producer of MTV's *Making the Band*. In 2018, *Forbes* estimated his net worth at $825 million, making him the second-richest hip-hop recording artist.

Sergey Mikhaylovich Brin (August 21, 1973) is an American computer scientist and Internet entrepreneur. Together with Larry Page, he co-founded Google. Brin is the president of Google's parent company Alphabet Inc. As of October 2018, Brin is the 13th-richest person in the world, with an estimated net worth of $50.6 billion. Brin immigrated to the United States with his family from the Soviet Union at the age of 6. He earned his bachelor's degree at the University of Maryland, College Park, following in his father's and grandfather's footsteps by studying mathematics, as well as computer science. After graduation, he enrolled in Stanford University to acquire a PhD in computer science. There he met Page, with whom he later became friends.

Snoop Dogg born **Calvin Cordozar Broadus Jr.** (October 20, 1971), is an American rapper, singer, record producer, television personality, entrepreneur, and actor. Among his other business ventures, on March

311

30, 2016, Snoop (Broadus) was reported to purchase the famed soul food restaurant chain Roscoe's House of Chicken and Waffles out of bankruptcy.

Tyler Perry, born **Emmitt Perry Jr.** (September 13, 1969) is an American actor, playwright, filmmaker and comedian. In 2011, *Forbes* listed him as the highest paid man in entertainment, earning $130 million USD between May 2010 and 2011. In 2015, Perry acquired the 330-acre former military base Fort McPherson, which he converted to studios. The studios were used to film the HBO Films/OWN film version of *The Immortal Life of Henrietta Lacks*, and is currently in ongoing use for the television series *The Walking Dead*. Along with various sets, Tyler Perry Studios also host 12 sound stages. The blockbuster Marvel film, Black Panther, was the first to be filmed on one the new stages.

Tyra Banks (December 4, 1973) born **Tyra Lynne Banks** is an American television personality, producer, businesswoman, actress, author, former model and occasional singer. Born in Inglewood, California, she began her career as a model at the age of 15, and was the first woman of African American descent to be featured on the covers of *GQ* and the *Sports Illustrated Swimsuit Issue*, on which she appeared twice. She was a Victoria's Secret Angel from 1997 to 2005. By the early 2000s, Tyra was one of the world's top-earning models. She began acting on television in 1993 on *The Fresh Prince of Bel-Air*, and made her film debut in *Higher Learning* in 1995. In 2000 she had a major role in the box-office hit *Coyote Ugly, and later appeared in several* other films and television series. In 2003, Tyra created, executive produced and hosted *America's Next Top Model*, and later she had her own talk show, *The Tyra Banks Show*, which aired on The CW for five seasons and won two Daytime Emmy awards for Outstanding Talk Show Informative. She also hosted *America's Got Talent* for its 12th season.

INVENTORS AND SCIENTISTS
WHO MAKE THE GRADE ....

Creativity is the lifeblood of successful entrepreneurs. It breeds new ideas, fosters new relationships and, day by day, changes the world. We are featuring a small percentage of the brilliant men and women who have created, contributed to and improved upon some of the world's greatest and most important inventions for many past centuries leading up to the present and opening the doors for the future.

George Edward Alcorn Jr. (March 22, 1940) is an American physicist and inventor who worked primarily for IBM and NASA. He was inducted into the National Inventors Hall of Fame in 2015.

Alexander Miles (1838 – 1918) is the 19th Century African-American inventor known best for patenting his design for improving the automatically opening and closing elevator doors. The patent was issued on October 11, 1887.

André Pinto Rebouças (January 13, 1838 – April 9, 1898) was a Brazilian military engineer, abolitionist and inventor, Serving as a military engineer during the Paraguayan War in Paraguay, Rebouças successfully developed a torpedo.

Andrew Jackson Beard (1849–1921) was an African-American inventor, born in Alabama. He was inducted into the National Inventors Hall of Fame in Akron, Ohio for his work on railroad coupler design. He was also able to develop and champion his first invention (a plow).

Archibald Alphonso Alexander (May 14, 1888 – January 4, 1958) was an African-American mathematician and engineer. He was an early African-American graduate of the University of Iowa and the first to graduate from the University of Iowa's College of Engineering. He was also responsible for the construction of many roads and bridges, including the an extension to the Baltimore-Washington Parkway. Also, with his business partner, Alexander designed the Tuskegee Airfield and the Iowa State University heating and cooling system.

Benjamin Thornton Montgomery (1819–1877) was an influential African-American inventor, landowner, and freedman in Mississippi. He was taught to read and write, and became manager of supply and shipping for Joseph Emory Davis at Hurricane Plantation at Davis Bend.

Bessie Coleman (January 26, 1892 – April 30, 1926) was an American civil aviator. She was the first woman of African-American descent and the first of Native American descent, to hold a pilot license.

Bill Gates, born **William Henry Gates III** (October 28, 1955) is an American business magnate, investor, author, philanthropist, and humanitarian. He is best known as the principal founder of Microsoft Corporation. During his career at Microsoft, Gates held the positions of chairman, CEO and chief software architect, while also being the largest individual shareholder until May 2014. On June 15, 2006, Gates announced that over the next two years he would transition out of his day-to-day role to dedicate more time to philanthropy. He divided his responsibilities between two successors when he placed Ray Ozzie in charge of day-to-day management and Craig Mundie in charge of long-term product strategy Gates married Melinda French on January 1, 1994. Barack Obama honored Bill and Melinda Gates with the Presidential Medal of Freedom for their philanthropic efforts in 2016, and François Hollande awarded Bill and Melinda in the following year with France's highest national award – the Legion of Honour for their charity efforts.

Charles Henry Turner (February 3, 1867 – February 14, 1923) was an American research biologist, educator, zoologist, and comparative psychologist born in Cincinnati, Ohio. Turner was the first African American to receive a graduate degree at the University of Cincinnati and a PhD from the University of Chicago. He is known for his studies in comparative psychology and on insect behavior, particularly bees and ants.

David Nelson Crosthwait Jr. (May 27, 1898 - February 25, 1976) was an African American electrical and mechanical engineer and one of the leaders in the United States in the field of heat transfer, ventilation and air conditioning. His achievements include the receipt of 39 U.S. patents and 80 foreign patents for his inventions. Mr. Crosthwait Jr. also designed the heating systems for Radio City Music Hall and Rockefeller Center in New York City.

Dorothy Johnson Vaughan (September 20, 1910 – November 10, 2008) was an African American mathematician and human computer who worked for the National Advisory Committee for Aeronautics (NACA), and NASA, at Langley Research Center in Hampton, Virginia. In 1949, she became supervisor of the West Area Computers, the first African-American woman to supervise a group of staff at the center. During her 28-year career, Vaughan taught herself and her staff computer programming language and headed the programming section of the Analysis and Computation Division (ACD) at Langley.

Elijah J. McCoy (May 2, 1844 – October 10, 1929) was a Canadian-born African American inventor and engineer who was notable for his 57 U.S. patents, most having to do with the lubrication of steam engines. Born free in Canada, he came to the United States as a young child, becoming a U.S. resident and citizen. This popular expression (the Real McCoy), typically meaning *the real thing*, has been associated with Elijah McCoy's oil-drip cup invention.

Earnest Everett Just (August 14, 1883 – October 27, 1941) was an African-American biologist and educator best known for his pioneering work in the physiology of development, especially in fertilization.

Frederick McKinley Jones (May 17, 1893 – February 21, 1961) was an African-American inventor, entrepreneur, winner of the National Medal of Technology, and inductee of the National Inventors Hall of Fame. His innovations in refrigeration brought great improvement to the long-haul transportation of perishable goods. He co-founded Thermo King.

Garrett Augustus Morgan, Sr. (March 4, 1877– July 27, 1963) was an important inventor, businessmen of both African American and Native American heritages, as well as an influential political leader. Morgan's most notable invention was the gas mask originally named "smoke hood". Morgan also discovered and developed a chemical hair-processing and straightening solution. He created a successful company based on the discovery along with a complete line of hair-care products

George Edward Alcorn Jr. (March 22, 1940) is an American physicist and inventor who worked primarily for IBM and NASA. He was inducted into the National Inventors Hall of Fame in 2015. During the summers of 1962 and 1963, he worked as a research engineer for the Space Division of North American Rockwell. He was involved with the computer analysis of launch trajectories and orbital mechanics for Rockwell missiles, including the Titan I and II, the Saturn and the Nova.

George Robert Carruthers (October 1, 1939) is an award-winning African-American inventor, physicist, and space scientist. Carruthers invented the ultraviolet camera/spectograph for NASA to use when it launched Apollo 16 in 1972. His work also demonstrated that molecular hydrogen exists in the interstellar medium. In 2003, Carruthers was inducted into the National Inventor's Hall of Fame. He received an honorary doctorate for Engineering from Michigan Technological University.

George Speck, also called **George Crum** (circa 1824– July 22, 1914) was an American chef and creator of the "potato chip." He worked as a hunter, guide, and cook in the Adirondack mountains, and became renowned for his culinary skills after being hired at Moon's Lake House on Saratoga Lake, near Saratoga Springs, New York.

Dr. George F. Grant (1846-1910) was a dentist by trade but also distinguished himself as an educator, scholar, and inventor. Grant earned acclaim as both an innovator in dental practice and as a frequent and vocal commentator on the development of dentistry. Even at leisure, his active mind never stopped working overtime: he filed the first U.S. patent for a golf tee.

George Murray (September 1853 – April 1926) was, without a doubt, one of the most remarkable citizens of his time. Born in Sumter County, South Carolina, George was a teacher, farmer, land developer and federal customs inspector. The former slave would go on to become a United States Congressman and a noted inventor.

George Washington Carver (c. 1864 to January 5, 1943) was born into slavery and went on to become a botanist and one of the most prominent scientists and inventors of his time as well as a teacher at the Tuskegee Institute. Carver devised over 100 products using one major crop — the peanut — including dyes, plastics and gasoline.

Granville T. Woods (April 23, 1856 to January 30, 1910) was born in Columbus, Ohio, to free African-Americans. Known as "Black Edison," he invented 15 appliances for electric railways and received nearly 60 patents, many of which were assigned to the major manufacturers of electrical equipment that are a part of today's daily life, including: a telephone transmitter, a trolley wheel and the multiplex telegraph.

James Forten (1766 – 1842) was born as a free Black man in Philadelphia, Pennsylvania. Forten began experimenting with different types of sails for ships and finally invented one that he found was better suited for maneuvering and maintaining greater speeds. Although he did not patent the sail, he was able to benefit financially, and he made a great impact upon the fortunes of industries and the lives of his fellow man.

James West, born **James Edward Maceo West** (February 10, 1931) in Farmville, Prince Edward County, Virginia is an African American inventor and acoustician. James West developed polymer foil electret transducers (now used in 90 percent of all contemporary microphones) and he holds over 250 foreign and U.S. patents for the production and design of microphones.

Jan Ernst Matzeliger, (September 15, 1852 - Aug. 24, 1889) is the son of a Dutch father and a Black Surinamese mother, Matzeliger, who was born in Dutch Guiana, the South American country now called Suriname. He is an inventor best known for his shoe-lasting machine that mechanically shaped the upper portions of shoes.

John P. Parker (1827 – January 30, 1900) was an American abolitionist, inventor, iron moulder and industrialist. Parker, who was African American, helped hundreds of slaves to freedom in the Underground Railroad resistance movement based in Ripley, Ohio. He was one of the few Blacks to patent his inventions before 1900. In

1865 with a partner, he bought a foundry company, which manufactured engines, Dorsey's patent reaper and mower, and sugar mill. In 1876 he brought in a partner to manufacture threshers, and the company became Belchamber and Parker.

Joseph Dickinson (1855 - January 12, 1921). was born in Canada and moved to Michigan in 1870. He learned about various types of organs while working for the Clough and Warren Organ Company in Detroit in 1872. One of the organs he designed was awarded a prize at the Centennial Exposition in Philadelphia, Pennsylvania in 1876 and Dickinson was quickly hired to build organs for major customers, including the Royal Family of Portugal. He was not the first inventor of the player piano, but he did patent an improvement that allowed the piano to start playing at any position on the music roll.

Joseph Lee (1849 – 1905) was born in and lived most of his life in Boston, Massachusetts. Lee decided that instead of simply throwing stale bread away, he would use it to make bread crumbs. He invented a device that could automate tearing, crumbling and grinding the bread into crumbs and patented the invention on June 4, 1895. He sold the rights to his bread crumbling machine and the Royal Worcester Bread Crumb Company of Boston soon had the devices in major restaurants around the world. Lee then invented an automatic bread-making machine and received a patent for it, which is the basis for machines still in use today.

Katherine Johnson, born **Katherine Coleman Goble Johnson** (August 26, 1918) is an African-American mathematician whose calculations of orbital mechanics as a NASA employee were critical to the success of the first and subsequent U.S. manned spaceflights. During her 35-year career at NASA and its predecessor, she earned a reputation for mastering complex manual calculations and helped the space agency pioneer the use of computers to perform the tasks.

Johnson's work included calculating trajectories, launch windows and emergency return paths for Project Mercury spaceflights, including those of astronauts Alan Shepard and John Glenn as well as rendezvous paths for the Apollo lunar lander and command module on flights to the Moon. Her calculations were also essential to the beginning of the Space Shuttle program and she worked on plans for a mission to Mars. In 2015, President Barack Obama awarded Johnson the Presidential Medal of Freedom.

Lewis Howard Latimer (September 4, 1848 - December 11, 1928) was born in Chelsea, Massachusetts to parents who had fled slavery. Latimer learned the art of mechanical drawing while working at a patent firm. He was an inventor and draftsman best known for his contributions to the patenting of the light bulb and the telephone. Latimer worked closely with Thomas Edison and Alexander Graham Bell, in addition to designing his own inventions, which included an improved railroad car bathroom and an early air conditioning unit.

Lewis Temple (October 1, 1800 – May 5, 1854) was an American blacksmith, abolitionist, and inventor. He was born in slavery in Richmond, Virginia. Lewis Temple was a skilled blacksmith, who is the creator of a whaling harpoon, known as "Temple's Toggle" and "Temple's Iron" that became the standard harpoon of the whaling industry in the middle of the 19th century. Temple never patented his invention which resulted in others copying his work and selling it as their own.

Lloyd Augustus Hall (June 20, 1894 – January 2, 1971) was an African American chemist, who contributed to the science of food preservation. By the end of his career, Hall had amassed 59 United States patents, and a number of his inventions were also patented in other countries. Among his many inventions, Lloyd Hall devoted much of his life and efforts to food science, particularly to improving a curing salt marketed by Griffith Laboratories known as flash-drying. Hall and Griffith later promoted the use of ethylene oxide for the sterilization of medical equipment. He was awarded several honors during his lifetime, and in 2004 he was inducted into the National Inventors Hall of Fame for his work.

Lonnie George Johnson (born October 6, 1949) is an American inventor and engineer who holds more than 120 patents. He is the inventor of the Super Soaker water gun, which has been among the world's bestselling toys every year since its release. Johnson discovered he was underpaid royalties for the Super Soaker and several "Nerf line of toys, specifically the N-Strike and Dart Tag brands." In November 2013, Johnson was awarded nearly $73 million in royalties from Hasbro Inc. in arbitration. According to Hasbro, the Super Soaker is approaching sales of $1 billion.

Marjorie Stewart Joyner (October 24, 1896 – December 27, 1994) was an American businesswoman. After graduation, she opened a salon on South State Street in Chicago, where she met Madam C.J. Walker. Joyner went to work for Walker and became the national adviser to her company, overseeing 200 beauty schools. Marjorie invented the Permanent Wave Machine thus ensuring her place in cosmetology history. She helped write the first cosmetology laws for Illinois and founded the United Beauty School Owners and Teachers Association with Mary Bethune McLeod in 1945. Over her 50-year career, Joyner taught around 15,000 stylists. In 1987, the Smithsonian Institution in Washington opened an exhibit featuring Joyner's invention and a replica of her original salon.

Mark E. Dean (born March 2, 1957) is an American inventor and computer engineer. He was part of the team that developed the interior architecture (ISA systems bus), that enables multiple devices, such as modems and printers, to be connected to personal computers and he led a design team for making a one-gigahertz computer processor chip. He holds three of nine PC patents for being the co-creator of the IBM personal computer released in 1981. Dean now holds more than 20 patents.

Mary Winston Jackson (April 9, 1921 – February 11, 2005) was an African American mathematician and aerospace engineer at the National Advisory Committee for Aeronautics (NACA), which in 1958 was succeeded by the National Aeronautics and Space Administration (NASA). She worked at Langley Research Center in Hampton, Virginia, for most of her career. She started as a human computer at the segregated West Area Computing division. She took advanced engineering classes and, in 1958, became NASA's first black female engineer.

Matthew Alexander Henson (August 8, 1866 – March 9, 1955) was an American explorer who accompanied Robert Peary on seven voyages to the Arctic over a period of nearly 23 years. They spent a total of 18 years on expeditions together. He is best known for his participation in the 1908-1909 expedition that claimed to have reached the geographic North Pole on April 6, 1909. Henson said he was the first of their party to reach the pole.

Michael Blakey (born February 23, 1953) is an American anthropologist who specializes in physical anthropology and its connection to the history of African Americans. Since 2001, he has been a National Endowment for the Humanities professor at the College of William & Mary, where he directs the Institute for Historical Biology. Previously, he was a professor at Howard University and the curator of Howard University's Montague Cobb Biological Anthropology Laboratory. Blakey was the director of research for the New York African Burial Ground Project, now the Burial Ground National Monument. According to Blakey, the existence of this burial ground in what is now Lower Manhattan (where between 10 and 20 thousand people of African descent were buried in the eighteenth century) was evidence of "false historical representation" and exposed as a myth the idea that New York and the northern states were not slave-owning areas.

Miriam E. Benjamin (September 16, 1861 – 1947) was an American school teacher and inventor from Washington, D.C. On July 17, 1888 she became the second Black woman to obtain a patent for her invention, the Gong and Signal Chair for Hotels. The system was adopted and installed within the United States House of Representatives and was the predecessor of the signaling system used today on airplanes for passengers to seek assistance from flight attendants.

Norbert Rillieux (March 17, 1806 – October 8, 1894) was an American inventor who was widely considered one of the earliest chemical engineers and noted for his pioneering invention of the multiple-effect evaporator. This invention was an important development in the growth of the sugar industry. In his honor, a bronze memorial was erected in the Louisiana State Museum with the inscription: "To honor Norbert Rillieux, born at New Orleans, Louisiana, March 17, 1806, and died at Paris, France, October 8, 1894. Inventor of Multiple Evaporation and Its Application to the Sugar Industry."

Otis Frank Boykin (August 29, 1920 – March 13, 1982) born in Dallas, Texas, was an African-American inventor and engineer. Boykin is best known for inventing an improved electrical resistor used in computers, radios, television sets and a variety of electronic devices, as well as a variable resistor used in guided missile parts. His most famous invention was a control unit for the pacemaker.

Ironically, Boykin died in Chicago in 1982 as a result of heart failure. Upon his death, he had 26 patents to his name.

Patricia Bath (November 4, 1942) born in Harlem, New York, became the first African American to complete a residency in ophthalmology in 1973. Two years later, she became the first female faculty member in the Department of Ophthalmology at UCLA's Jules Stein Eye Institute. In 1976, Bath co-founded the American Institute for the Prevention of Blindness, which established that "eyesight is a basic human right." In 1986, Bath invented the Laserphaco Probe, improving treatment for cataract patients. She patented the device in 1988, becoming the first African-American female doctor to receive a medical patent.

Philip Emeagwali (August 23, 1954) is a computer scientist, who was born in Akure, Nigeria. Dr. Emeagwali has been cited as "The Bill Gates of Africa." Emeagwali, won the 1989 Gordon Bell Prize ($1,000) for price-performance in high-performance computing applications, in an oil reservoir modeling calculation using a novel mathematical formulation and implementation. Emeagwali used 65,000 processors to invent the world's fastest computer which performs at 3.1 billion calculations per second. By discovering a practical application for utilizing supercomputers, he opened up a whole new market for them.. Former United States President Bill Clinton summed up worldwide sentiment by declaring Emeagwali "One of the great minds of the Information Age."

Richard Bowie Spikes (October 2, 1878 - January 22, 1963) was an African-American inventor. The holder of a number of United States patents, his inventions (or mechanical improvements on existing inventions) include a beer tap, automobile directional signals, the automatic gear shift device based on automatic transmission for automobiles and other motor vehicles and a safety braking system for trucks and buses.

Robert Pelham, Jr (January 4, 1859 – June 12, 1943) was a journalist and civil servant in Detroit, Michigan and Washington, D.C.. He served in a number of public positions in Michigan, and later worked at the United States Census in Washington, D.C. While working there as a clerk Pelham felt as though his job could be a whole lot easier which inspired him to invent and patent a pasting apparatus in 1905 and to engineer a tallying machine in 1913.

Sarah Elisabeth Goode (1855 – April 8, 1905) was an entrepreneur and inventor, born in Toledo, Ohio. She was the first African-American woman to receive a United States patent, which she received in 1885. The first African-American woman to receive a patent was Judy W. Reed on September 23, 1884, but Reed only signed her patent with her mark (an X) and not her signature. Goode invented a folding cabinet bed which helped people who lived in tight housing to utilize their space efficiently. When the bed was folded up, it looked like a desk, with room for storage. She received a patent for it on July 14, 1885. Her invention was the precursor to the Murphy bed, which was patented in 1900.

Thomas Elkins (1818 - August 10, 1900) designed a device that helped with the task of preserving perishable foods by way of refrigeration. Elkins patented this refrigerated apparatus on November 4, 1879 and had previously patented several other inventions including: a chamber commode in 1872 and a dining, ironing table and quilting frame combined in 1870. An inventor, abolitionist, and trained medical professional, Dr. Thomas Elkins was born in New York State. Elkins also studied surgery and dentistry, and operated a pharmacy in Albany for several decades.

Thomas O. Mensah (1950) is a Ghanaian-American chemical engineer and inventor. His works are in fields relating to the development of fiber optics and nanotechnology. He has 14 patents, 7 of which awarded within a period of six years and was inducted into the US National Academy of Inventors in 2015. Mensah is President and CEO of Georgia Aerospace Systems that manufactures nano composite structures used in missiles and aircraft for the US Department of Defense.

Valerie Thomas (May 1943) was born in in Maryland. Thomas is an African-American scientist and inventor best known for her patented illusion transmitter and contributions to NASA research. In 1980, Thomas received a patent for an illusion transmitter. The device produces optical illusion images via two concave mirrors. This technology was subsequently adopted by NASA and has since been adapted for use in surgery as well as the production of television and video screens.

ATHLETES WHO MAKE THE GRADE ....

Nearly every professional and amateur sport has an African American star athlete. Some have set new records for athletic achievement. Others also are remembered for courageously breaking longstanding racial barriers in their sport. We have featured a small percentage of athletes – role models and mentors - who have made us proud as a people.

Althea Gibson, (August 25, 1927 - September 28, 2003) was born in Silver, South Carolina and died in East Orange, New Jersey. Gibson grew up in New York City, where she began playing tennis at an early age under the auspices of the New York Police Athletic League. In 1942 she won her first tournament, which was sponsored by the American Tennis Association (ATA), an organization founded by African American players. In 1947 she captured the ATA's women's singles championship, which she would hold for 10 consecutive years. Althea dominated women's competition in the late 1950s. She was the first African American player to win the French (1956), Wimbledon (1957–58), and U.S. Open (1957–58) singles championships.

Arthur Ashe (July 10, 1943 - February 6, 1993) was born in Richmond, Virginia. Arthur Ashe became the first and is still the only African-American male tennis player to win the U.S. Open and Wimbledon. He is also the first African-American man to be ranked as the No. 1 tennis player in the world. Always an activist, when Ashe learned that he had contracted AIDS via a blood transfusion, he turned his efforts to raising awareness about the disease, before finally succumbing to it.

Charles Wade Barkley (born February 20, 1963) is an American retired professional basketball player who is currently an analyst on *Inside the NBA*. Nicknamed "Chuck", "Sir Charles", and "The Round Mound of Rebound," Barkley established himself as one of the National Basketball Association's most dominant power forwards. An All-American center at Auburn, he was drafted as a junior by the Philadelphia 76ers with the 5th pick of the 1984 NBA draft. He was selected to the All-NBA First Team five times, the All-NBA Second Team five times, and once to the All-NBA Third Team. He earned eleven NBA All-Star Game appearances and was named the All-Star MVP in 1991. In 1993 with the Phoenix Suns, he was voted the league's Most Valuable Player and during the NBA's 50th anniversary, named one of the 50 Greatest Players in NBA History.

Douglas Lee Williams (August 9, 1955) is a former American football quarterback and former head coach of the Grambling State Tigers football team. Williams is known for his remarkable performance with the Washington Redskins in Super Bowl XXII against the Denver Broncos. Williams, who was named the Super Bowl MVP, passed for a Super Bowl record 340 yards and four touchdowns, with one interception. He was the first African-American starting quarterback to win a Super Bowl. Williams also became the first player in Super Bowl history to pass for four touchdowns in a half, and the only quarterback to throw for four touchdowns in a single quarter. Williams is now a team executive for the Redskins, being hired for that role in 2014.

Dr. J, born **Julius Erving** (February 22, 1950) in Roosevelt, New York is a Hall of Fame basketball forward. "Dr. J" was an acrobatic player in the NBA and ABA who became known for his style and grace, on and off the court, during his 16-year professional basketball career. In 1968, Erving, who was not recruited by many big basketball programs, enrolled at the University of Massachusetts. He played just two seasons for the school—freshmen were ineligible to play varsity, and Erving left before his senior season—but he left his mark on the program. At UMass, he averaged 32.5 points and 20.2 rebounds a game, one of only five players at the time to ever average more than 20 points and 20 rebounds a game. In 1971 Erving left college and joined the Virginia Squires, of the American Basketball Association (ABA), as an undrafted free agent. Playing forward, he transitioned quickly to the pro game. In the spring of 1972 Erving was selected 12th overall by the Milwaukee Bucks of the National Basketball Association (NBA), he instead signed a contract with the Atlanta Hawks and joined the team for pre-season workouts. He was barred from playing in the NBA and returned to play the 1972-73 season with the Squires and then joined the New York Nets. Dr. J helped the New York Nets win the ABA championship in 1974 and 1976 and also received the Most Valuable Player award for each of those seasons. When the ABA was folded into the NBA in 1976, the cash-strapped Nets sold Erving to the Philadelphia 76ers for $3 million. In 1983 he helped lead the 76ers to a world championship. Upon retiring in 1987, he had played in more than 800 games, scoring an average of 22 points per game.

Hank Aaron (February 5, 1934), born **Henry Louis Aaron** and nicknamed "Hammer" or "Hammerin' Hank" is the Baseball legend who broke Babe Ruth's hallowed mark of 714 home runs and finished his career with numerous big-league records. Aaron is a retired American Major League Baseball (MLB) right fielder who has been the Senior Vice President of Atlanta National League Baseball Club, Inc. since 1998. He played 21 seasons for the Milwaukee/Atlanta Braves in the National League (NL) and two seasons for the Milwaukee Brewers in the American League (AL), from 1954 through 1976. Aaron held the MLB record for career home runs for 33 years, and he still holds several MLB offensive records. He hit 24 or more home runs every year from 1955 through 1973 and is one of only two players to hit 30 or more home runs in a season at least fifteen times. In 1999, *The Sporting News* ranked Aaron fifth on its "100 Greatest Baseball Players" list. Hank Aaron was the last player to appear in both the Negro Leagues and the Major Leagues.

Hank Carter grew up in the Queensbridge Projects, Long Island City, New York. He was educated in the public-school system and attended Baruch College. He served in Vietnam, and was awarded the Army's Good Conduct Medal, a Bronze Star, and other military honors. After Vietnam, Hank began working as a teller in a bank. In 1970, through the Jacob Riis Community Center he started an organization in his spare time known as United Queens. The intent was to get kids involved in basketball and get them off the streets and away from a life of crime and fight the drug dealers. Carter spent his time raising money to purchase basketball uniforms and other equipment for kids in the Queensbridge community. When he visited the hospital on Roosevelt Island, he noticed that scores of paralyzed patients had no wheelchairs. Carter then began a campaign to raise money to buy wheelchairs for the hospital. Cookie sales and other fundraisers became part of his program. Over the years Wheelchair Charities, Inc. has purchased more than 560 motorized wheelchairs, many of which cost as much as $36,000. Then he thought about charity basketball games. Thus, the Wheelchair Basketball Classic, a tournament featuring teams from all five boroughs, was born. In that first game, Bernard King scored the first-ever jump shot. The Wheelchair Basketball Classic has become an annual event. Carter then talked Madison Square Garden into sponsoring an annual All-Star game featuring NBA stars. Howard White, an executive at Nike, became involved and still remains involved today. The first vans came rolling in, enabling the hospital patients to leave the island to attend Broadway shows and do other activities. Over the years, Carter and his friends, NBA stars and Nike have contributed millions of dollars, for a variety of equipment and programs for patients and residents with profound disabilities, including thousands of manual and motorized wheelchairs, specially equipped buses, modified beds, and other equipment. Hank Carter is the first African-American to have a hospital in New York City named after him.

Jacqueline "Jackie" Joyner-Kersee (born March 3, 1962) is an American retired track and field athlete, ranked among the all-time greatest athletes in the heptathlon as well as long jump. She won three gold, one silver, and two bronze Olympic medals, in those two events at four different Olympic Games. *Sports Illustrated for Women* magazine voted Joyner-Kersee the Greatest Female Athlete of All-Time. She is on the Board of Directors for USA Track & Field (USATF), the national governing body of the sport.

Jack Johnson (March 31, 1878 – June 10, 1946), born **John Arthur Johnson** and nicknamed the "Galveston Giant", was an American boxer who, at the height of the Jim Crow era, became the first African American world heavyweight boxing champion (1908–1915). Among the period's most dominant champions, Johnson remains a boxing legend, with his 1910 fight against James J. Jeffries dubbed the "fight of the century". According to filmmaker Ken Burns, "for more than thirteen years, Jack Johnson was the most famous and the most notorious African-American on Earth." Transcending boxing, he became part of the culture and the history of racism in America.

Jackie Robinson (January 31, 1919 – October 24, 1972) named **Jack Roosevelt Robinson** was an American professional baseball player who became the first African American to play in Major League Baseball (MLB) in the modern era. Robinson broke the baseball color line when the Brooklyn Dodgers started him at first base on April 15, 1947. When the Dodgers signed Robinson, they heralded the end of racial segregation in professional baseball that had relegated black players to the Negro leagues since the 1880s. Robinson was inducted into the Baseball Hall of Fame in 1962.

Jesse Owens (September 12, 1913 to March 31, 1980) was an American track-and-field athlete who won four gold medals. Jesse Owens, also known as "The Buckeye Bullet," broke two world records at the 1936 Berlin Olympic Games. His long jump world record stood for 25 years.

Joe Louis, born **Joseph Louis Barrow** (May 13, 1914 – April 12, 1981) was an American professional boxer who competed from 1934 to 1951. He reigned as the world heavyweight champion from 1937 to 1949, and is considered to be one of the greatest heavyweight boxers of all time. Nicknamed the "Brown Bomber," Louis' championship reign lasted 140 consecutive months, during which he participated in 26 championship fights. The 27th fight, against Ezzard Charles in 1950, was a challenge for Charles' heavyweight title and so is not included in Louis' reign. He was victorious in 25 title defenses, second only to Julio César Chávez with 27. In 2005, Louis was ranked as the best heavyweight of all time by the International Boxing Research Organization, and was ranked number one on *The Ring* magazine's list of the "100 greatest punchers of all time."

Kareem Abdul-Jabbar born **Ferdinand Lewis Alcindor Jr.** (April 16, 1947) is an American retired professional basketball player who played 20 seasons in the National Basketball Association (NBA) for the Milwaukee Bucks and the Los Angeles Lakers. During his career as a center, Abdul-Jabbar was a record six-time NBA Most Valuable Player (MVP), a record 19-time NBA All-Star, a 15-time All-NBA selection, and an 11-time NBA All-Defensive Team member. A member of six NBA championship teams as a player and two more as an assistant coach, Abdul-Jabbar twice was voted NBA Finals MVP. In 1996, he was honored as one of the 50 Greatest Players in NBA

History. NBA coach Pat Riley and players Isiah Thomas and Julius Erving have called him the greatest basketball player of all time.

Katelyn Michelle Ohashi (April 12, 1997) is an American artistic gymnast. Currently, she competes for the University of California, Los Angeles and is a two-time All-American. Previously, she was a four-time member of USA Gymnastics' Junior National Team, the 2011 junior national champion and the winner of the 2013 American Cup. She was trending globally on various social media networks in January 2019 for her perfect 10 score at the 2019 Collegiate Challenge, the third perfect 10 floor routine of her career.

Kobe Bryant, in full **Kobe Bean Bryant**, (August 23, 1978) was born in Philadelphia, Pennsylvania. Kobe was an American professional basketball player, who helped lead the Los Angeles Lakers of the National Basketball Association (NBA) to five championships (2000–02, 2009–10). Bryant's father, Joe ("Jelly Bean") Bryant, was a professional basketball player who spent eight seasons in the NBA and eight more playing in Italy, where Kobe went to school. When his family returned to the United States, Kobe played basketball at Lower Merion High School in Ardmore, Pennsylvania, where he received several national Player of the Year awards and broke the southeastern Pennsylvania scoring record set by Wilt Chamberlain with 2,883 points. Kobe opted to forgo college and declared himself eligible for the NBA draft when he graduated from high school. The Charlotte Hornets chose him with the 13th pick of the 1996 draft. He was traded to the Lakers shortly thereafter and became the second youngest NBA player in history when the 1996–97 season opened. He quickly proved his merit with the Lakers and was selected for the NBA All-Star Game in just his second season, becoming the youngest all-star. Bryant led the league in scoring during the 2005–06 and 2006–07 seasons, and in 2008 he was named the league's MVP for the first time in his career. Bryant won his fourth NBA title in 2009, and he was named the finals

MVP after averaging a stellar 32.4 points per game in the series. He led the Lakers to their third straight Western Conference championship in 2009–10, and was once more named NBA finals MVP after the Lakers defeated the Boston Celtics in a seven-game series. Bryant ruptured his Achilles tendon in April 2013, causing him to miss the rest of the season. He returned to the court in December 2013 but after six games he fractured his kneecap, and then in January 2016, he tore his rotator cuff. Kobe retired following the last regular-season game of the 2015–16 season. In 2015 Kobe wrote the poem "Dear Basketball," and two years later it served as the basis for a short film of the same name, which he also narrated. The work won an Academy Award for best animated short film.

Lebron James, born **LeBron Raymone James Sr.,** (December 30, 1984) is an American professional basketball player for the Los Angeles Lakers of the National Basketball Association (NBA). Often considered the best basketball player in the world and regarded by some as the greatest player of all time, James' accomplishments are extensive and include four NBA Most Valuable Player Awards, three NBA Finals MVP Awards, two Olympic gold medals, three All-Star Game MVP awards, and an NBA scoring title. He is the all-time NBA playoffs scoring leader and has amassed fourteen NBA All-Star Game appearances, twelve All-NBA First Team designations, and five All-Defensive First Team honors. A prep-to-pro, James played high school basketball for St. Vincent–St. Mary High School in his hometown of Akron, Ohio, where he was heavily touted in the national media as a future NBA superstar. He joined the Cleveland Cavaliers in 2003 as the first overall draft pick. James concluded his first season by winning the NBA Rookie of the Year Award. He was given the NBA Most Valuable Player Award in 2009 and 2010. James departed Cleveland in 2010 as a free agent to sign with the Miami Heat. In Miami, James won his first NBA championship in 2012, and followed that with another title a year later. He was named league MVP and NBA Finals

MVP in both championship years. In 2014, James opted out of his contract with Miami, after four seasons, to re-sign with the Cavaliers. In 2016, James led the Cavaliers to their first NBA championship by defeating the Golden State Warriors to end Cleveland's 52-year professional sports title drought. In 2018, he opted out of his Cleveland contract to sign with the Lakers.

Leon Spinks (July 11, 1953) is an American boxer who won an Olympic gold medal in 1976 and was the world heavyweight champion in 1978. He and Michael Spinks became the first brothers to win gold medals in the same sport at the same Olympics and, as professional champions, the first brothers in boxing history to win world titles. Spinks, a light heavyweight, had a successful amateur boxing career. In 1977 Spinks began to fight professionally, moving up to the heavyweight division. On February 15, 1978, in only his eighth professional fight, Spinks outpointed Muhammad Ali over 15 rounds to capture the world heavyweight title. In New Orleans seven months later, however, Ali won a rematch. Spinks retired from professional boxing in 1995, having won 26 of his 46 bouts, 14 of which were by knockouts.

Marvelous Marvin Hagler (May 23, 1954) born **Marvin Nathaniel Hagler** is an American former professional boxer who competed from 1973 to 1987. He reigned as the undisputed middleweight champion from 1980 to 1987, making twelve defenses of that title, and currently holds the highest knockout percentage of all undisputed middleweight champions, at 78%, while also holding the second longest unified championship reign in boxing history at twelve consecutive defenses. At six years and seven months, his reign as undisputed middleweight champion is the second longest of the last century, behind only Tony Zale, who reigned during World War II. In 1982, annoyed that network announcers often did not refer to him by his nickname, "Marvelous", Hagler legally changed his name to Marvelous Marvin Hagler.

Michael Jordan (February 17, 1963), born **Michael Jeffrey Jordan** also known by his initials, MJ, is an American former professional basketball player. He played 15 seasons in the National Basketball Association (NBA) for the Chicago Bulls and Washington Wizards. His biography on the official NBA website states: "By acclamation, Michael Jordan is the greatest basketball player of all time." Jordan was one of the most effectively marketed athletes of his generation and was considered instrumental in popularizing the NBA around the world in the 1980s and 1990s. He is currently the principal owner and chairman of the NBA's Charlotte Hornets.

Mike Tyson (June 30, 1966) born **Michael Gerard Tyson** is an American former professional boxer who competed from 1985 to 2005. He reigned as the undisputed world heavyweight champion and holds the record as the youngest boxer to win a heavyweight title at 20 years, four months and 22 days old. Tyson won his first 19 professional fights by knockout or stoppage, 12 of them in the first round. He won the WBC title in 1986 after stopping Trevor Berbick in the second round, and added the WBA and IBF titles after defeating James Smith and Tony Tucker in 1987. This made Tyson the first heavyweight boxer to simultaneously hold the WBA, WBC and IBF titles, and the only heavyweight to successively unify them.

Muhammad Ali (January 17, 1942 – June 3, 2016) born **Cassius Marcellus Clay Jr.** was an American professional boxer, activist, and philanthropist. Nicknamed "The Greatest," he is widely regarded as one of the most significant and celebrated sports figures of the 20th century and one of the greatest boxers of all time. As a Muslim, Ali was initially affiliated with Elijah Muhammad's Nation of Islam (NOI) and advocated their black separatist ideology, but he later disavowed the NOI. After retiring from boxing in 1981, at age 39, Ali focused on religion and charity. In 1984, he was diagnosed with Parkinson's syndrome and was cared for by his family until his death on June 3, 2016, in Scottsdale, Arizona.

Reggie Jackson (May 18, 1946) born **Reginald Martinez Jackson** is an American former professional baseball right-fielder who played 21 seasons for the Kansas City / Oakland Athletics, Baltimore Orioles, New York Yankees, and California Angels of Major League Baseball (MLB). Jackson was inducted into the National Baseball Hall of Fame in 1993.

Satch Sanders (November 8, 1938) born **Thomas Ernest Sanders** is an American retired college and professional basketball player and coach. He was a 6'6", 210 lb power forward. There aren't many native New Yorkers who become sports heroes in the city of Boston; but Celtics Legend Tom "Satch" Sanders is a member of that exclusive group. Sanders went on to play all 13 of his NBA seasons with the Celtics as a forward. He is tied for third for most NBA championships in a career and is one of three NBA players with an unsurpassed 8–0 record in NBA Finals series outcomes. The Boston Celtics had won the league's two previous championships before it drafted Sanders and then went on to win the next six with him on board. He walked into a developing Celtics dynasty and became a key piece of the franchise's ongoing success. He retired following the 1972-73 season. Sanders was elected to the 2011 class to enter the Naismith Basketball Hall of Fame as a contributor.

Shaquille Rashaun O'Neal, (March 6, 1972), nicknamed **"Shaq"** is an American retired professional basketball player who is a sports analyst on the television program *Inside the NBA* on TNT. He is widely considered one of the greatest players in the history of the National Basketball Association (NBA). At 7 ft 1 in tall and 325 pounds, he was one of the tallest and heaviest players in the history of the NBA. O'Neal played for six teams throughout his 19-year career. Following his time at Louisiana State University, O'Neal was drafted by the Orlando Magic with the first overall pick in the 1992 NBA draft. He quickly became one of the best centers in the league, winning Rookie of the Year in 1992–93 and leading his team to the 1995 NBA Finals. After four years with the Magic, O'Neal signed as a free agent with the Los Angeles Lakers. They won three consecutive championships in 2000, 2001, and 2002. O'Neal was traded to the Miami Heat in 2004, and his fourth NBA championship followed in 2006. Midway through the 2007–2008 season he was traded to the Phoenix Suns. After a season-and-a-half with the Suns, O'Neal was traded to the Cleveland Cavaliers in the 2009–10 season. O'Neal played for the Boston Celtics in the 2010–11 season before retiring. O'Neal is one of only three players to win NBA MVP, All-Star game MVP and Finals MVP awards in the same year (2000).

Serena Jameka Williams (September 26, 1981) is an American professional tennis player. The Women's Tennis Association (WTA) ranked her world No. 1 in singles on eight separate occasions between 2002 and 2017. She reached the No. 1 ranking for the first time on July 8, 2002. On her sixth occasion, she held the ranking for 186 consecutive weeks, tying the record set by Steffi Graf. In total, she has been No. 1 for 319 weeks, which ranks third in the "Open Era" among female players behind Graf and Martina Navratilova. Williams holds the most Grand Slam titles in singles, doubles, and mixed doubles combined among active players. Her 39 major titles puts her joint-third on the all-time list and second in the Open Era: 23 in singles, 14 in women's doubles, and two in mixed doubles. She is the most recent female player to have held all four Grand Slam singles titles simultaneously (2002–03 and 2014–15) and the third player to achieve this twice, after Rod Laver and Graf. Serena is also the most recent player to have won a Grand Slam title on each surface (hard, clay and grass) in one calendar year. She is also, together with her sister Venus, the most recent player to have held all four Grand Slam women's doubles titles simultaneously (2009–10). When the children were young, the Williams family moved to Compton, California, where Serena started playing tennis at the age of three. Her father home-schooled Serena and her sister, Venus. While Mr. and Mrs. Williams have been the official coaches, other mentors who helped the girls learn the game included Richard Williams, a Compton (not related) who would go on to found The Venus and Serena Williams Tennis/Tutorial Academy. When Williams was nine, she and her family moved from Compton to West Palm Beach, Florida, so that she and Venus could attend the tennis academy of Rick Macci; In 1995 Mr. Williams pulled the girls out of the academy and took over their coaching again. In August 2009, Williams and her sister Venus became minority owners of the Miami Dolphins after purchasing a small stake in the team. They live near each other in Palm Beach Gardens, Florida, which is about an hour's drive from the Dolphins' stadium. They are the first Black women to hold any amount of ownership in an NFL franchise.

Stephen Curry, born **Wardell Stephen Curry II** (March 14, 1988) is an American professional basketball player for the Golden State Warriors of the National Basketball Association (NBA). Many players and analysts have called him the greatest shooter in NBA history. He is credited with revolutionizing the game of basketball by inspiring teams to regularly employ the three-point shot as part of their winning strategy. In 2014–15, Curry won the NBA Most Valuable Player Award and led the Warriors to their first championship since 1975. The following season, he became the first player in NBA history to be elected MVP by a unanimous vote and to lead the league in scoring while shooting above 50–40–90. That same year, the Warriors broke the record for the most wins in an NBA season enroute to reaching the 2016 NBA Finals, which they lost to the Cleveland Cavaliers. Curry helped the Warriors return to the NBA Finals in 2017 and 2018, where they won back-to-back titles.

"Sugar" Ray Leonard (May 17, 1956), born **Ray Charles Leonard** is best known as an American former professional boxer, motivational speaker, and occasional actor. Often regarded as one of the greatest boxers of all time, he competed from 1977 to 1997, winning world titles in five weight divisions; the lineal championship in three weight divisions; as well as the undisputed welterweight title. Leonard was part of "The Fabulous Four," a group of boxers who all fought each other throughout the 1980s, consisting of himself, Roberto Durán, Thomas Hearns and Marvin Hagler.

Sugar Ray Robinson, born **Walker Smith Jr.**; (May 3, 1921 – April 12, 1989) was an American professional boxer who competed from 1940 to 1965. Robinson's performances in the welterweight and middleweight divisions prompted sportswriters to create "pound for pound" rankings, where they compared fighters regardless of weight. He was inducted into the International Boxing Hall of Fame in 1990. He is widely regarded as the greatest boxer of all time, and in 2002, Robinson was ranked number one on *The Ring*magazine's list of "80 Best Fighters of the Last 80 Years." Robinson was 85–0 as an amateur with 69 of those victories coming by way of knockout, 40 in the first round. He turned professional in 1940 at the age of 19 and by 1951 had a professional record of 128–1–2 with 84 knockouts. From 1943 to 1951 Robinson went on a 91 fight unbeaten streak, the third longest in professional boxing history. Robinson held the world welterweight title from 1946 to 1951 and won the world middleweight title in the latter years. He retired in 1952, only to come back two and a half years later and regain the middleweight title in 1955. He then became the first boxer in history to win a divisional world championship five times (a feat he accomplished by defeating Carmen Basilio in 1958 to regain the middleweight championship).

Tiger Woods (born December 30, 1975) **Eldrick Tont Woods** is an American professional golfer who is among the most successful golfers of all time, and one of the most popular athletes of the 21st century. He was one of the highest-paid athletes in the world for several years. Woods is generally considered one of the greatest golfers of all time.

Tony Dungy, born **Anthony Kevin Dungy** (October 6, 1955) is a former professional American football player and coach in the National Football League (NFL). Dungy was head coach of the Tampa Bay Buccaneers from 1996 to 2001, and head coach of the Indianapolis Colts from 2002 to 2008. Dungy became the first African American head coach to win the Super Bowl when his Colts defeated the Chicago Bears in Super Bowl XLI. Dungy set a new NFL record for consecutive playoff appearances by a head coach in 2008 after securing his tenth straight playoff appearance with a win against the Jacksonville Jaguars. Dungy announced his retirement as coach of the Indianapolis Colts on January 12, 2009 following the Colts' loss in the playoffs. The Colts qualified for the playoffs in every season they were coached by Dungy. Since retirement, Dungy has served as an analyst on NBC's *Football Night in America.* He is also the national spokesman for the fatherhood program All Pro Dad. Dungy was elected to the Pro Football Hall of Fame on February 6, 2016.

Venus Williams, born **Venus Ebony Starr Williams** (June 17, 1980) is an American professional tennis player who is currently ranked No. 38 in the WTA singles rankings. She is generally regarded as one of the all-time greats of women's tennis and, along with younger sister Serena Williams, is credited with ushering in a new era of power and athleticism on the women's professional tennis tour. Venus has been ranked world No. 1 by the Women's Tennis Association on three occasions, for a total of 11 weeks. She first reached the No. 1 ranking on February 25, 2002, the first African American woman to do so in the Open Era, and the second all time since Althea Gibson. Williams' seven Grand Slam singles titles are tied for 12th on the all-time list, and 8th on the Open Era list, more than any other active female player except Serena. She has reached 16 Grand Slam finals, most recently at Wimbledon in 2017. She has also won 14 Grand Slam Women's doubles titles, all with Serena; the pair is unbeaten in Grand Slam doubles finals. At the 2018 US Open, Williams extended her record as the all-time leader, male or female, in Grand Slams played, with 80. With her run to the 2017 Wimbledon singles final, she broke the record for longest time between first and most recent grand slam singles finals appearances.

Wilt Chamberlain (August 21, 1936 – October 12, 1999) born **Wilton Norman Chamberlain** was an American basketball player who played center position and is considered one of the most prominent and dominant players in NBA history. He played for the Philadelphia/San Francisco Warriors, the Philadelphia 76ers, and the Los Angeles Lakers of the National Basketball Association (NBA). He played for the University of Kansas and also for the Harlem Globetrotters before playing in the NBA. Chamberlain stood 7 ft 1 in tall, and weighed 250 pounds as a rookie before bulking up to 275 and eventually to over 300 pounds with the Lakers.

ACTORS WHO MAKE THE GRADE ....

Whether performing on stage, in films, or on TV, African Americans have entertained the populace of the United States for centuries. Some, like Sidney Poitier, challenged racial attitudes with his role in popular films like "Guess Who's Coming to Dinner," while others, such as Oprah Winfrey, have expanded upon their careers to become media moguls and cultural icons.

Antonio Fargas, born **Antonio Juan Fargas** (August 14, 1946) is an American actor known for his roles in 1970s blaxploitation movies, His breakout role began in the late 1960s comedy, *Putney Swope*, today a cult film. After starring in a string of blaxploitation movies in the early 1970s, such as his role as Link Brown in the movie *Foxy Brown* and in *Across 110th Street*, he gained recognition as streetwise informant "Huggy Bear" in the mid-1970s television series *Starsky & Hutch*.

Denzel Hayes Washington Jr. (December 28, 1954) is an American actor, director, and producer. He has received three Golden Globe awards, one Tony Award and two Academy Awards: Best Supporting Actor for the historical war drama film *Glory* (1989) and Best Actor for his role as corrupt detective Alonzo Harris in the crime thriller *Training Day* (2001

Dorothy Dandridge (November 9, 1922 – September 8, 1965) born **Dorothy Jean Dandridge** was an American film and theatre actress, singer, and dancer. She is perhaps one of the most famous African-American actresses to have a successful Hollywood career and the first nominated for an Academy Award for Best Actress for her performance in the 1954 film *Carmen Jones*. Dandridge performed as a vocalist in venues such as the Cotton Club and the Apollo Theater. During her early career, she performed as a part of The Wonder Children, later The Dandridge Sisters, and appeared in a succession of films, usually in uncredited roles.

Eddie Murphy (April 3, 1961) was born **Edward Regan Murphy** in Brooklyn, New York, to Lillian (Laney), a telephone operator, and Charles Edward Murphy, a transit police officer who was also an amateur comedian and actor. **Murphy** is an American comedian, actor, screen writer, singer, and film producer. He was a regular cast member on *Saturday Night Live* from 1980 to 1984. He has worked as a stand-up comedian and was ranked #10 on Comedy Central's list of the 100 Greatest Stand-ups of All Time. In films, Murphy has received Golden Globe Award nominations for his performances in *48 Hrs.*, the *Beverly Hills Cop* series, *Trading Places*, and *The Nutty Professor*. In 2007, he won the Golden Globe for Best Supporting Actor and received a nomination for the Academy Award for Best Supporting Actor for his portrayal of soul singer James "Thunder" Early in *Dreamgirls*.

Gabourey Sidibe (May 6, 1983) is an American actress. Sidibe made her acting debut in the 2009 film *Precious*, a role that earned her the Independent Spirit Award for Best Female Lead in addition to nominations for the Golden Globe and Academy Award for Best Actress. Her other film roles include *Tower Heist* (2011), *White Bird in a Blizzard* (2014), and *Grimsby* (2016). From 2010 to 2013, she was a main cast member of the Showtime series *The Big C* and was featured as "Queenie" in the television series *American Horror Story* between 2013 and 2016. Gabourey is currently starring in the Fox musical drama series *Empire* as Becky Williams.

Halle Berry (August 14, 1966) born **Maria Halle Berry,** is an American actress. Berry won the 2002 Academy Award for Best Actress for her performance in the romantic drama *Monster's Ball* (2001). As of 2018, she is the only woman of African-American descent to have won the award.

James Earl Jones (January 17, 1931) is an American actor. His career has spanned more than 60 years, and he has been described as "one of America's most distinguished and versatile" actors and "one of the greatest actors in American history." Since his Broadway debut in 1957, Jones has won many awards, including a Tony Award for his role in *The Great White Hope*, which also earned him a Golden Globe Award and an Academy Award nomination for Best Actor in a Leading Role for the film version of the play. Jones has won three Emmy Awards, including two in the same year in 1990. He is also known for his voice roles as Darth Vader in the *Star Wars* film series and Mufasa in Disney's *The Lion King*, as well as many other film, stage and television roles.

Jamie Foxx (December 13, 1967) was born **Eric Marlon Bishop.** He is an American actor, singer, songwriter, record producer, and comedian. For his portrayal of Ray Charles in the 2004 biographical film *Ray*, he won an Academy Award for Best Actor, BAFTA Award for Best Actor in a Leading Role, and a Golden Globe Award for Best Actor – Motion Picture Musical or Comedy. That same year, he was nominated for the Academy Award for Best Supporting Actor for his role in the crime film *Collateral*. Since spring 2017, Foxx has served as the host and executive producer of the Fox game show *Beat Shazam*

Lena Horne (June 30, 1917 – May 9, 2010) born **Lena Mary Calhoun Horne** was an American singer, dancer, actress, and civil rights activist. Lena's career spanned over 70 years, appearing in film, television, and theater. Lena joined the chorus of the Cotton Club at the age of 16 and became a nightclub performer before moving to Hollywood, where she had small parts in numerous movies, and more substantial parts in the 1943 films *Cabin in the Sky* and *Stormy Weather*. Because of her political activism, Horne found herself blacklisted and unable to get work in Hollywood.

Marla Gibbs (June 14, 1931) born **Margaret Theresa Bradley**, is an American actress, comedian, singer, writer and television producer, whose career spans five decades. Gibbs is known for her role as George Jefferson's maid, Florence Johnston, in the CBS sitcom, *The Jeffersons* (1975–85), for which she received five nominations for Primetime Emmy Award for Outstanding Supporting Actress in a Comedy Series. Gibbs has won a total of seven NAACP Image Awards.

Jackie "Moms" Mabley, born **Loretta Mary Aiken** (March 19, 1894 – May 23, 1975), was an American standup comedian. A veteran of the Chitlin' Circuit of African-American vaudeville, she later appeared on the *Ed Sullivan Show* and *The Smothers Brothers Comedy Hour*. Nonetheless, she persisted for more than sixty years. At the height of her career, she was earning $10,000 a week at Harlem's Apollo Theater. She made her New York City debut at Connie's Inn in Harlem. Mabley was billed as "The Funniest Woman in the World". She tackled topics too edgy for most mainstream comics of the time, including "racism" and "young men."

Morgan Freeman (June 1, 1937) is an American actor, producer, and narrator. Freeman won an Academy Award in 2005 for Best Supporting Actor with *Million Dollar Baby* (2004), and he has received Oscar nominations for his performances in *Street Smart* (1987), *Driving Miss Daisy* (1989), *The Shawshank Redemption* (1994), and *Invictus* (2009). He has also won an Award and a Screen Actors Guild Award.

Mr. T (May 21, 1952) born **Laurence Tureaud** is an American actor, bodyguard, television personality, and retired professional wrestler, known for his roles as B. A. Baracus in the 1980s television series *The A-Team* and as boxer Clubber Lang in the 1982 film *Rocky III*. Mr. T is known for his distinctive hairstyle inspired by warriors of Mandinka nation in West Africa, his gold jewelry, and his tough-guy image.

Redd Foxx, born **John Elroy Sanford** (December 9, 1922 – October 11, 1991), was an American stand-up comedian and actor, best remembered for his explicit comedy records and his starring role on the 1970s sitcom *Sanford and Son*. Foxx gained notoriety with his raunchy nightclub acts during the 1950s and 1960s. Known as the "King of the Party Records," he performed on more than 50 records in his lifetime. He also starred in TV shows *Sanford*, *The Redd Foxx Show* and *The Royal Family*. His film projects included *All the Fine Young Cannibals* (1960), *Cotton Comes to Harlem* (1970), *Norman... Is That You?* (1976) and *Harlem Nights* (1989).

Richard Thomas Pryor (December 1, 1940 – December 10, 2005) born **Richard Franklin Lennox Thomas Pryor** was an American stand-up comedian, actor, and social critic. Pryor was known for uncompromising examinations of racism and topical contemporary issues, which employed vulgarities and profanity, as well as racial epithets. He reached a broad audience and is widely regarded as one of the greatest and most influential stand-up comedians of all time.

Samuel Leroy Jackson (born December 21, 1948) is an American actor and film producer. He achieved prominence and critical acclaim in the early 1990s with films such as *Goodfellas* (1990), *Jungle Fever* (1991), *Patriot Games* (1992), *Amos & Andrew* (1993), *True Romance* (1993), *Jurassic Park* (1993) and his collaborations with director Quentin Tarantino including *Pulp Fiction* (1994), *Jackie Brown*

(1997), *Django Unchained* (2012), and *The Hateful Eight* (2015). He is a highly prolific actor, having appeared in over 100 films.

Sidney Poitier (February 20, 1927) was born in Miami, Florida. After a delinquency-filled youth and a short stint in the U.S. Army, Poitier moved to New York to pursue an acting career. He joined the American Negro Theater and later began finding roles in Hollywood. Following his performance in the 1963 film *Lilies of the Field*, he became the first African-American to win an Academy Award for Best Actor. He also directed several films, including *Buck and the Preacher* and *Stir Crazy*. The acclaimed actor was knighted in 1974 and honored with the Presidential Medal of Freedom in 2009.

DANCERS WHO MAKE THE GRADE ....

W*hat would the world be without the language of the dance?* For centuries dance has brought people together – every ethnicity in every corner of the globe. Dancing is a form of artistic expression as well as sensual, evocative art. The art of dance uses movement to communicate meaning about the human experience. It is far more than exercise or entertainment. It is a powerful medium to express one's values, thoughts, and aspirations about the lives we live and the world in which we live. We find dance in all aspects of culture: in gestures we use every day, in religious ceremony, in mating rituals, in popular culture, in entertainment, in fitness, and in fine art. Here we have featured a few of the world's best dancers who have contributed to our culture.

Alvin Ailey (January 5, 1931 – December 1, 1989) was an African-American choreographer and activist who founded the Alvin Ailey American Dance Theater and the Ailey School in New York City. He is credited with popularizing modern dance and revolutionizing African-American participation in 20th-century concert dance. His company gained the nickname "Cultural Ambassador to the World" because of its extensive international touring. Ailey's choreographic masterpiece *Revelations* is believed to be the best known and most often seen modern dance performance. In 1977, Ailey was awarded the Spingarn Medal from the NAACP. He received the Kennedy Center Honors in 1988. In 2014, President Barack Obama selected Ailey to be a posthumous recipient of the Presidential Medal of Freedom.

Carmen de Lavallade (March 6, 1931) is an American actress, dancer and choreographer. Carmen de Lavallade's career spans sixty years and encompasses all aspects of the performing arts. She has appeared in films and television and on Broadway but is best known for her work in the realm of dance. Considered one of the most beautiful dancers to ever grace the stage, de Lavallade has been described by critics with such terms as completely magical, a goddess, and a living treasure. She has been a muse to choreographers such as Lester Horton, Alvin Ailey, and Donald McKayle, and she is a pioneer who began to change the aesthetics of ballet and who has helped establish a link between contemporary forms of dance and styles from the era of Katherine Dunham and Josephine Baker.

Gregory Hines (February 14, 1946 - August 9, 2003) was born **Gregory Oliver Hines** in New York, New York and died in Los Angeles, California. Hines was an American tap dancer, actor, and choreographer who was a major figure in the revitalization of tap dancing in the late 20th century. By the age of four, Gregory and his older brother Maurice were taking tap lessons with renowned dancer and choreographer Henry Le Tang. The brothers soon formed the Hines Kids, a song-and-dance act that appeared in clubs across the United States. When Gregory was six years old the duo performed at the world-famous Apollo Theater in Harlem, New York.

Judith Jamison (May 10, 1943) was born in Philadelphia, Pennsylvania. She established her own 12-member troupe, the Jamison Project, in 1988. After Ailey's death in 1989, Jamison became artistic director of the Ailey troupe and its school. In doing so, she became the first African American woman to direct a major modern dance company. The recipient of numerous awards, Jamison received a Kennedy Center Honor in 1999 and the National Medal of Arts in 2001. She became the Ailey troupe's artistic director emeritus in 2011.

Josephine Baker (June 3, 1906 – April 12, 1975) born **Freda Josephine McDonald,** was an entertainer, activist, and French Resistance agent. Her career was centered primarily in Europe, mostly in her adopted France. During her early career she was renowned as a dancer and was among the most celebrated performers to headline the revues of the Folies Bergère in Paris. Her performance in the revue Un Vent de Folie in 1927 caused a sensation in Paris. Her costume, consisting of only a girdle of bananas, became her most iconic image and a symbol of the Jazz Age and the 1920s.

Katherine Mary Dunham (June 22, 1909 – May 21, 2006) also known as **Kaye Dunn** was an African American dancer, choreographer, author, educator, and social activist. Dunham had one of the most successful dance careers in African American and European theater of the 20th century and directed her own dance company for many years. She has been called the "matriarch and queen mother of black dance.

Misty Copeland, born **Misty Danielle Copeland** (September 10, 1982) is an American ballet dancer for American Ballet Theatre (ABT), one of the three leading classical ballet companies in the United States.. In 1997, Copeland won the Los Angeles Music Center Spotlight Award as the best dancer in Southern California. After two summer workshops with ABT, she became a member of ABT's Studio Company in 2000 and its corps de ballet in 2001, and became an ABT soloist in 2007. As a soloist from 2007 to mid-2015, she was described as having matured into a more contemporary and sophisticated dancer. On June 30, 2015, Copeland became the first African American woman to be promoted to principal dancer in ABT's 75-year history. In 2015, Misty was named one of the 100 most influential people in the world by *Time* magazine, appearing on its cover

Sammy Davis Jr. (December 8, 1925 – May 16, 1990) born **Samuel George Davis Jr.** was an American singer, musician, dancer, actor, vaudevillian and comedian. He was noted for his impressions of actors, musicians, and other celebrities. At the age of three, Davis began his career in vaudeville with his father, Sammy Davis Sr. and the Will Mastin Trio, which toured nationally. After military service, Davis returned to the trio and became a recording artist. Davis became an overnight sensation following a nightclub performance at Ciro's (in West Hollywood) after the 1951 Academy Awards. In 1954, he lost his left eye in a car accident, and later converted to Judaism, finding commonalities between the oppression experienced by African-American and Jewish communities.

SINGERS AND MUSICIANS
WHO MAKE THE GRADE ....

There would be no jazz music today were it not for the contributions of artists like Miles Davis or Louis Armstrong, who were instrumental in the evolution of this uniquely American music genre. But African Americans have been essential to all aspects of music, from opera singer Marian Anderson, to the Queen of Soul Aretha Franklin, to pop icon Michael Jackson and beyond.

Alicia Keyes (January 25, 1981) was born **Alicia Augello Cook.** She is a 15-time Grammy® Award-winning singer/songwriter/producer, an accomplished actress, a *New York Times* best-selling author, an entrepreneur and a powerful force in the world of philanthropy and in the global fight against HIV and AIDS. Keys became a Coach on NBC's "The Voice" for its 11th season and returned as a Coach on the hit show's 12th season. As a devoted and influential activist, in September 2014, Keys launched We Are Here, a movement that empowers the global community around a host of issues and initiatives building a better world where all people are heard, respected, equal, and treated with dignity. Alicia is also the co-founder of Keep a Child Alive (KCA), a non-profit organization that partners with grass-roots organizations to combat the physical, social, and economic impact of HIV on children, their families and their communities in Africa and India. Keys made her directorial debut for Lifetime's *Five* and most recently served as Executive Producer of the critically-acclaimed film *The Inevitable Defeat of Mister & Pete*. In 2011, she made her producorial debut with Lydia R. Diamond's play *Stick Fly* for the Cort Theater, which Keys also composed the original music for. Keys currently resides in the New York City area with her husband, producer Swizz Beatz, and their children.

Aretha Franklin (March 25, 1942 – August 16, 2018) born **Aretha Louise Franklin** was an American singer, songwriter, civil rights activist, actress, and pianist. Franklin began her career as a child singing gospel at New Bethel Baptist Church in Detroit, Michigan, where her father C. L. Franklin was minister. At the age of 18, she embarked on a secular career recording for Columbia Records. However, she achieved only modest success. She found acclaim and commercial success after signing with Atlantic Records in 1966. Hit songs such as "Respect", "Chain of Fools", "Think", "(You Make Me Feel Like) A Natural Woman", "I Never Loved a Man (The Way I Love You)", and "I Say a Little Prayer", propelled her past her musical peers. By the end of the 1960s, Aretha Franklin had come to be known as "The Queen of Soul."

Berry Gordy, Jr., (born November 28, 1929, Detroit, Michigan, U.S.), American businessman, founder of the Motown Record Corporation (1959), which became the most successful black-owned music company in the United States. Through Motown, he developed the majority of the great rhythm-and-blues (R&B) performers of the 1960s and '70s, including Diana Ross and the Supremes, Smokey Robinson and the Miracles, the Marvelettes, Stevie Wonder, Marvin Gaye, the Temptations, and Michael Jackson and the Jackson Five. Gordy was said to have masterminded the popular "Motown sound," a ballad-based blend of traditional Black harmony and gospel music with the lively beat of R&B. In the early 1970s Gordy relocated the company to Hollywood and began producing films, including *Lady Sings the Blues* (1972), featuring Ross in her film debut as Billie Holiday. By the mid-1980s the company boasted annual revenues in excess of $100 million, and Motown acts had recorded more than 50 number one hits on the *Billboard* pop singles chart. Gordy sold the record company in 1988. He was honored for lifetime achievement at the American Music Awards in 1975, was inducted into the Rock and Roll Hall of Fame in 1988, received the President's Merit Award from the Recording Academy in 2008 and was awarded the National Medal of Arts in 2016.

Big Daddy Kane, born **Antonio Hardy** (September 10, 1968) is a Grammy Award-winning American rapper and actor who started his career in 1986 as a member of the rap collective the Juice Crew. He is widely considered to be one of the most influential and skilled MCs in hip hop. *Rolling Stone* magazine ranked Big Daddy Kane's song "Ain't No Half-Steppin'" #25 on its list of *The 50 Greatest Hip-Hop Songs of All Time*, calling him "a master wordsmith of rap's late-golden age and a huge influence on a generation of MCs."

Biggie Smalls, born **Christopher George Latore Wallace** (May 21, 1972 – March 9, 1997 was an American rapper. He is considered by many to be one of the greatest rappers of all time. In 1996, while recording his second album, Wallace was heavily involved in the growing East Coast–West Coast hip hop feud. He was murdered by an unknown assailant in a drive-by shooting in Los Angeles on March 9, 1997. His second album, *Life After Death* (1997), released sixteen days later, rose to number one on the U.S. album charts. In 2000, it became one of the few hip-hop albums to be certified Diamond.

Billie Holiday (April 7, 1915 – July 17, 1959) born **Eleanora Fagan** , was an American jazz singer with a career spanning nearly thirty years. Nicknamed "**Lady Day**" by her friend and music partner Lester Young, Holiday had a seminal influence on jazz music and pop singing. Her vocal style, strongly inspired by jazz instrumentalists, pioneered a new way of manipulating phrasing and tempo. She was known for her vocal delivery and improvisational skills, which made up for her limited range and lack of formal music education

Chuck Berry (October 18, 1926 – March 18, 2017) born **Charles Edward Anderson Berry** was an American singer, songwriter, and one of the pioneers of rock and roll music. With songs such as "Maybellene" (1955), "Roll Over Beethoven" (1956), "Rock and Roll Music" (1957) and "Johnny B. Goode" (1958), Berry refined and developed rhythm and blues into the major elements that made rock and roll distinctive. Writing lyrics that focused on teen life and consumerism, and developing a music style that included guitar solos and showmanship, Berry was a major influence on subsequent rock music.

Chuck D, born **Carlton Douglas Ridenhour** (August 1, 1960), is an American rapper, author, and producer. As the leader of the rap group Public Enemy, he helped create politically and socially conscious hip hop music in the mid-1980s. *The Source* ranked him at No. 12 on their list of the Top 50 Hip-Hop Lyricists of All Time.

Cuba Gooding Sr. (April 27, 1944 – April 20, 2017) was an American singer and actor. He was the most successful lead singer of the soul group The Main Ingredient, replacing former lead singer Donald McPherson who died unexpectedly of leukemia in 1971. According to *Billboard*, as the lead vocalist he scored five top 10 hits most notably, "Everybody Plays the Fool" (1972), peaking at No. 2 for three weeks, and peaking at No. 3 on *Billboard*'s all-genre Hot-100 list. "Just Don't Want to Be Lonely" (1974), "Happiness Is Just Around the Bend" and "Rolling Down a Mountainside" were also top 10 hits on *Billboard* charts.

DJ Kool Herc, born **Clive Campbell** (born April 16, 1955), is a Jamaican–American DJ who is credited with helping originate hip hop music in The Bronx, New York City, in the 1970s. Known as the "Founder of Hip-Hop" and "Father of Hip-Hop", Campbell began playing hard funk records of the sort typified by James Brown as an alternative, both to the violent gang culture of the Bronx and to the nascent popularity of disco in the 1970s.

Diana Ross (March 26, 1944) is an American singer, actress, and record producer. Born and raised in Detroit, Michigan, Ross rose to fame as the lead singer of the vocal group the Supremes, which, during the 1960s, became Motown's most successful act, and are the best charting girl group in US history, as well as one of the world's best-selling girl groups of all time. The group released a record-setting twelve number-one hit singles on the US *Billboard* Hot 100, including "Where Did Our Love Go", "Baby Love", "Come See About Me", "Stop! In the Name of Love", "You Can't Hurry Love", "You Keep Me Hangin' On", "Love Child", and "Someday We'll Be Together.

Dizzy Gillespie (October 21, 1917 - January 6, 1993) was born **John Birks Gillespie** in Cheraw, South Carolina and died in Englewood, New Jersey. Dizzy was an American jazz trumpeter, composer, and bandleader who was one of the seminal figures of the bebop movement. He was a trumpet virtuoso and improviser, building on the virtuoso style of Roy Eldridge' but adding layers of harmonic and rhythmic complexity previously unheard in jazz. In the 1940s Gillespie, with Charlie Parker, became a major figure in the development of bebop and modern jazz.

Donna Summer, born **LaDonna Adrian Gaines** (December 31, 1948 – May 17, 2012) was an American singer, songwriter and actress. She gained prominence during the disco era of the late 1970s. A five-time Grammy Award winner, Summer was the first artist to have three consecutive double albums reach number one on the United States *Billboard* 200 chart and charted four number-one singles in the US within a 12-month period. Summer has reportedly sold over 100 million records worldwide, making her one of the world's best-selling artists of all time. She also charted two number-one singles on the Hot

R&B/Hip-Hop Songs chart in the US and a number-one single in the United Kingdom. Summer returned to the United States in 1975, and she recorded hits such as "Last Dance", "MacArthur Park", "Heaven Knows", "Hot Stuff", "Bad Girls", "Dim All the Lights", and "On the Radio." She became known as the Queen of Disco, while her music gained a global following. Summer died on May 17, 2012, from lung cancer, at her home in Naples, Florida.

Doug E. Fresh, born **Douglas Davis,** (born September 17, 1966), is a Barbadian-American rapper, record producer and beatboxer, also known as the "Human Beat Box." The pioneer of 20th-century American beatboxing, Fresh is able to accurately imitate drum machines and various special effects using only his mouth, lips, gums, throat, tongue and a microphone.

Duke Ellington, born **Edward Kennedy Ellington** (April 29, 1899 – May 24, 1974) was an American composer, pianist, and leader of a jazz orchestra, which he led from 1923 until his death over a career spanning more than fifty years. Born in Washington, D.C., Ellington was based in New York City from the mid-1920s onward and gained a national profile through his orchestra's appearances at the Cotton Club in Harlem. In the 1930s, his orchestra toured in Europe. Although widely considered to have been a pivotal figure in the history of jazz, Ellington embraced the phrase "beyond category" as a liberating principle and referred to his music as part of the more general category of American Music rather than to a musical genre such as jazz.

Funkmaster Flex, born **Aston George Taylor Jr.** (August 5, 1967), is an American disc jockey, rapper, record producer, actor, and host on New York City's Hot 97 radio station. In 1992, he became host of the first hip hop radio show on Hot 97 in New York, which was a pop radio station at the time. By the mid-1990s, Flex was signed by a major record label, Loud Records, for a series of mixtapes entitled *60*

Minutes of Funk. All four were certified gold by the RIAA in the US. In 1995 he formed The Flip Squad along with seven of New York City's most respected disc jockeys, including Biz Markie, "BounceMasta" Doo Wop, Big Kap, DJ Enuff, Mister Cee, Frankie Cutlass, DJ Riz, Cipha Sounds and Mark Ronson. Their self-titled debut LP was released on MCA in late 1998. In 1999, he released The Tunnel with Def Jam, which included songs by artists Dr. Dre, Jay-Z, Eminem, LL Cool J, DJ Myth, Method Man, DMX, Nas and Snoop Dogg.

Gladys Maria Knight, born **Gladys Maria Knight** (May 28, 1944), known as the "Empress of Soul," is an American singer, songwriter, actress, businesswoman and author. A seven-time Grammy Award-winner, Knight is best known for the hits she recorded during the 1960s, 1970s, and 1980s with her group Gladys Knight & the Pips, which included her brother Merald "Bubba" Knight and her cousins Edward Patten and William Guest. Knight has recorded two number-one Billboard Hot 100 singles ("Midnight Train to Georgia" and "That's What Friends Are For"), eleven number-one R&B singles, and six number-one R&B albums. She has won seven Grammy Awards and is an inductee into the Rock and Roll Hall of Fame along with The Pips. She also recorded the theme song for the 1989 James Bond film *License To Kill.* Knight is also listed as one of *Rolling Stone* magazine's 100 Greatest Singers of All Time.

Harry Belafonte (born **Harold George Bellanfanti Jr.** (March 1, 1927) is an American singer, songwriter, activist and actor. One of the most successful Jamaican-American pop stars in history, he was dubbed the "King of Calypso" for popularizing the Caribbean musical style (originating in Trinidad & Tobago) with an international audience in the 1950s. His breakthrough album *Calypso* (1956) is the first million-selling LP by a single artist. Belafonte is perhaps best known for singing "The Banana Boat Song", with its signature lyric

"Day-O". He has recorded in many genres, including blues, folk, gospel, show tunes, and American standards. He has also starred in several films, most notably in Otto Preminger's hit musical *Carmen Jones* (1954), *Island in the Sun* (1957), and Robert Wise's *Odds Against Tomorrow* (1959).

Ice Cube, born **O'Shea Jackson Sr.** (born June 15, 1969), is an American rapper, writer and actor. Ice Cube initially gained recognition as a member of the hip hop group C.I.A. in 1984, which disbanded three years later. Ice Cube, alongside Dr. Dre and Eazy E, then formed the group N.W.A, where he gained extreme notoriety as the group's primary songwriter and performer, noted for becoming one of the founding artists of gangsta rap. Ice Cube transitioned into film, where his popularity was further enhanced by his starring role in *Boyz n the Hood* (1991), followed by several other films performance which he acted in and produced. As a businessman, Ice Cube has founded his clothing line, Solo by Cube, as well as the 3 on 3 basketball league BIG3, which predominately features retired NBA players.

Ice T, born **Tracy Lauren Marrow** (February 16, 1958), is an American musician, rapper, songwriter, actor, record producer, record executive and author. He began his career as an underground rapper in the 1980s and was signed to Sire Records in 1987, when he released his debut album *Rhyme Pays*. The following year, he founded the record label Rhyme $yndicate Records and released another album, *Power*, which went on to go Platinum. He co-founded the heavy metal band Body Count, which he introduced on his 1991 rap album *O.G.: Original Gangster*, In 1992. Ice-T encountered controversy over his track "Cop Killer", and asked to be released from his contract with Warner Bros. Records. Since 2000, he has portrayed NYPD Detective/Sergeant Odafin Tutuola on the NBC police drama *Law & Order: Special Victims Unit*.

James Brown, born **James Joseph Brown** (May 3, 1933 – December 25, 2006) was an American singer-songwriter, dancer, musician, record producer and bandleader. A progenitor of funk music and a major figure of 20th-century music and dance, he is often referred to as the "Godfather of Soul." In a career that lasted 50 years, he influenced the development of several music genres. Brown recorded 17 singles that reached number one on the *Billboard* R&B charts. He also holds the record for the most singles listed on the *Billboard* Hot 100 chart which did not reach number one. Brown has received honors from many institutions, including inductions into the Rock and Roll Hall of Fame and Songwriters Hall of Fame.

Jimi Hendrix (November 27th, 1942 – September 18, 1970) born Johnny Allen Hendrix, was an American rock guitarist, singer, and songwriter, widely recognized as one of the most creative and influential musicians of the 20th century. Jimi Hendrix pioneered the explosive possibilities of the electric guitar. Hendrix's innovative style of combining fuzz, feedback and controlled distortion created a new musical form. Because he was unable to read or write music, it is nothing short of remarkable that Jimi Hendrix's meteoric rise in the music took place in just four short years. His musical language continues to influence a host of modern musicians. Hendrix is widely regarded as one of the most influential electric guitarists in the history of popular music, and one of the most celebrated musicians of the 20th century. The Rock and Roll Hall of Fame describes him as "arguably the greatest instrumentalist in the history of rock music.

John Cheatdom (July 7, 1938), is a Doo Wop master. John originally came from the Bedford-Stuyvesant area of Brooklyn along with Jerome "Romeo" Ramos, Marvin Holland and Sammy Gardner where they formed **"The Velours"**, an American R&B vocal group and had two hits in the US in the late 1950s, "Can I Come Over Tonight" and "Remember". They relocated to England in the late 1960s, changed their name to "The Fantastics", and had a top ten hit in the UK in 1971 with "Something Old, Something New". Remaining in England, John formed "The Realistics" in 1976. The group broke up in 1983, when John then joined various unofficial line-ups of "The Platters", aka "The Magic Platters", who toured internationally. John is still performing live today and has just released his autobiography 'Keeping Doo Wop Alive, One Man's Story of Strength, Stamina and Survival as an International Entertainer."

Kurtis Blow born Kurtis Walker (August 9, 1959), is an American rapper, singer, songwriter, record/film producer, b-boy, DJ, public speaker and minister. He is the first commercially successful rapper and the first to sign with a major record label. "The Breaks," a single from his 1980 self-titled debut album, is the first certified gold record rap song for Hip Hop. Throughout his career he has released 15 albums and is currently an ordained minister.

Louie Armstrong (August 4, 1901 – July 6, 1971) nicknamed "Satchmo," "Pops" and, later, "Ambassador Satch," was born Louis Daniel Armstrong in 1901 in New Orleans, Louisiana. An all-star virtuoso, he came to prominence in the 1920s, influencing countless musicians with both his daring trumpet style and unique vocals. Armstrong was an American trumpeter, composer, vocalist and occasional actor and comedian, who was one of the most influential artists in jazz history. Known for songs like "Star Dust," "La Vie En Rose" and "What a Wonderful World," Armstrong's career spanned five decades, from the 1920s to the 1960s. In 2017, he was inducted into the Rhythm & Blues Hall of Fame.

Luther Vandross, born **Luther Ronzoni Vandross Jr.** (April 20, 1951 – July 1, 2005) was an American singer, songwriter and record producer. Throughout his career, Vandross was an in-demand background vocalist for several different artists including Todd

Rundgren, Judy Collins, Chaka Khan, Bette Midler, Diana Ross, David Bowie, Barbra Streisand, Ben E. King, and Donna Summer. He later became a lead singer of the group Change, which released its gold-certified debut album, *The Glow of Love*, in 1980 on Warner Bros. Records. After Vandross left the group, he was signed to Epic Records as a solo artist and released his debut solo album, *Never Too Much*, in 1981. During his career, Vandross sold over 35 million records worldwide, and received eight Grammy Awards including Best Male R&B Vocal Performance four different times. He won a total of four Grammy Awards in 2004 including the Grammy Award for Song of the Year for a song recorded not long before his death, "Dance with My Father."

Mahalia Jackson; (October 26, 1911 – January 27, 1972) was an American gospel singer. Possessing a powerful contralto voice, she was referred to as "The Queen of Gospel". Mahalia became one of the most influential gospel singers in the world and was heralded internationally as a singer and civil rights activist. She was described by entertainer Harry Belafonte as "the single most powerful Black woman in the United States" Mahalia recorded about 30 albums (mostly for Columbia Records) during her career, and her 45 rpm records included a dozen "golds"—million-sellers.

Marian Anderson (February 27, 1897 – April 8, 1993) was an American singer. She was one of the most celebrated singers of the twentieth century. Music critic Alan Blyth said: "Her voice was a rich, vibrant contralto of intrinsic beauty." Most of her singing career was spent performing in concert and recital in major music venues and with famous orchestras throughout the United States and Europe between 1925 and 1965. She made many recordings that reflected her broad performance repertoire of everything from concert literature to opera to traditional American songs and spirituals.

Maurice Starr (1953) born **Larry Curtis Johnson,** is an American musician, songwriter, and record producer. He is best known for his work creating songs and albums with pop and soul bands such as Con Funk Shun, New Edition, and the New Kids on the Block In 1982, Starr discovered the band New Edition on his talent show. He co-wrote and co-produced their debut album with the hits, "Candy Girl", "Is This The End", and "Popcorn Love". Subsequent to the album's success, creative differences resulted in Starr and New Edition parting ways. The group continued to produce a number of U.S. Top 10 R&B hit singles throughout the '80s. In 1984, Starr created New Kids on the Block, a band consisting of five male teenagers, brothers Jordan Knight and Jonathan Knight, with Danny Wood, Donnie Wahlberg and Joey McIntyre. By 1989, New Kids on The Block was the fastest-rising act in the United States. Starr's biography is chronicled in Tony Rose's book "Before the Legend: The Rise of New Kids on the Block and a Guy Named Maurice Starr (The Early Years)" published by Colossus Books.

Michael Jackson, born **Michael Joseph Jackson** (August 29, 1958 – June 25, 2009) was an American singer, songwriter and dancer. Dubbed the "King of Pop", he is regarded as one of the most significant cultural icons of the 20th century and is also regarded as one of the greatest entertainers of all time. As a child, Jackson became the lead singer of his family's popular Motown group, the Jackson 5. Michael Jackson enjoyed a chart-topping career both with the Jackson 5 and as a solo artist. He went on to a solo career of astonishing worldwide success, delivering No. 1 hits from the albums *Off the Wall*, and *Bad,* and he released the best-selling album in history, 'Thriller,' in 1982. Jackson's contributions to music, dance, and fashion, along with his publicized personal life, made him a global figure in popular culture for over four decades.

Miles Davis (May 26, 1926 – September 28, 1991) born Miles Dewey Davis III was an American jazz trumpeter, bandleader, and composer. Instrumental in the development of jazz, Miles Davis is considered one of the top musicians of his era. Born in Illinois in 1926, he traveled at age 18 to New York City to pursue music. He is among the most influential and acclaimed figures in the history of jazz and 20th century music. Throughout his life, He adopted a variety of musical directions in a five-decade career that kept him at the forefront of many major stylistic developments in jazz and was at the helm of a changing concept of jazz. The winner of eight Grammy awards, Miles Davis died in 1991 from respiratory distress in Santa Monica, California.

Nat King Cole (March 17, 1919 – February 15, 1965) was born **Nathaniel Adams Cole** in Montgomery, Alabama and died in Santa Monica, California. Cole was an American jazz pianist and vocalist, who recorded over one hundred songs that became hits on the pop charts. His trio was the model for small jazz ensembles that followed. Cole also acted in films and on television and performed on Broadway. He was the first Black man to host an American television series. Cole was hailed as one of the best and most influential pianists and small-group leaders of the swing era. He attained his greatest commercial success, however, as a vocalist specializing in warm ballads and light swing.

Queen Latifah (March 18, 1970) whose birthname is **Dana Elaine Owens** was born in Newark, New Jersey. She is an American rapper, songwriter, singer, actress, and producer. Queen Latifah signed with Tommy Boy Records in 1989 and released her debut album *All Hail the Queen* the same year, featuring the hit single "Ladies First". *Nature of a Sista* (1991) was her second and final album with Tommy Boy Records. She has long been considered one of hip-hop's pioneer feminists. Queen Latifah received a star on the Hollywood Walk of Fame in 2006. Her work in music, film and television has earned her a Grammy Award, an Emmy Award, a Golden Globe Award, three Screen Actors Guild Awards, two NAACP Image Awards, an Academy Award nomination and sales of over two million records.

Ray Charles (September 23, 1930 - June 10, 2004) was born **Ray Charles Robinson** in Albany, Georgia and died in Beverly Hills, California. Charles, a pianist, singer, composer, and bandleader, was a leading Black entertainer billed as "the Genius." Charles was credited with the early development of soul music, a style based on a coming together of gospel, rhythm and blues, and jazz music. Ray Charles was the musician most responsible for developing soul music. devising a new form of Black pop by merging '50s R&B with gospel-powered vocals.

Renee Minus White is one of the original member of **The Chantels**, the famed female rhythm and blues group. The Chantels rocked the world and the music industry during the late 1950s with hits including "Maybe," "He's Gone," "The Plea," "I Love You So," and "Look In My Eyes" and many other chart toppers. Renee grew up in the Bronx during the 1950s. Her father, Leroy Minus, was a jazz pianist who fell in love and married Thelma Minus, a jazz singer. Both parents retired their show business careers to raise their seven children. Renee attended St. Anthony of Padua's Grammar School. White met four young girls, Arlene Smith, Jackie Landry, Millicent Goring and Lois Harris. The girls became good friends and formed The Chantels. Decades later, The Chantels are still singing and entertaining audiences throughout the country.

Robert Leroy Johnson (May 8, 1911 – August 16, 1938) was an American blues singer-songwriter and musician. His landmark recordings in 1936 and 1937 display a combination of singing, guitar skills, and songwriting talent that has influenced later generations of musicians.

As an itinerant performer who played mostly on street corners, in juke joints, and at Saturday night dances, Johnson had little commercial success or public recognition in his lifetime. But, after the reissue of his recordings in 1961, on the LP *King of the Delta Blues Singers,* his work reached a wider audience. Johnson is now recognized as a master of the blues, particularly of the Mississippi Delta blues style. He is credited by many rock musicians as an important influence. Johnson was inducted into the Rock and Roll Hall of Fame in its first induction ceremony, in 1986, as an early influence on rock and roll. In 2003, David Fricke ranked Johnson fifth in *Rolling Stone* magazine's "100 Greatest Guitarists of All Time."

Stevie Wonder (May 13, 1950) born Stevland Hardaway Morris is an American singer, songwriter, musician, record producer, and multi-instrumentalist. A child prodigy, Wonder is considered to be one of the most critically and commercially successful musical performers of the late 20th century. Wonder signed with Motown's Tamla label at the age of 11, and he continued performing and recording for Motown into the 2010s. He has been blind since shortly after his birth. Among Wonder's works are singles such as "Signed, Sealed, Delivered I'm Yours," "Superstition," "Sir Duke," "You Are the Sunshine of My Life," and "I Just Called to Say I Love You," and albums such as *Talking Book, Innervisions*, and *Songs in the Key of Life.* He has recorded more than 30 U.S. top ten hits and received 25 Grammy Awards, one of the most-awarded male solo artists, and has sold over 100 million records worldwide, making him one of the top 60 best-selling music artists. Wonder is also noted for his work as an activist for political causes, including his 1980 campaign to make Martin Luther King Jr.'s birthday a holiday in the United States. In 2009, Wonder was named a United Nations Messenger of Peace. In 2013, *Billboard* magazine released a list of the *Billboard Hot* 100 All-Time Top Artists to celebrate the US singles chart's 55th anniversary, with Wonder at number six.

Tupac Shakur, born **Lesane Parish Crooks**, (June 16, 1971 – September 13, 1996), also known by his stage names **2Pac** and **Makaveli,** he was an American rapper and actor. Shakur is one of the best-selling music artists of all time having sold over 75 million records worldwide. Much of Shakur's work has been noted for addressing contemporary social issues that plagued inner cities, and he is considered a symbol of resistance and activism against inequitie. Shakur lived with Kidada Jones, his fiancée, daughter of Quincy Jones and actress Peggy Lipton, for several months until his death. Jones was waiting for Shakur in their Las Vegas hotel room when she was notified that he was shot. She rushed to the hospital and remained with him until he died from his injuries six days later.

AUTHORS WHO MAKE THE GRADE ....

No survey of American literature would be complete without major contributions from Black writers. Books like Ralph Ellison's "Invisible Man" and "Beloved" by Toni Morrison are masterpieces of fiction, while Maya Angelou and Alex Haley have made major contributions to literature, poetry, autobiography, and history.

Alex Haley (1921-1992) was best known for works depicting the struggles of African Americans. Raised in Henning, Tennessee, he began writing to help pass the time during his two decades with the U.S. Coast Guard. After conducting interviews with Malcolm X for Playboy magazine, he turned the material into his first book, "The Autobiography of Malcolm X" (1965). Haley's subsequent novel, "Roots" (1976), was a fictionalized account of his own family's history, traced through seven generations. It was adapted into a 1977 miniseries that became the most-watched broadcast in TV history, a record it would hold for years.

Alice Walker (February 9, 1944) is an American novelist, short story writer, poet, and activist. She wrote the novel *The Color Purple* (1982), for which she won the National Book Award for hardcover fiction, and the Pulitzer Prize for Fiction. She also wrote the novels *Meridian* (1976) and *The Third Life of Grange Copeland* (1970), among other works. An avowed feminist, Walker coined the term "womanist" to mean "A black feminist or feminist of color" in 1983.

Camille Yarbrough (January 8, 1938) is an American musician, actress, poet, activist, television producer, and author. Camille was born in 1938 and raised in the South Side of Chicago. She was the seventh and youngest child in her family. She is best known for "Take Yo' Praise", which Fatboy Slim sampled in his track "Praise You" in 1998. "Take Yo' Praise" was originally recorded in 1975 for Yarbrough's first album, *The Iron Pot Cooker*, released on Vanguard Records. The album was based on the 1971 stage dramatization of Yarbrough's one-woman, spoken word show, *Tales and Tunes of an African American Griot*. She toured nationally with this show during the 1970s and 1980s. Yarbrough's second album, *Ancestor House*, is a spoken word/soul/blues album that she released on her own record label, Maat Music, in 2003. *Ancestor House* was recorded live at Joe's Pub in New York City. *Tales and Tunes of an African American Griot* was produced at La MaMa Experimental Theatre Club in the East Village of Manhattan in 1973. Journalist Kevin Powell wrote, regarding her first album: "Without question, *The Iron Pot Cooker* is a precursor to Lauryn Hill's best-seller *The Mis-Education of Lauryn Hill*." Other reviews of this album include Billboard: "Yarbrough has stylish traces of Nina Simone and Gil Scott-Heron but her own style of singing and recitation... are outstanding. Her songs are all thought provoking" and SPIN: "Nana Camille is a 'hip-hop foremother'" Camille Yarbrough currently resides in New York City.

Henry Louis Gates, Jr., (September 16, 1950) is an American literary critic, teacher, historian, filmmaker and public intellectual who currently serves as the Alphonse Fletcher University Professor and Director of the Hutchins Center for African and African American Research at Harvard University and the director of the W. E. B. Du Bois Institute for African and African American Research at Harvard University. He is editor in chief of the Oxford African American Studies Center and of the daily online magazine *The Root*. He has received more than forty honorary degrees from institutions the world over. In 2010, Gates wrote an op-ed in *The New York Times* that discussed the role played by Africans in the slave trade. In an article for *Newsweek*, which begins and ends with the observation that it is very difficult to decide whether or not to give reparations to the descendants of American slaves, whether they should receive compensation for their ancestors' unpaid labor and lack of rights.

Iyanla Vanzant, born **Rhonda Eva Harris** (September 13, 1953) is an American inspirational speaker, lawyer, New Thought spiritual teacher, author, life coach and television personality. She is known primarily for her books, her eponymous talk show, and her appearances on *The Oprah Winfrey Show*. She can currently be seen on television as the host of *Iyanla: Fix My Life*, on OWN: Oprah Winfrey Network.

James Baldwin (August 2, 1924 – December 1, 1987), born James Arthur Baldwin established his reputation with his first novel, *Go Tell It on The Mountain* (1953), an autobiographical tale of growing up in Harlem. James Baldwin's also wrote the novel *if Beale Street Could Talk,* which became a 2018 American romantic drama film directed and written by Barry Jenkins *and was* released in the United States on December 14, 2018 by Annapurna Pictures. The film received numerous accolades and nominations, including winning Best Supporting Actress for Regina King at the 76th Golden Globe Awards, Baldwin became one of the leading African-American authors of his generation, known for novels and essays that tackled black-white and hetero-homosexual relationships. He was particularly a noted essayist during the Civil Rights movement of the 1960s.

Jewell Parker Rhodes (1954) born in Pittsburgh, Pennsylvania, is an American bestselling novelist and educator. Rhodes is the author of five middle grade novels, including the New York Times bestseller and #1 Kids' Indie Best Pick *Ghost Boys*, as well as *Towers Falling*, *Ninth Ward*, *Sugar*, and *Bayou Magic*. Rhodes has published six novels for adults, including *Voodoo Dreams*, the Marie Laveau trilogy, and the American Book Award winner *Douglass' Women*, as well as two writing guides and a memoir. Rhodes is the Founding Artistic Director and the Piper Endowed Chair of the Virginia G. Piper Center for Creative Writing at Arizona State University. She is also a professor of Creative Writing and American Literature and the former Director of the Master of Fine Arts Program in Creative Writing.

Langston Hughes (February 1, 1902 – May 22, 1967) was an American poet, born James Mercer **Langston Hughes.** He published more than three dozen books during his life, starting out with poetry and then expanding into novels, short stories, and plays. He is closely associated with the Harlem Renaissance, the flowering of African-American literature and music in New York City following World War One, but he wrote poetry, books, and newspaper columns right through into the 1960s. Hughes's work often spoke plainly about the lives of ordinary black people, which in later years earned him a reputation as one of the major black voices of the 1900s.

Lerone Bennett Jr., (October 17, 1928 – February 14, 2018) was a historian and journalist who wrote extensively on race relations and black history and was a top editor at Ebony magazine for decades. Mr. Bennett was both lyrical and outspoken in his writing, arguing that the history of Black people in the United States had been ignored or told only through a white filter. His best-known book was "Before the Mayflower," drawn from a series of articles for Ebony and first published in 1962. (Revised editions were still being published decades later.) In it he noted that the first Blacks arrived in the colonies in 1619, the year before the Mayflower did, on a ship that reached Jamestown, Virginia. He wrote of that same arrival in a 1992 article in Ebony.

Maya Angelou (April 4, 1928 - May 28, 2014) named **Marguerite Annie Johnson** was born in St. Louis, Missouri and died in Winston-

Salem, North Carolina. Maya was an American poet, author, historian, songwriter, playwright, dancer, stage and screen producer, director, performer, singer, and civil rights activist, best known for her seven autobiographical books which explore the themes of economic, racial, and sexual oppression. In 1993, Angelou wrote and delivered a poem, "On the Pulse of the Morning," at the inauguration for President Bill Clinton at his request. In 2000, she received the National Medal of Arts, and in 2010 she was awarded the Presidential Medal of Freedom by President Barack Obama.

Nikki Giovanni (June 7, 1943) is one of America's foremost poets. Over the course of a long career, Giovanni has published numerous collections of poetry—from her first self-published volume *Black Feeling Black Talk* (1968) to *New York Times* best-seller *Bicycles: Love Poems* (2009)—several works of nonfiction and children's literature, and multiple recordings, including the Emmy-award nominated *The Nikki Giovanni Poetry Collection* (2004). Her most recent publications include *Chasing Utopia: A Hybrid* (2013) and, as editor, *The 100 Best African American Poems* (2010). A frequent lecturer and reader, Giovanni has taught at Rutgers University, Ohio State University, and Virginia Tech, where she is a University Distinguished Professor.

Phillis Wheatley (1753 – December 5, 1784) although she was an African slave, was the first published African-American female poet and one of the best-known poets in pre-19th century America. Born in West Africa, she was sold into slavery at the age of seven or eight and transported to North America. She was purchased by the Wheatley family of Boston, who taught her to read and write and encouraged her poetry when they saw her talent. Educated and enslaved in the household of prominent Boston commercialist John Wheatley. Phillis was the abolitionists' illustrative testimony that blacks could be both artistic and intellectual. Her name was a household word among literate colonists and her achievements a catalyst for the fledgling antislavery movement.

Ralph Ellison (March 1, 1913 – April 16, 1994) was a scholar and writer. He was born Ralph Waldo Ellison in Oklahoma City, Oklahoma, named by his father after Ralph Waldo Emerson. Ellison was best known for his novel *Invisible Man*, which won the National Book Award in 1953. He also wrote *Shadow and Act* (1964), a collection of political, social and critical essays, and *Going to the Territory* (1986). For *The New York Times*, the best of these essays in addition to the novel put him "among the gods of America's literary Parnassus." A posthumous novel, *Juneteenth*, was published after being assembled from voluminous notes he left after his death.

Richard Wright (September 4, 1908.- November 25, 1960) was born **Richard Nathan Wright** in Natchez, Mississippi and died in Paris, France. The works of Richard Wright include a 1940 novel *Native Son* which was a best-seller and is still considered a classic of modern American literature. One of the most influential African-American writers of the 20th century, Wright grew up in Mississippi and Tennessee, then ended up in Chicago at the age of 19. Self-educated, he turned to writing poetry and short stories. He received critical attention for his first book, *Uncle Tom's Children* (1938). After World War II, Wright, disillusioned with race relations in the U.S., settled permanently in France. His other works include *Black Boy* (1945), *The Outsider* (1953) and a posthumously published collection of stories, *Eight Men* (1960).

Zora Neale Hurston (January 7 1891 – January 28, 1960) was born in Notasulga, Alabama, Zora became a fixture of New York City's Harlem Renaissance. The Harlem newcomer turned heads and raised eyebrows as she claimed four awards: a second-place fiction prize for her short story "Spunk," a second-place award in drama for her play

Color Struck, and two honorable mentions. Upon receiving a Guggenheim fellowship, Hurston traveled to Haiti and wrote what would become her most famous work: *Their Eyes Were Watching God* (1937). The novel tells the story of Janie Mae Crawford, who learns the value of self-reliance through multiple marriages and tragedy. She was also an outstanding folklorist and anthropologist who recorded cultural history, as illustrated by her *Mules and Men*. Hurston died in poverty in 1960, before a revival of interest led to posthumous recognition of her accomplishments.

PUBLISHERS WHO MAKE THE GRADE ....

While African-American publishers have been active in the United States   Black-owned newspaper and magazine publishers and presses have long been a part of the American publishing industry. However, the 1960s, 1970s, 1980s and 1990s especially saw a massive boom in black-owned book publishers, with presses—both general and specialized—springing up in cities across the country. Though many of these small, independent, black-owned newspaper publishing houses have since ceased to operate, some are still thriving today. We have featured just a few of those publishers in this section.

Alain Leroy Locke (September 13, 1885 – June 9, 1954) was an American writer, philosopher, educator, and patron of the arts. Distinguished as the first African-American Rhodes Scholar in 1907, Locke was the philosophical architect —the acknowledged "Dean"— of the Harlem Renaissance. *The New Negro* was published in 1925 and had a significant impact on the dialogue of Black cultural achievements, which brought him national recognition. In *The New Negro*, Locke examined the famous Harlem Renaissance for the general reading public. It also became a platform where he attacked the legacy of European supremacy by pointing out the great achievements of Africans. The publication of the book and its acclaim would place Locke at the forefront of "The New Negro Movement." As a result, popular listings of influential African Americans have repeatedly included him. On March 19, 1968, the Rev. Dr. Martin Luther King, Jr. proclaimed: "We're going to let our children know that the only philosophers that lived were not Plato and Aristotle, but W. E. B. Du Bois and Alain Locke came through the universe."

Carl Weber is president, CEO and Publisher of Urban Books LLC, the largest African American owned urban genre publishing companies in the world. Weber, a New York Times bestselling author has personally written and published over twenty novels. He has also branched out into screen writing and has written and produced three of his bestselling novels; *The Man in 3B*, *The Preacher's Son*, and *The Choir Director* into independent films with his production company, Urban Books Media LLC. Weber ran the Urban Knowledge chain of bookstores. Weber is a graduate of Virginia State University and holds an MBA in marketing from University of Virginia.

Cloves C. Campbell, Jr., is the Publisher of the **Arizona Informant**. It all started in 1971 when two brothers "Cloves C. Campbell, Sr., and Dr. Charles R. Campbell realized there was something missing in Arizona. The family-owned and operated newspaper continues to provide an important voice for the African-American community in Arizona. Currently, Cloves Campbell, Jr. serves as Board Chair of the National Newspaper Publishers' Association (NNPA). He served in the State House of Representatives for District 16 from 2007-2010 fulfilling duties on the Appropriations, Banking and Insurance, and House Ethics committees. With an extensive background in marketing communications, media/public relations and advertising sales, Cloves has also lent his expertise as Vice-Chair of Arizona African-American Democratic Caucus as well as being a board member of several organizations.

Cynthia Horner was named Publisher of **Right On magazine,** which was purchased by the owners of Word Up. The magazine provides expertise in the young adult entertainment field, which includes editorial responsibilities at Word Up! Publications. Cynthia is a writer, magazine editor, and entertainment industry entrepreneur. Her Independent Production Services (Cinnamon CHIPS), based in New York City, is a media relations company under which she spearheads public relations projects, particularly in the non-profit sector, literary projects for herself and others, artist development, marketing and writing/editing projects for teen and adult music and general interest publications.

Earl Gilbert Graves Sr. is an American entrepreneur, publisher, businessman, philanthropist, and advocate of African-American businesses. A graduate of Morgan State University, he is the founder of *Black Enterprise* magazine and chairman of the media company Earl G. Graves, Ltd. In August 1970, the first issue of *Black Enterprise* magazine hit newsstands. Earl G. Graves, Ltd. grew to include a number of divisions including publishing, marketing, radio, television and event coordinating arms. The firm is the co-owner of the private equity fund Black Enterprise Greenwich Street Corporate Growth Fund, an equity partnership formed with Travelers Group, Inc., which aims to invest and promote minority operated businesses.

Haki R. Madhubuti is the founder, publisher, and chairman of the board of **Third World Press** (established in 1967), which today is the largest and oldest independent publisher of Black thought and literature in the country. Madhubuti (then known as Don Luther Lee), with early support from Johari Amini and Carolyn Rodgers, launched Third World Press Foundation from his basement apartment on the South Side of Chicago. With Madhubuti's $400 honorarium received from a poetry reading, a used mimeograph machine, and individuals committed to the local and national Black Arts and empowerment movements, the Press produced its first publications. Madhubuti is a much sought-after poet and lecturer, and has convened workshops and served as guest/keynote speaker at thousands of colleges, universities, libraries and community centers in the U.S. and abroad.

John Harold Johnson (January 19, 1918 – August 8, 2005) was an American businessman and publisher. He was the founder of the **Johnson Publishing Company**. In 1982, he became the first African American to appear on the Forbes 400. Johnson's *Ebony* (founded 1945) and *Jet* (founded 1951) magazines were among the most influential African-American businesses in media in the second half of the twentieth century In 1951, Johnson launched *Tan* (a "true confessions"-type magazine). In 1951, *Jet*, a weekly news digest, began. Later publications included *African American Stars* and *Ebony Jr.*, a children's magazine. Everything in the magazine was addressed to the African-American consumer. Johnson maintained that *Ebony's* success was due to the positive image of African Americans that it offered. In its 40th year of publication, *Ebony* had a circulation of 2,300,000 which was the primary reason that Johnson was considered one of the 400 richest individuals in the United States. *June 2016* marked the end of an era for the historic Chicago-based Johnson Publishing Co. After a 71-year run, Johnson Publishing, the family-owned business sold *Ebony and the* digital-only *Jet* magazine to Clear View Group, a private equity firm in Texas that has been described as African-American-owned.

Kassahun Checole is the founder and publisher of **Africa World Press** and the **Red Sea Press**. Mr. Checole was born in what is today Eritrea. While in secondary school in Keren, Eritrea, he enjoyed organizing a musical group and wrote poetry in his school's first newsletter. Later, he started attending Haile Selassie University in Addis Ababa, Ethiopia, but due to political demonstrations in 1969 in the University, Mr. Checole left school and started working at a clearinghouse in the port city of Massawa, Eritrea. In the early 1980s, in his late 40s, Mr. Checole did something to solve the problem of the scarcity of publishing outlets on topics related to Africa by founding the Africa World Press, Inc. (AWP), in 1983, with a mission to "provide high quality literature on the history, culture, and politics of

Africa and the African Diaspora." AWP first started publishing in early 1984. I9t was producing a handful of books per year. In the present day, AWP publishes more than 120 books each year. It has offices in the U.S., England (in London), Eritrea, Ethiopia, and Ghana.

Melvin B. Miller, a graduate of Harvard College and Columbia Law School, is Publisher and Founder of the **Bay State Banner**, an African American owned news weekly. The Bay State Banner reports on the political, economic, social and cultural issues that are of interest to African American and English-speaking Latinos in Boston and throughout New England. In addition to the weekly newspaper, the Banner has daily updated content on their digital platform, as well as specialty publications *Be Healthy* and *Banner Biz*. Be Healthy has won national awards for excellence in health care coverage. Started in 1965, the Banner provides its estimated 120,000 weekly print readers and 300,000 online readers with reports on a mix of local, national, international news and cultural events. The Banner is the newspaper of record for Boston community and has chronicled the struggles and successes of the people since its inception.

Pat Stevenson is the Founder and Publisher of **Harlem News Group.** Pat has been publishing community newspapers for more than 22 years. Prior to embarking upon her publishing venture, Pat had a successful career for more than a decade in advertising with executive positions in several advertising agencies working on fortune 500 accounts including Anheuser Busch, General Foods, General Motors and Avon. The Harlem New Group, Inc. publishes four weekly newspapers: Harlem Community News, Queens Community News, Brooklyn Community News and Bronx Community News. The publications are free to readers and they currently distribute 50,000 weekly copies in malls, supermarkets, retail outlets, apartment buildings, banks, colleges, YMCA's, libraries and cultural institutions in the communities that they serve. The Harlem News Group's motto is "Good News You Can Use." Harlem News Group's editorial features *only* positive news and information. They also provide a positive environment in which businesses and corporations can advertise and promote their products and services.

Tony Rose is the Publisher, Founder and CEO of **Amber Communications Group, Inc.** (ACGI). Since 1998, ACGI has been the nation's largest African-American book publisher of Self-Help Books and Music Biographies. Imprints include: Amber Books Publishing; Amber Classics Books; Colossus Books; Desmoon Books; Joyner/Amber Books - Co-Published with the Tom Joyner Foundation; and Amber/Wiley Books - Co-Published with John Wiley & Sons Inc. *Rose is noted as the first African American Independent Publisher to ink a multi-book, multi-year, Co-Publishing/Imprint deal with a major book publisher.* Tony Rose is the recipient of numerous publishing awards, including: The NAACP Image Award for outstanding Literature for "Obama Talks Back: Global Lessons - A Dialogue with America's Young Leaders" - Best Literary Work Youth / Teens and "The Harlem Book Fair / Phillis Wheatley Book Awards - African American Book Publisher of the Year." He has also written several award-winning books, including: "African American History in the United States of America"; "How to Be in the Entertainment Business"; and "The Autobiography of an American Ghetto Boy— The 1950's and 1960's—From the Projects to NAACP Image Award Winner, Volume One." In 2001 Tony Rose founded Quality Press, the nation's largest "African American Book Packager" to accommodate authors who wished to self-publish their books. Visit: WWW.QUALITYPRESS.INFO; WWW.AMBERBOOKSPUBLISHING.COM and TONYROSEENTERPRISES.COM

W. Paul Coates is the founder and director of **Black Classic Press,** which specializes in republishing obscure and significant works by and about people of African descent. A leader in the field of small publishers, Coates founded BCP Digital Printing in 1995 to produce books and documents using digital print technology. Paul Coates was a Vietnam vet who rolled with the Black Panthers, an old-school disciplinarian and new-age believer in free love. He launched a publishing company in his basement dedicated to telling the true history of African civilization.

Wade Hudson (publisher) and **Cheryl Hudson** (editorial director) founded **Just Us Books** in 1988. Just Us Books, Inc. is an independent publishing company that focuses on Black interest books for children and young adults. The company's main goal is to provide African-American children with positive images of themselves in books and learning materials.

Zane is the pseudonym of **Kristina Laferne Roberts.** Zane is the publisher of Strebor Books/Atria Books/Simon and Schuster where she publishes 36–60 books a year by other authors, as well as her own erotic fiction novels. Zane is the *New York Times* bestselling author of several titles, including: *Afterburn, The Heat Seekers and Dear G-Spot;* and she is best known for her novel *Addicted,* which is a major motion picture released by Lionsgate on October 10, 2014. In 1997, Zane began writing erotic stories to pass the time after her children went to bed. She was living in North Carolina and working as a sales representative. The stories developed a following on the Internet and she self-published *The Sex Chronicles* before landing a deal with Simon & Schuster. Her work was also the basis for the Cinemax program *Zane's Sex Chronicles*. Her latest project, *Zane's The Jump Off*, premiered March 29, 2013, on Cinemax.

MEDIA AND PUBLIC RELATIONS EXPERTS
WHO MAKE THE GRADE ....

A public relations specialist or publicist is a person whose job is to generate and manage publicity for a company, a brand, or public figure- especially a celebrity- or for a work such as a book, film or album. They have the role to maintain and represent the images of individuals, as well as an entire corporation or business. Publicists are also hired by public figures who want to maintain or protect their image. Publicists brand their clients by getting magazine, TV, newspaper, and website coverage. Most top-level publicists work in private practice, handling multiple clients. In order to succeed, Publicists must have good working relationships with media professionals, such as: journalists, TV news producers, radio producers and program directors. In order to have these relationships, publicists usually network with these media professionals. Here are some of the most notable media and public relations professionals in the U.S.

Angelo Ellerbee, the CEO of Double XXposure Public Relations firm is a veteran of the entertainment business, whose expertise in the industry turned into a full-service public relations, image consulting and artist development company. He has represented such clients as Michael Jackson, Lionel Richie, Mary J. Blige, DMX, Ginuwine, Shabba Ranks, Gang Starr and many others. Ellerbee's professional direction is rooted in the old-school principle of ensuring the all-around preparedness of the artist. He has taken his cue from Motown Records impresario Berry Gordy and has adapted that winning strategy to serve contemporary artists. Angelo Ellerbee has few peers when it comes to creating impactful images, and has made his image-making skills available to TV outlets such as CNN and The Maury Povich Show, just to name a couple

Ann Tripp currently provides the twice-hourly "news and views" on nationally syndicated "Steve Harvey Morning Show" on WBLS. She is also the host of "Healthful Solutions" (on cable), a narrator of certain SHOWTIME television specials, and is the executive producer, researcher and "voice" of the nationally-syndicated Black History Minute (United Stations Radio Network), where she profiles the historic, cultural, political and social milestones of African-Americas. Ann is a member of the National Academy of Television Arts and Sciences, the New York Press Club and the National Association of Negro Business and Professional Women Clubs, Inc.

Bill Tatum, born **Wilbert Arnold Tatum** (January 23, 1933 - February 26, 2009) the former publisher and editor of the Harlem-based Amsterdam News, was a powerful voice for the African-American community during his 40-year career in journalism. Mr. Tatum bought the newspaper in 1971 with a group of prominent investors that included Percy E. Sutton, the former Manhattan borough president, and H. Carl McCall, the former New York State comptroller. Mr. Tatum assumed control of the paper in 1983 and bought out the last investor in 1996. Tatum stepped down in 1997 and named his daughter Elinor Tatum, then 26 years old and a graduate of New York University's postgraduate journalism program, to serve as publisher and editor-in-chief of the paper. He retained his position as chairman of the board until his death.

Doug Banks, born **Calvin Douglas Banks Jr.** (June 9, 1958 – April 11, 2016) was an American radio personality. He began his radio career broadcasting on his high school's radio station. Local station WDRQ offered him a spot as a temporary late-night weekend disc jockey for a country music station, then, he got a permanent multi-year gig at KDAY in Los Angeles, California. Soon after, in April 1979 he started at KMJM-Majic 108, as "The Unknown DJ." Banks then moved on to the LA station KFI, KDIA in Oakland, California, and WBMX (now WVAZ) in Chicago, Illinois. From 1986 to 1995, Banks did nights, mornings, and afternoons for WGCI-FM in Chicago. Next, the ABC Radio Network offered Banks the opportunity to do a nationally syndicated show, hosted by Banks along with new sidekick DeDe McGuire, which rose to become one of the top-rated syndicated urban programs in America. In July 2010, Banks moved his show to American Urban Radio Networks and renamed it *The Doug Banks Show*.

Frankie "Hollywood" Crocker (December 18, 1937 – October 21, 2000) was a disc jockey who helped grow WBLS, the music radio station in New York. Crocker was the master of ceremonies of shows at the Apollo Theater in Harlem and was one of the first VJs on VH-1, the cable music video channel, in addition to hosting the TV series *Solid Gold* and NBC's *Friday Night Videos*. As an actor, Crocker appeared in five films, including *Cleopatra Jones* (1973) and *Five on the Black Hand Side* (1973). He is credited with introducing as many as 30 new artists to the mainstream. When Studio 54 was at the height of its popularity, Crocker rode in through the front entrance on a white stallion. Crocker, a native of Buffalo, coined the phrase "urban contemporary" in the 1970s, a label for the eclectic mix of songs that he played.

Imhotep Gary Byrd is a New York City-based radio talk show host and executive producer, radio DJ, poet, songwriter, music recording artist and producer, rapper, writer and community advocate/activist. Byrd began his career as a radio DJ in Buffalo at age 15. In 2015, he celebrated 50 years as a radio personality. Since the 1980s he's been a talk show host on WLIB, WBLS and WBAI. During the 1980s, Byrd was also a radio and television personality in England, hosting shows on the BBC and other British networks. His 1984 BBC television special with Gil Scott Heron and James Brown earned national awards. . During the 1990s, he created the "Global Black Experience," a live broadcast for the Apollo Theater. Currently, Byrd can also be heard nationally as "The Voice" of Sirius XM's "Soul Town" Channel ("Classic Soul & Motown.") His New York City public broadcasting program on Pacifica, "Radio GBE," a weekly talk and music program, is on WBAI-FM and at WBAI.org .

Gayle King is an American television personality and journalist, who is co-anchor of the CBS News morning show *CBS This Morning,* a position she has held since its debut in 2012. She is also an editor-at-large for *O, The Oprah Magazine.*

Hoda Kotb is an American broadcast journalist, television personality, and author. She is of Egyptian descent and is a main co-anchor of the NBC News morning show *Today,* and co-host of its entertainment-focused fourth hour. Kotb formerly served as a correspondent for the television news magazine program *Dateline NBC.*

Ken 'Spider' Webb is one of New York's most popular morning radio personalities. Since the late 1960's native New Yorkers depended heavily on his voice to get them going early every morning with classic soul music, 'the color of the day', plenty of laughs and family humor. Ken has made radio his life-long profession, beginning his on-air career in amateur radio at the age of 13. After 6 years as a Television Broadcast Engineer/Instructor at Brooklyn College (CUNY), in July of 1971 Ken became the very first radio 'morning man' for Inner City Broadcasting's flagship station, WBLS-FM (NYC) where he raised WBLS-FM morning ratings to the #1 position. In 1983, Ken moved to RKO Broadcasting's WRKS-FM and brought its morning ratings to the #1 position for the very first time in that station's history, where it remained until 1995 when he returned to WBLSWLIB-AM, WWRL-AM and WQCD-NY (CD101.9). In the area of community service, Ken founded the WBLS Sure Shots Benefit Basketball team in 1972 and the KISS Kards Benefit Basketball team in 1983. In 1985 Ken began syndicating his 2-hour weekly radio jazz show, "Jazz From the City" from his own studio in Long Island New York. The 2-hour weekly jazz show aired in Japan on the 40-station network, The Tokyo FM Network], the Philippines, the Caribbean and 150 stations in the US. He has also developed an internet radio marketing and advertising company, Webb Internet Radio Network and hosts his daily Sirius/XM Satellite Radio show, 'Soul Town."

Lee Louis Daniels is an American producer, director and writer. He produced *Monster's Ball* and directed *Precious*, which received six Academy Award nominations, including Best Director; it won two of the awards. In 2012, Daniels directed *The Butler*, a historical fiction drama featuring an ensemble cast portraying unique events on the 20th century presidents of the United States at the White House. Daniels is also a co-creator, executive producer, and director of the television series *Empire* and *Star*, which debuted in 2015 and 2016, respectively.

Lisa Evers (born June 15, 1953) is an American general assignment reporter for FOX 5 News, host of the *Street Soldiers with Lisa Evers* TV and radio show in New York City, a former high-ranking Guardian Angel, and a long-time community volunteer for urban, youth and children's charities. Evers is seen daily on FOX 5 News in New York reporting on a wide variety of hard news stories from local issues like police-community relations to counter-terrorism. She recently went inside the NYPD's bomb squad for an exclusive look at their work. Evers has interviewed such celebrities as Derek Jeter, Jay-Z, and 50 Cent. In addition to television, Evers hosts a weekly #1 rated community affairs talk show on New York's Hot 97-FM radio station. Prior to FOX 5, Evers was a general assignment reporter for 1010

WINS, the nation's #1 news radio station. She reported live from Ground Zero on September 11, 2001.

Sarah-Ann Shaw is an American-born journalist and television reporter with WBZ-TV from 1969 to 2000. She is most prominently renowned as the first female African-American reporter to be televised in Boston. Shaw is also known for her presence in civil rights movements and as a volunteer in education programs. Her recognition is widespread, including awards from the National Association for the Advancement of Colored People (NAACP), Rosie's Place, the Museum of Afro-American History and Action for Boston Community Development (ABCD).

Shonda Lynn Rhimes is an American television producer, screenwriter, and author. She is best known as the showrunner—creator, head writer, and executive producer—of the television medical drama *Grey's Anatomy*, its spin-off *Private Practice*, and the political thriller series *Scandal*. Rhimes has also served as the executive producer of the ABC television series *Off the Map*, *How to Get Away with Murder*, and *The Catch*. In 2007, Rhimes was named one of *TIME* magazine's 100 People Who Help Shape the World.

Spike Lee (March 20, 1957) born **Shelton Jackson Lee,** is an American film director, producer, writer, and actor. His production company, 40 Acres and a Mule Filmworks, has produced over 35 films since 1983. He made his directorial debut with *She's Gotta Have It* (1986), and has since directed such films as *Do the Right Thing* (1989), *Malcolm X* (1992), *The Original Kings of Comedy* (2000), *25th Hour* (2002), *Inside Man* (2006), *Chi-Raq* (2015), and *BlacKkKlansman* (2018). In January 2019 Lee landed his first directing Academy Award nomination for "BlacKkKlansman," about a black cop who infiltrated the Ku Klux Klan in the 1970s. The film won six nominations altogether, including best picture and best adapted screenplay. Lee has also acted in 10 of his own films. Lee's films have examined race relations, colorism in the black community, the role of media in contemporary life, urban crime and poverty, and other political issues. He has won numerous accolades for his previous work, including two Academy Award nominations, a Student Academy Award, and an Academy Honorary Award from the Academy of Motion Picture Arts and Sciences, two Emmy Awards, and two Peabody Awards, among others.

Terrie Williams founded The Terrie Williams Agency (TTWA), a public relations firm, in 1988. Her first clients were Miles Davis and comedian Eddie Murphy. The firm provides employee training and motivational speaking for various corporations, community-based organizations and universities. Over the years, it has represented public figures such as Prince, Chris Rock, Janet Jackson, Louis Gossett Jr., the Reverend Al Sharpton, Sean "Diddy" Combs, MoNique, Ntozake Shange, and the late Johnnie L. Cochran. Corporate clients include HBO, Revlon, Time Warner, *Essence* magazine and Forest City Ratner Companies. Terrie's work in public relations has been referenced in textbooks, business guides, print editorials, social media, and pop culture. Since its creation in 1988, The Terrie Williams Agency has provided many of its services on a pro bono basis to underserved communities

Tom Joyner is an American radio host, host of the nationally syndicated *The Tom Joyner Morning Show*, as well as the founder of Reach Media Inc., the Tom Joyner Foundation, and BlackAmericaWeb.com. In 1994, Joyner was signed by ABC Radio Networks to host a nationally syndicated program, *The Tom Joyner Morning Show*, featuring Joyner and a team of comedians and commentators reporting and discussing the latest news and sports of the day, and playing popular R&B songs from the 1970s through the 1990s as well as contemporary R&B hits. Decades later, Tom Joyner continues to be an influential broadcaster; the *TJMS* is heard live in over 100 cities, both on-air and via streaming audio, through its syndicator, Reach Media.

Troy Johnson founded and launched ALBC.com in 1998. The African American Literature Book Club, is a website dedicated to books and film by and about African Americans and people of African descent with content also aimed at African-American bookstores. AALBC.com publishes book and film reviews, author profiles, resources for writers and related articles. It features all genres of books but targets primarily a middle-aged African-American female demographic.

Vaughn Harper (March 1, 1945 – July 9, 2016[) was an American broadcast announcer and DJ, an actor and musician who voiced himself as host of The Vibe 98.8 radio station in Grand Theft Auto IV. A native New Yorker, Harper's on-air style was as smooth as the soulful slow jams he played on his pioneering show. He was best known as a DJ for New York station WBLS from 1975 to 2008, most famously hosting its Quiet Storm late-night program which played slow jams and R & B. Harper passed away on July 9, 2016 at the age of 71.

Wendy Williams, media mogul, entrepreneur, performer and best-selling author, is best known for her long-running talk show. The Wendy Williams Show includes a diverse mix of interviews with celebrity guests from television, film, music, and sports. In 2015, both Wendy and the show earned Daytime Emmy® nominations for "Best Talk Show Host" and "Best Entertainment Talk Show. "The Wendy Williams Show is taped live in New York City. A reflection of Wendy's entertaining personality and distinctive sense of humor, the show has memorabilia in the Smithsonian Museum, and is broadcast in 53 countries.

POLITICIANS, LAWYERS, AND OTHER LEADERS WHO MAKE THE GRADE ....

African Americans have served with distinction in all three branches of government, in the military, and in legal practice. Thurgood Marshall, a leading civil rights lawyer, ended up on the U.S. Supreme Court. Others, like Gen. Colin Powell, are notable political and military leaders.

Andrew Young (March 13, 1932) helped change the course of history as a leader in the Civil Rights movement. He built a remarkable legacy as a civic activist, elected official, groundbreaking ambassador, social entrepreneur, and adviser to presidents. Young was elected Mayor in 1981 and re-elected in 1985 with nearly 85 percent of the vote. Hartsfield International Airport, whose development he championed, made it possible for Atlanta to attract 1,100 new businesses, $70 billion in foreign direct investment, and 1 million new jobs to the region during his tenure. It is now the busiest airport in the world. The city hosted the Democratic National Convention in 1988. Young also led the successful effort to bring the 1996 Olympic Games to Atlanta. Today, he leads the Andrew J. Young Foundation's efforts to develop and support new generations of visionary leaders. Young is the recipient of the Presidential Medal of Freedom and the French Legion d'Honneur and has received honorary degrees from more than 100 colleges and universities. Young was instrumental in the building of modern-day Atlanta.

Charles Bernard Rangel (June 11, 1930) is an American politician who was a U.S. Representative for districts in New York from 1971 to

2017. A member of the Democratic Party, he was the second-longest serving incumbent member of the House of Representatives at the time of his retirement, serving continuously since 1971. As its most senior member, he was also the Dean of New York's congressional delegation. Rangel was the first African-American Chair of the influential House Ways and Means Committee. He is also a founding member of the Congressional Black Caucus. Rangel was born in Harlem in Upper Manhattan and lives there to this day. He earned a Purple Heart and a Bronze Star for his service in the U.S. Army during the Korean War, where he led a group of soldiers out of a deadly Chinese army encirclement during the Battle of Kunu-ri in 1950. Rangel graduated from New York University in 1957 and St. John's University School of Law in 1960. He then worked as a private lawyer, Assistant U.S. Attorney, and legal counsel during the early-mid-1960s. He served two terms in the New York State Assembly, from 1967 to 1971, and then defeated long-time incumbent Congressman Adam Clayton Powell, Jr. in a primary challenge on his way to being elected to the House of Representatives. Rangel rose rapidly in the Democratic ranks, His long-time concerns with battling the importation and effects of illegal drugs led to his becoming chair of the House Select Committee on Narcotics, where he helped define national policy on the issue during the 1980s. As one of Harlem's "Gang of Four", he also became a leader in New York City and State politics. He played a significant role in the creation of the 1995 Upper Manhattan Empowerment Zone Development Corporation and the national Empowerment Zone Act, which helped change the economic face of Harlem and other inner-city areas.

Clarence Thomas (June 23, 1948) grew up in rural Georgia, attended Conception Seminary and Holy Cross College, then graduated from Yale Law School in 1974. He practiced law for a short time in Missouri, then was an assistant to the attorney general and a corporate attorney before becoming an aide to Senator John Danforth (1979-81).

Thomas caught the eye of the administration of President Ronald Reagan and ended up as the chairman of the Equal Employment Opportunity Commission (EEOC) from 1982 until he was appointed in 1990 by President George Bush to the U.S. Court of Appeals. In 1991 he was nominated to the Supreme Court by President Bush, to fill the seat left by retiring justice Thurgood Marshall. Justice Thomas is now the most senior justice on the bench.

Colin Powell (April 5, 1937), born **Colin Luther Powell** in Harlem, New York, was the son of Jamaican immigrants. He was raised in the South Bronx and graduated from Morris High School in 1954 and then went to City College of New York, where he studied geology. He joined Reserve Officers' Training Corps (ROTC) and soon became commander of his unit. In 1989, President George H. W. Bush appointed General Colin Powell as Chairman of the Joint Chiefs of Staff. The post is the highest military position in the Department of Defense, and Powell was the first African-American officer to receive that distinction. General Powell became a national figure during Desert Shield and Desert Storm operations in Iraq. As chief military strategist, he developed what became known as the "Powell Doctrine," an approach to military conflicts that advocates using overwhelming force to maximize success and minimize casualties. He continued as chairman of the Joint Chiefs in the first few months of the Clinton administration and publicly disagreed with the president on the issue of admitting gays into the military, although he eventually agreed to the "don't ask, don't tell" compromise. For the remainder of Bush's first term, Colin Powell tried to establish an international coalition to assist in the rebuilding of Iraq. In September 2004, he testified before Congress that the intelligence sources he used in his February presentation to the United Nations were "wrong" and it was unlikely that Saddam had any stockpiles of weapons of mass destruction. In 2004, Powell announced his resignation as secretary of state.

Condoleezza Rice (November 14, 1954) is an American political scientist and diplomat. Rice became one of the most influential women in the world of global politics when President George W. Bush named her as his national security adviser in December of 2000, making her the first woman to serve in that position. In 2004, when Colin Powell resigned his position, Rice served as the 66th United States Secretary of State, becoming the second person to hold that office in the administration of President George W. Bush. In addition, Condoleezza Rice made history as the first *female* African-American Secretary of State, as well as the second African-American Secretary of State (after Colin Powell), and the second female Secretary of State (after Madeleine Albright). The fourth year of the Bush Administration was a difficult one for Rice and other top White House and Pentagon personnel. Though Hussein had been captured and the war in Iraq was officially declared over, U.S. troops stationed in Iraq had become the target of repeated attacks by insurgents, and American military operatives had yet to capture Bin Laden. Rice's role became extremely important after the September 11, 2001, attacks on New York City and the Pentagon in Washington. Rice played a crucial part in shaping the most aggressive U.S. foreign policy in modern history, with wars launched against Afghanistan and Iraq during her time in office. In April of 2004 Rice was called to testify before a special panel that had been set up to investigate the 9/11 attacks. Rice held her ground.

David Dinkins, born **David Norman Dinkins** (July 10, 1927) is an American politician, lawyer, and author who served as the 106th Mayor of New York City, from 1990 to 1993. He was the first and, to date, the only African American to hold that office. He began his political career by serving in the State Assembly (1966), eventually advancing to Manhattan borough president before becoming mayor. Under the Dinkins administration, crime in New York City decreased more dramatically and more rapidly than at any time in previous New York City history. Dinkins entered office in January 1990 pledging racial healing, and famously referred to New York City's demographic diversity as a "gorgeous mosaic." The rates of most crimes, including all categories of violent crime, made consecutive declines during the last 36 months of his four-year term, ending a 30-year upward spiral and initiating a trend of falling rates that continued beyond his term. Before entering politics, Dinkins was among the more than 20,000 Montford Point Marines, the first African-American U.S. Marines (trained 1942–1949; Dinkins' service was 1945–1946); he graduated *cum laude* from Howard University; and he received his law degree from Brooklyn Law School (1956). While maintaining a private law practice from 1956 to 1975, Dinkins rose through the Democratic Party organization in Harlem, beginning at the Carver Democratic Club under the aegis of J. Raymond Jones. He became part of an influential group of African American politicians that included Denny Farrell, Percy Sutton, Basil Paterson, and Charles Rangel; the latter three together with Dinkins were known as the "Gang of Four." As an investor, Dinkins was one of fifty African American investors who helped Percy Sutton found Inner City Broadcasting Corporation in 1971.

Jesse Jackson (October 8, 1941) was born **Jesse Louis Burns** in Greenville, South Carolina. He is an American civil rights leader, Baptist minister, and politician. Jesse adopted the name of his stepfather, Charles Jackson, at about age 15. He attended the University of Illinois (1959–60) on a football scholarship, then transferred to the predominantly black Agricultural and Technical College of North Carolina in Greensboro and received a B.A. in sociology (1964). He did graduate work at the Chicago Theological Seminary and was ordained a Baptist minister in 1968. Jesse became involved in the civil rights movement, became a worker in King's Southern Christian Leadership Conference (SCLC), and helped found the Chicago branch of Operation Breadbasket. In 1971 Jesse founded Operation PUSH (People United to Save Humanity), a Chicago-based organization in which he advocated black self-help and in 1984 he established the National Rainbow Coalition, which sought equal rights for African Americans, women, and homosexuals. These two organizations merged in 1996 to form the Rainbow/PUSH Coalition. Jesse Jackson's bids for the U.S. presidency (in the Democratic Party's nomination races in 1983–84 and 1987–88) were the most successful by an African American until 2008, when Barack Obama captured the Democratic presidential nomination. Highlights of his career include participating in civil rights demonstrations with the Rev. Martin Luther King Jr., negotiating successfully for the release of three US soldiers who had been held in Yugoslavia and receiving the Presidential Medal of Freedom from President Bill Clinton.

Kweisi Mfume, born Frizzell Gerald Gray (October 24, 1948) is an American politician and the former President/CEO of the National Association for the Advancement of Colored People (NAACP), as well as a five-term Democratic Congressman from Maryland's 7th congressional district, serving in the 100th through 104th Congress. In 1978, Kweisi Mfume was elected to the Baltimore City Council, serving there until 1986. Serving in Maryland's 7th Congressional district for five terms, Kweisi made himself known as a Democrat with an apparent balance between strong progressive ideologies and a capacity for practical compromise. In February 1996, Mfume left the House to accept the presidency of the National Association for the Advancement of Colored People (NAACP), stating that he could do more to improve American civil rights there than in the Congress. He reformed the association's finances to pay off its considerable debt while pursuing the cause of civil rights advancement for African Americans. Though many in Baltimore wanted Mfume to run for mayor in the 1999 election, Mfume stayed with the NAACP. Mfume served this position for nine years before stepping down in 2004 to pursue other interests. On September 12, 2006, he lost a primary campaign for the United States Senate seat that was being vacated by Maryland U.S. Senator Paul Sarbanes.

Les Brown born **Leslie Calvin Brown** (February 17, 1945) is an American motivational speaker, author, radio DJ, former television host, and former politician. As a politician, he is a former member of the Ohio House of Representatives. After leaving the Ohio state legislature, he decided to get into television and eventually ended up on PBS. He also formed Les Brown Enterprises in order to support his newest career as a motivational speaker and was on KFWB in California on a daily syndicated radio program from 2011 to 2012. As a premier Keynote Speaker and leading authority on achievement for audiences as large as 80,000—Les Brown energizes people to meet the challenges of the world around them. He is committed to motivating and training today's generation to be achievers and leaders

Maxine Moore Waters (August 15, 1938) born Maxine Carr, served in the California State Assembly, to which she was first elected in 1976. A member of the Democratic Party, Waters is currently in her 15th term in the House, having served since 1991. She previously represented the state's 29th district (1991–1993) and 35th district (1993–2013) and has chaired the Congressional Black Caucus from 1997 to 1999. Before becoming a U.S. Representative, as an Assemblywoman, she advocated divestment from South Africa's apartheid regime. Waters is the most senior of the twelve black women currently serving in Congress, She has been serving as the U.S. Representative for California's 43rd congressional district since 2013 and had been an outspoken opponent of the Iraq War and of Republican Presidents George H. W. Bush, George W. Bush and Donald Trump.

Thurgood Marshall (July 2, 1908 - January 24, 1993) was born in Baltimore, Maryland. After completing high school in 1925, Thurgood attended the historically black Lincoln University in Chester County, Pennsylvania. After amassing an impressive record of Supreme Court challenges to state-sponsored discrimination, including the landmark Brown v. Board decision in 1954, President John F. Kennedy appointed Thurgood Marshall to the U.S. Court of Appeals for the Second Circuit. In this capacity, he wrote over 150 decisions including support for the rights of immigrants. In 1965 President Lyndon Johnson appointed Judge Marshall to the office of U.S. Solicitor General. Before his subsequent nomination to the United States Supreme Court in 1967, Thurgood Marshall won 14 of the 19 cases he argued before the Supreme Court on behalf of the government. Until his retirement from the highest court in the land, Justice Marshall established a record for supporting the voiceless American.

MILITARY NOTABLES
WHO MAKE THE GRADE ....

When you think about Heroes and Sheroes, there are so many to learn about and remember. These great people have put their lives on the line and many have sacrificed their lives to protect the people and their rights as well as those in leadership roles in our country.

Austin Dabney was a slave who became a private in the Georgia militia and fought against the British during the Revolutionary War (1775-83). He was the only African American to be granted land by the state of Georgia in recognition of his bravery and service during the Revolution and one of the few to receive a federal military pension. Born in Wake County, North Carolina, in the 1760s, Austin Dabney moved with his master, Richard Aycock, to Wilkes County, Georgia, in the late 1770s. In order to avoid military service himself, Aycock sent Dabney to join the Georgia militia as a substitute. Serving as an artilleryman under Elijah Clarke, Dabney is believed to have been the only black soldier to participate in the Battle of Kettle Creek, one of the most significant battles in Georgia, which took place near Washington on February 14, 1779. He was severely wounded in the thigh during the fighting, and Giles Harris, a white soldier, took Dabney to his home to care for the wound. Dabney remembered Harris's kindness and worked for the Harris family for the rest of his life.

Benjamin Oliver Davis Sr. (1880 – November 26, 1970) was a United States Army officer. After graduating from high school, in response to the start of the Spanish–American War, Davis entered the military service on July 13, 1898, as a temporary first lieutenant in the 8th United States Volunteer Infantry, an all-black unit. This regiment was stationed at Chickamauga Park, Georgia, from October 1898 until the unit was disbanded in March 1899. During the war, Davis briefly served in Company D, 1st Separate Battalion of the Washington D.C. National Guard. He became the first African-American to rise to the rank of Brigadier General in the U.S. military in 1940. He was the father of Air Force General Benjamin O. Davis Jr. On July 20, 1948, after fifty years of military service, Davis retired in a public ceremony with President Harry S. Truman presiding. 6 days later on July 26, 1948, President Truman issued executive order 9981 which abolished racial discrimination in the armed forces. From July 1953 through June 1961, he served as a member of the American Battle Monuments Commission. Davis died on November 26, 1970, at Great Lakes Naval Hospital in Chicago, Illinois, and was buried at Arlington National Cemetery.

Daniel "Chappie" James Jr. (February 11, 1920 – February 25, 1978) was an American fighter pilot in the U.S. Air Force, who in 1975 became the first African American to reach the rank of four-star in the forces. He attended the famous Tuskegee Institute and instructed African American pilots during World War II. Chappie flew combat missions during the Korean War and Vietnam War, and received the Defense Distinguished Service Medal, two Air Force Distinguished Service Medals, two Legion of Merits, three Distinguished Flying Crosses, Meritorious Service Medal and fourteen Air Medals. On September 1, 1975, Chappie was promoted to the four-star rank of General (O-10) and assigned as commander in chief of NORAD/ADCOM at Peterson Air Force Base, Colorado. In these dual capacities he had operational command of all United States and

Canadian strategic aerospace defense forces. On December 6, 1977, he assumed duty as special assistant to the Chief of Staff, U.S. Air Force. General James retired from the Air Force on January 31, 1978.

Doris "Dorie" Miller (October 12, 1919 – November 24, 1943) was an American Messman Third Class in the United States Navy. During the attack on Pearl Harbor on December 7, 1941 Miller manned anti-aircraft guns, (despite having no formal training in their use), and attended to the wounded. For his actions, he was recognized by the Navy and awarded several medals. He was the first African American to be awarded the Navy Cross, the third highest honor awarded by the US Navy at the time, after the Medal of Honor and the Navy Distinguished Service Medal. Miller's acts were heavily publicized in the black press, making him an iconic emblem of the war for Black Americans. Nearly two years after Pearl Harbor, he was killed in action when his ship, *Liscome Bay,* was sunk by a Japanese submarine during the Battle of Makin.

Colonel **Frederick D. Gregory** (January 7, 1941) became the first Black to pilot a space shuttle when he led the *Challenger* on a seven-day mission in 1985. As an astronaut he has spent more than 455 hours in outer space, and he commanded three major space missions from 1985 to 1991. Colonel Gregory was a decorated helicopter pilot during the Vietnam War and a jet test pilot prior to working with the National Aeronautics and Space Administration (NASA). From 2002 to 2005, Gregory held the second highest administration position, deputy administrator, with NASA. In 2005 he briefly rose to the top spot as acting administrator, becoming the first African American to lead NASA.

Guy Bluford, born Guion Bluford (November 22, 1942) is a member of the SDS-8 space shuttle Challenger crew. In 1983, Bluford was the first African American in space. Bluford became the only Black engineering student at Pennsylvania State University in 1960. He graduated with a degree in aerospace engineering in 1964 and went through pilot training at Williams Air Force Base in Arizona where he received his pilot wings one year later. He flew 144 combat missions with the 557th Squadron in Vietnam. After serving his tour of duty in Vietnam, Bluford worked as a flight instructor at Sheppard Air Force Base in Texas and started graduate studies at the Air Force Institute of Technology in 1972. He received a M.S. in aerospace engineering in 1974 and a Ph.D. in 1978. The same year, he was one of the thirty-five selected for the National Aeronautics and Space Administration (NASA) astronaut training program out of 10,000 applicants. On August 30, 1983, he flew the space shuttle, conducted experiments and helped launch a $45 million satellite to provide communications and weather information for India. Bluford flew a total of four missions in space and continued with NASA until 1993. He received an M.B.A from the University of Houston while still serving in 1987, and became the Vice President of a computer software company in Maryland after retiring. Bluford broke the color line of space.

Henry Ossian Flipper (March 21, 1856 – April 26, 1940) was an American soldier, former slave, and the first African American to graduate from the United States Military Academy at West Point in 1877, earning a commission as a 2nd lieutenant in the US Army. Following Flipper's commission, he was transferred to one of the all-Black regiments serving in the US Army which were historically led by white officers. Assigned to 'A' Troop under the command of Captain Nicholas M. Nolan, he became the first nonwhite officer to lead buffalo soldiers of the 10th Cavalry.

Joycelyn Elders, (August 13, 1933) the former U.S. Surgeon General, was born **Minnie Lee Jones** in Schaal, Arkansas. She added the name Joycelyn when she was in college. She received a B.S. in biology from Philander Smith College in 1952. Upon graduating from college in

1952, Elders enlisted in the Army and became a physical therapist. After ending her military career in 1956 Joycelyn enrolled in medical school; she received an M.D. from the University of Arkansas Medical School in 1960. In 1993, President Bill Clinton nominated Elders to the highest medical office in the land, U.S. Surgeon General. She withstood difficult Senate confirmation hearings and became the first woman and first Black U.S. Surgeon General on September 8, 1993. The Surgeon General holds the military rank of Vice Admiral in the United States Navy. Although personally against abortion, she publicly advocated pro-choice policies and because of several controversies with conservatives in Congress and religious groups, President Clinton was prompted to demand her resignation. Dr. Elders remained active in public health policy after her resignation. She worked as special assistant to the intergovernmental affairs director of the U.S. Education Department until her retirement.

Private Peter Salem (October 1, 1750–August 16, 1816) was an African American from Massachusetts who served as a soldier in the American Revolutionary War. Born into slavery in Framingham, Massachusetts, he was freed by a later master, Major Lawson Buckminster, to serve in the local militia. He then enlisted in the Continental Army, serving for nearly five years during the war. Afterwards, he married and worked as a cane weaver. A monument was erected to him in the late 19th century at his grave in Framingham, Massachusetts.

Roscoe Conkling Brown Jr. (March 9, 1922 – July 2, 2016) was one of the Tuskegee Airmen and a squadron commander of the 100th Fighter Squadron of the 332nd Fighter Group. He was appointed to this position in June, 1945, which was after V-E Day (May 8, 1945). During combat, he served as a flight leader and operations officer. He graduated from the Tuskegee Flight School on March 12, 1944 as member of class 44-C-SE and served in the U.S. Army Air Forces in

Europe during World War II. During this period, Captain Brown shot down an advanced German Me 262 jet fighter and a FW-190 fighter. He was awarded the Distinguished Flying Cross. Brown was born in Washington, D.C. in 1922. His father, Roscoe C. Brown Sr. (1884–1963), was a dentist and an official in the United States Public Health Service who was born as George Brown and had changed his name to honor Roscoe Conkling, a strong supporter of the rights of African Americans during Reconstruction. His mother was the former Vivian Berry, a teacher. Prior to his wartime service, he graduated from Springfield College, Springfield, Massachusetts, where he was valedictorian of the Class of 1943. After the war, Captain Brown resumed his education. His doctoral dissertation was on exercise physiology; and he became a professor at New York University and directed their Institute of Afro-American Affairs.

ABOUT THE AUTHOR
DOCTOR BOB LEE

Doctor **Bob Lee** is a man who brings back the fruits of his success to the youth and disenfranchised of communities in need. His posture of humility and quiet attentiveness precedes the underlying wealth of knowledge, creativity and experience just below the surface waiting to spring forth.

His impressive profile reads like that of an elder statesman who has reached the proverbial mountaintop. The rise above the pitfalls faced by an inner-city youth from an overcrowded, low-income household was all too common for the times. The struggle was not devoid of its share of bumps and bruises, encounters with law enforcement, drug-filled atmospheres and serious bodily injuries. But through it all, a small blessing of a childhood deal with an older sister would put the wheels of progress in motion. The good Doctor tells a story of how his sister shrewdly offered him a job opportunity, which in reality was a well-devised plan to keep young Bob occupied, useful and monitored as she and her friends entertained themselves. Resolve came in a way that her young brother would become a 'junior partner' commissioned to be the disc jockey at neighborhood parties. The music was managed through a simple system. The 45s had color-coded spindle adapters to identify the fast from the slow songs. When the color Red or Yellow was called out, he knew when the crowd wanted to hear a fast or slow song. Bob viewed himself as the most important person in the room. The plan worked well for all and the seeds of a career had been planted.

Then there's the story of how he acquired the title "Doctor", at such a young age. Bob had accompanied his father to the doctor's office one day and was fascinated by the doctor's white coat hanging on the door and microscope on the desk. Doing what young boys do, Bob donned the oversized coat and peered through the lens of the microscope to see the unexpected-microorganisms that actually had names and purposes in life. He was hooked to the extent that the encounter carried over to his curiosity about how life works. His knack for precision became a part of his personality. Hence, his friends dubbed him as the "Doctor."

The "Doctor" as a young man was no stranger to sports. He played football, baseball and basketball, but it was amateur boxing that showed him the importance of preparedness. Survival in the hood required the ability to talk the talk and walk the walk. At both, Bob was able to hold his own. But he quickly learned that resting on one's laurels is no substitute of preparation for a task. A bout with a formidable opponent tested the limits of his ability when he failed to properly get in shape. He paid for it dearly, but then came to know the value of being prepared when you walk in the door.

Music played an important role in the development of adolescents from the Queensbridge area of New York City in the early 1970's, and Bob Lee was no exception. He found that his creative mind was well-received by his peers when he manned the turntables as a DJ for house parties, festivals, schools, and charity work at hospitals under the mentorship of a neighborhood icon he looked up to: Mr. Hank Carter. It was through this friendship and the linking of the two unlikely entities - music and community service - it all began to make sense to him. Both were satisfying and important parts of his life and would launch a journey that would benefit others as well as himself.

Bob Lee went on to pursue his B.A. and M.A. degrees in Communications from New York Institute of Technology while disc jockeying for WTNY-88.7 radio. His popularity began to flourish on a grander scale as he reached a wider more diverse listening audience. By 1980 the momentum of his career was beginning to escalate. He was accepted as an intern at N.Y.'s hottest R&B radio station, WBLS, under the legendary Frankie Crocker and Hal Jackson. By 1986, he became a staple on the weekend edition of the "Quiet Storm" with the smooth baritone voicings of Vaughn Harper. Not long after, he became an integral part of the highly popular "Morning Show" with Ken Webb in which he developed the "On Time" program spotlighting positive outlooks at community schools and healthy food programs. All these shows became models for urban listening programs in cities across the nation.

In the years to follow Doctor Bob Lee's career continued to skyrocket. The doors began to open to his own creative juices. He hosts BLS – Bob Lee Show, a music-intensive radio series. For more than ten years, Lee has hosted the weekly live television program "Open," which broadcasts on BronxNet, a world-wide cable television station. The program features news and topics affecting the community and also treats viewers to new and established musical guests. In addition to his on-air roles, Bob manages community affairs and government relations for WBLS.

Bob is also the President & CEO of Bob Lee Enterprises, an umbrella for his many talents, including: motivational speaking and coaching, deejaying and consulting for companies who want to do grassroots promotions.

The marriage of entertainment and community service provided a suitable foundation in the building of Doctor Bob Lee. It's earned him his own unique place amongst today's stars of Hip Hop, R&B and Soul. He maintains a rigorous schedule of Radio, TV, DJing, book signings, speaking engagements and appearances. Though he's come a long way, Doctor Bob Lee maintains his never-ending quest to build a better future for today's youth.

Doctor Bob Lee is the President, Founder & CEO of the Make The Grade Foundation for education. Make The Grade Foundation is a 501(c)(3) non-profit organization that facilitates and encourages academic achievement.

People to Know in Black History - Honoring the Heroes and Sheroes Who Make the Grade is Bob Lee's fourth published book. His previous books include: *7 Ways to Make the Grade: A Living Guide to Your Community's Success: Parents, Teachers, Students, Community, Clergy, Health & Financial Literacy; Your Daily Dose of Quotes and Anecdotes – Featuring Words of Wisdom to Help You Make the Grade and Your Daily Dose of Quotes and Anecdotes II – Featuring Words of Wisdom to Help You Make the Grade – With Bonus Section.*

Follow Doctor Bob Lee on: Facebook, Twitter, and Instagram.

IN CONCLUSION

The list is expansive, but not nearly complete. I am pleased to tell you that ***People to Know for Black History and Beyond - Recognizing the Heroes and Sheroes Who Make the Grade*** is just the first volume of a multi-volume set.

Now that you have finished reading this book, ask yourself, "What common characteristics do all these people have?" They are people just like us with the burning desire to discipline themselves and do the things necessary to become successful.

**WHO ARE SOME OF THE PEOPLE YOU CAN
THINK OF THAT MAKE THE GRADE?
Tell us their story, Email: Makethegrade4u@gmail.com**

REFERENCES

www.wikipedia.org

www.legacy.com

www.history.com

www.brittanica.com

www.biography.com

www.myheritage.com

www.patents.justia.com

www.americanthinker.com

www.famousblackinventors.com

INDEX